Prospects for democratic consolidation in East-Central Europe

MANCHESTER
UNIVERSITY PRESS

Prospects for democratic consolidation in East-Central Europe

edited by
Geoffrey Pridham *and* Attila Ágh

Manchester University Press
Manchester and New York

distributed exclusively in the USA by Palgrave

Copyright © Manchester University Press 2001

While copyright in the volume as a whole is vested in Manchester University Press, copyright in individual chapters belongs to their respective authors, and no chapter may be reproduced wholly or in part without the express permission in writing of both author and publisher.

Published by Manchester University Press
Oxford Road, Manchester M13 9NR, UK
and Room 400, 175 Fifth Avenue, New York, NY 10010, USA
http://www.manchesteruniversitypress.co.uk

Distributed exclusively in the USA by
Palgrave, 175 Fifth Avenue, New York,
NY 10010, USA

Distributed exclusively in Canada by
UBC Press, University of British Columbia, 2029 West Mall, Vancouver, BC, Canada V6T 1Z2

British Library Cataloguing-in-Publication Data
A catalogue record of this book is available from the British Library

Library of Congress Cataloging-in-Publication Data applied for

ISBN 07190 6057 5 *hardback*

First published 2001

10 09 08 07 06 05 04 03 02 01   10 9 8 7 6 5 4 3 2 1

Typeset in Monotype Times New Roman
by Servis Filmsetting Ltd, Manchester
Printed in Great Britain
by Bookcraft (Bath) Ltd, Midsomer Norton

Contents

List of figures and tables

Figures

Tables

Notes on contributors

Attila Ágh is Head of the Political Science Department at the Budapest University of Economics and Public Administration and Director of the Hungarian Centre for Democracy Studies. He has written widely on problems of democratic transition and consolidation in post-Communist Europe. Among his recent book publications are *The Politics of Central Europe* (London: Sage, 1998) and *Emerging Democracies in East-Central Europe and the Balkans* (Cheltenham: Edward Elgar, 1998).

Robert Bideleux is Reader in Politics at the University of Wales, Swansea. He is author of, among other things, *Communism and Development* (London: Methuen 1985, revised 1987) and, with Ian Jeffries, *A History of Eastern Europe* (London: Routledge, 1998). He is currently writing, again with Ian Jeffries, *The Balkans and East-Central Europe: A Contemporary History* (for Routledge) and a book on democracy, civil society and the state (also for Routledge).

Karen Henderson is Lecturer in Politics at the University of Leicester. She is author (with Neil Robinson) of *Post-Communist Politics* (Hemel Hempstead: Prentice Hall, 1997) and editor of *Back to Europe: Central and Eastern Europe and the European Union* (London: UCL Press, 1999). Her major research interests are democratisation in East-Central Europe, especially Slovakia and the Czech Republic, and the eastward enlargement of the European Union.

Paul Lewis is Reader in Central and East European Politics at the Open University. His publications range over diverse aspects of comparative and East European politics. His books include *Central Europe since 1945* (Harlow: Longman, 1994) and *Political Parties in Post-Communist Eastern Europe* (London: Routledge, 2000). Current research interests involve continuing work on party development in Central and Eastern Europe and the evolving character of the European Union in its relation to the post-Communist region.

Wolfgang Merkel is Professor of Political Science at the University of
Heidelberg and has written widely on comparative problems of regime
change. His publications include four (co)edited volumes called
Systemwechsel (Opladen: Leske and Budrich, 1994, 1996, 1997 and 1999)
as well as *Systemtransformation* (Opladen: Leske and Budrich, 1999). He
has also written articles on social democratic governments, political
systems in Western Europe and European integration.

Frances Millard is Reader in the Department of Government at the University
of Essex. Her main interests lie in the field of comparative Communist and
post-Communist politics. She is author of *The Anatomy of the New Poland*
(Cheltenham: Edward Elgar, 1994) and *Polish Politics and Society*
(London: Routledge, 1999) as well as numerous articles on political parties,
elections and aspects of social policy.

Fritz Plasser is Professor of Political Science at the University of Innsbruck
and works on comparative studies of voting behaviour and party system
change, the role of the mass media in political campaigns, political culture,
the democratic consolidation of post-Communist societies and worldwide
trends in election campaign practices. His recently published books include
*Parteien auf komplexen Wählermärkten: Reaktionsstrategien politischer
Parteien in Westeuropa*, which he co-edited with Peter Mair and Wolfgang
C. Müller (Vienna: Signum, 1999); 'Das Osterreichische Wahlverhalten',
co-edited with Peter A. Ulram and Franz Sommer (Vienna: Signum, 2000);
*Die Zukunft der österreichischen Demokratie: Trends, Prognosen und
Szenarien*, co-edited with Anton Pelinka and Wolfgang Meixner (Vienna:
Signum, 2000).

Geoffrey Pridham is Professor of European Politics and Director of the Centre
for Mediterranean Studies, University of Bristol. He has written widely on
problems of democratic transition and consolidation in both Southern
Europe and Central and Eastern Europe. His latest books include
*Stabilising Fragile Democracies: Comparing New Party Systems in Southern
and Eastern Europe*, co-edited with Paul Lewis (London: Routledge, 1996);
Experimenting with Democracy: Regime Change in the Balkans, co-edited
with Tom Gallagher (London: Routledge, 2000); and *The Dynamics of
Democratisation: A Comparative Approach* (London: Continuum, 2000).
He is currently working on a project on the relationship between EU
Eastern enlargement and domestic politics in post-Communist applicant
states with a Leverhulme Fellowship.

Peter A. Ulram is Assistant Professor of Political Science at the University of
Vienna and Senior Research Executive at the FESSEL-GfK Institute for
Market and Opinion Research in Vienna. His recent publications include
Democratic Consolidation in East-Central Europe, with F. Plasser and H.
Waldrauch (Macmillan, 1998); *On the Eve of EU Enlargement: Economic
Developments and Democratic Attitudes in East-Central Europe*, with J.
Stankovsky and F. Plasser (Vienna: Signum, 1998); and *Das*

Österreichische Wahlverhalten, with F. Plasser and F. Sommer (Vienna: Signum, 2000).

Klaus von Beyme is Professor of Political Science at Heidelberg University. His research interests lie within the field of comparative politics in Western and Eastern Europe. Recent publications include *Transition to Democracy in Eastern Europe* (London: Macmillan, 1996); *The Legislator: Parliament as a Decision-Making Centre* (Aldershot: Ashgate, 1998); and *Parliamentary Democracy, 1789–1999* (London: Macmillan, 2000).

Preface

The year of 1989 was a turning point in world history and was commemorated in 1999 by a series of conferences held under the predictable title of 'Ten years after'. Many such conferences had a marked political character, including public figures as speakers, and they often embraced all the post-Communist countries undergoing transformation. They also had a public function in conveying the importance of what happened in 1989 and providing an opportunity to assess – and, to some extent, also publicise – the achievements of the intervening decade despite all the difficulties that had been encountered. Among these conferences was one held in Budapest at the Budapest University of Economic Sciences and Public Administration, 17–19 June 1999, entitled 'Ten years after: democratic transition and consolidation in East Central Europe'. This conference was primarily a conference of scholars, and it focused exclusively on the East-Central European region.

This regional focus made it more possible to concentrate systematically on the basic question of democratic consolidation. There are altogether twenty-seven post-Communist countries, and it is difficult to make generalisations about them all since they have been confronting different problems and are at different stages of establishing their democratic polities and market economies. But the East-Central European countries, unlike those in the Balkans or post-Soviet republics, have essentially completed the period of democratic transition and have embarked upon the path towards democratic consolidation. Accordingly, democratic consolidation has now become a central topic in academic analyses of East-Central Europe, thus offering a new opportunity for comparative studies in the field of democratisation.

The Budapest conference was the occasion for twenty-two presentations on both political and economic aspects of this transformation by leading comparative scholars and area specialists. This edited volume is based on revised versions of a selection of papers from the Budapest conference dealing with political regime change. Its main purpose is not only to analyse patterns over the last decade in East-Central Europe but to provide some indication of the main tendencies that are likely to mark the course of democratic consolidation in the new decade. In selecting papers for inclusion, we gave preference to a balance between comparative and thematic contributions on the one side and country case-studies on the other. With respect to the latter we have concentrated on the so-called Visegrad states, but others from the same region are discussed in the comparative and thematic chapters. Among the themes, special attention has been given to international aspects of post-Communist transformation as well as to developments at the level of society, in addition to institutions and the role of political parties. Both these dimensions were considered particularly important from the start of this change and this evaluation has guided our choice. The different levels of the consolidation process are reviewed in general terms in the first chapter, which also introduces, in its conclusion, the various chapters in this book.

Geoffrey Pridham
University of Bristol
Attila Ágh
Budapest University of Economics

1 *Geoffrey Pridham*

Comparative reflections on democratisation in East-Central Europe: a model of post-communist transformation?

Introduction: focusing on East-Central Europe

It is more than a decade since the fall of Communism opened the way for regime change in Central and Eastern Europe as well as, eventually, in new states deriving from the former Soviet Union. The process of system change has been on a scale unprecedented in Europe when compared with earlier transitions in postwar, and later Southern, Europe. Political regime change – the main focus of earlier transitions – has been accompanied by economic transformation as well as, in a large number of cases, state and nation building. Already, this decade has witnessed more advances in system change than could realistically be expected at the time 'the walls came tumbling down'.[1] Furthermore, so many more national cases of system change have occurred simultaneously in the 1990s, far outnumbering those on previous occasions, and thus inviting systematic cross-national comparison.

A decennial anniversary is an obvious moment for assessing a major historical event. One may look back and reassess the evolution, dynamics and tentative outcomes of regime change and draw conclusions about the prospects for democratic consolidation. In experiences of regime change in Europe, a decade, and sometimes even less time, has normally seen the accomplishment of democratic transition and already movement through early consolidation. It is recognised, however, that regime change in Central and Eastern Europe may take rather longer and that, in some cases at least, transition may extend in time; not to mention that eventually some new regimes may not comfortably fit into the category of Western-style liberal democracies.

But such an anniversary does not necessarily connect with major signposts in the trajectory of regime change. Stripped of its historical symbolism, 'Ten years after' may be seen prosaically as simply one point in time for a panoramic review of the outcome thus far. While sufficient time has elapsed for interim judgements, and individual national cases may reveal the direction of their regime changes, it is questionable whether the democratisation process can be complete even adopting minimalist definitions of democratic consolidation and focusing on the more promising national cases – which those in East-Central Europe tend to be in the post-Communist world.

It became somewhat commonplace to categorise and grade the different regional groupings of countries in systemic change during the 1990s. Those located in East-Central Europe have been considered the most likely success cases in moving without serious diversion through democratic consolidation, all the more so when compared with the more fragile new regimes in the Balkans and, certainly, the more complicated regime changes in Russia and other countries formerly in the USSR. This progress is officially acknowledged by the explicit international recognition whereby all first-stage entrants in the European Union's eastward enlargement have been invited from East-Central Europe.

Nevertheless, there was some diversity of official judgement when Brussels applied economic and political accession criteria, reminding us of cross-national variation in the course of regime change. Indeed, such variation is highly probable and is likely to increase the further these countries from East-Central Europe move forward into consolidation. This is because that lengthier process involves levels of engagement not always evident in the often short phase of transition, since society-level factors as well as issues concerning political–cultural modernisation are more active in consolidation. These tend to highlight national peculiarities rather more than the elite focus and constitutional tasks usually characteristic of transition. Moreover, the different styles of early transition across Central and Eastern Europe in 1989–91, not to mention significant dissimilarities between the Communist regimes that collapsed beforehand, already demonstrated that regime-change trajectories could commence from varied starting positions. This was true also of East-Central Europe, where for example forms of pre-transition liberalisation occurred in Hungary and Poland in contrast to the hard-line Communist regime in Czechoslovakia.

Problems of the three transformations have interacted during the process of change in the countries of Central and Eastern Europe. But cross-national variation is again to the fore, both in the extent to which nation-building tasks have been on the agenda and in the strategies adopted for economic transformation. An important concern therefore is how far these other transformations have affected political regime change. In truth, multiple transformation – which broadly distinguishes regime change in Central and Eastern Europe from earlier 'waves' of democratisation in Europe since 1945 – argues strongly for embracing maximalist conceptions of democratic consolidation. While transition to democracy may in a few impressive instances be accomplished more speedily than elsewhere, its consolidation as well as the completion of economic transformation and especially nation building require a longer time frame – one probably closer to a generation than a decade. These two or –

where applicable, three – processes have acted upon one another sufficiently, if not profoundly and sometimes critically, so that overall consolidation may be in sight only when this kind of dynamic has begun to settle down. For this reason, democratic consolidation in East-Central Europe could take rather longer than is commonly supposed.[2]

It is generally open to question whether democratic consolidation can be fully achieved in much less than two or three decades, given the central task of acquiring regime legitimation and, with it, adequate progress towards a 'remaking' of political culture. Whether, in this new age of the information revolution, these deeper developments do indeed accelerate is a phenomenon to be watched, given the Internet's potential for affecting attitudes through interactive discussion of public issues and ready exchange of information across frontiers.

There are, admittedly, different levels of the consolidation process. Conceivably, some will register real progress in the first decade of regime change, especially when developing in parallel rather than in succession to transition. Identifying levels of consolidation is analytically convenient as it facilitates interim assessments of change in East-Central Europe. Furthermore, the way in which and the degree to which different levels of consolidation interplay reflects on the dynamics of regime change, and possibly, too, the chances of positive or negative outcomes. How, therefore, does the region of East-Central Europe look in this respect? Can it in any way be regarded as a model of post-Communist transformation, given its progress ahead of other regions formerly part of the Communist world?

We look first at this region in comparative perspective, drawing in particular on lessons from democratisation studies. Attention turns then to the record of the 1990s, examining more closely patterns and problems in East-Central Europe and whether these indicate a distinctive grouping of countries undergoing transformation. And, finally, conclusions are drawn about outstanding issues, the chances for completing democratisation and general prospects of this region.

Comparative perspectives: do regime-change studies help?

East-Central Europe (ECE) could of course be presented as a model of post-Communist transformation by default. Relative to other regions of the former Communist world, it does as a whole present the most hopeful of such groupings relative to the countries of the Balkans and above all to those of the defunct Soviet Union whose prospects for international integration are much weaker (with the exception of the Baltic republics). This trend of cross-regional variation has been apparent for some time, notwithstanding cross-national differences within each region. And it may be justified on economic and societal, as well as on political grounds, not to mention that ECE countries are better networked internationally and, insofar as historical influences and geo-political factors count, they benefit distinctly more from those than they are inhibited by them in their democratisation courses. One might also add they have been rather less burdened by nation-building difficulties than countries in the other two regions.

Countries in the Balkans have, as a whole, more complex historical legacies and, in general, have faced more momentous tasks of socio-economic modernisation than those in ECE; while in the region of the former USSR there is still high instability but also greater uncertainty about regime-change outcomes including those in the most important instance, that of Russia. As one indicator of the present state of post-Communist transformation, there is a larger number of hybrid regimes – mixing authoritarian practices with formal democracy – in these two regions than in East-Central Europe, where the only obvious case was Croatia, until after Tudjman it re-embarked on democratisation and sought integration at the European level in a very decided way. Earlier doubts about Slovakia's commitment to liberal democracy were largely dispelled by Mečiar's defeat in the 1998 parliamentary election, although that country's subsequent policy redirection remains to be confirmed by the next election. Clearly, the 'Latin American' scenario sometimes voiced with respect to more pessimistic outcomes in the post-Communist world does not apply to ECE.[3] In fact, that region differs from Latin America in several important respects, such as having institutionalised competitive party systems and reasonably active civil societies, where it approximates more to previous European democratisations.

One may summarise the difference between East-Central Europe and the other regions as follows: confident assessments of positive rather than negative dynamics in democratisation have been much more possible with the former; and this remains the case. In order to understand this phenomenon better, one may turn to regime-change studies and put East-Central Europe into theoretical as well as comparative perspective.

While 'transition' and 'consolidation' are generally seen as distinguishable phases of the overall democratisation process, they should be distinguished qualitatively and not necessarily in terms of chronology. They are not strictly divisible as successive phases although invariably consolidation is completed after transition if not long afterwards, since consolidation usually amounts to a much longer part of the process. Conceivably, consolidation will start at one or more levels while transition is still in progress. For instance, civil society may emerge as viable soon after authoritarian collapse due to historical factors as well as developments under the predecessor regime, while elites are still tussling with transition tasks. In any case, democratic consolidation is viewed as a multi-dimensional or multi-level process where different dimensions may develop at variable paces – and, notionally, consolidation may be achieved here at different points of time.

Democratic transition is seen as commencing at the point when the previous non-democratic regime begins to collapse, leading to a situation when, with a new constitution in place, the democratic structures are settled formally and political elites are prone to start adjusting their behaviour accordingly. Signs, therefore, of elite consensus or the formation of elite consensus are a significant indication of transition being accomplished. Transition tasks involve above all negotiating the constitutional settlement and setting the rules of procedure for political competition as well as for dismantling authoritarian agencies and abolishing laws unsuitable for democratic life. These attributes are seen as characteristics of transition, but not as absolutes. For example, delayed constitutional settlements may – or may not – bear witness to difficult transitions. In reality, as a very crude average, transitions have taken around half a decade – in some cases, rather less; but in others, evidently longer.

Democratic consolidation is not only a much lengthier process but one with wider and usually deeper effects. It involves, in the first instance, the gradual removal of the remaining uncertainties surrounding transition (e.g. constitutional, elite behaviour, resolution of civil–military relations). The way is then opened for the institutionalisation of the new democracy, the internalisation of rules and procedures and the dissemination of democratic values. In reality, democratic consolidation may take minimally a decade and maximally two or more decades. However, much depends on the case in question, including, in particular, the weight of historical inheritances and problems. It is particularly on these grounds that one may expect post-Communist countries, including those in East-Central Europe, to be maximal cases. Expectations of when consolidation is complete have also been affected by definitional differences between those who emphasise formal democratic requirements and others who argue – as do the contributors to this book – that consolidation can only be really achieved when the criteria for substantive democracy are also satisfied.

This argument is undoubtedly supported by the multi-transformation process that has taken and is still taking place in post-Communist states. Just focusing on political regime change is not going to explain democratisation completely, let alone the overall transformation of which democratisation forms a central part.[4] 'Transformation' refers to a fairly deep or fundamental process of change. This is likely to characterise democratisation the more it develops, i.e. transformation is more likely to arise from regime consolidation; although it is implicit in transition, for if you change a political system there will probably be some rather significant consequences. It is also likely to be a process that is distinctly more long than short term.

In light of this, it would appear that countries in East-Central Europe have worked through their democratic transitions – with the possible exception of Slovakia, where a firm cross-party elite consensus on democratic procedures and rules still has not emerged. Croatia is, given Tudjman's dominance during the past decade, obviously in early transition, although this may turn out to require somewhat less time than elsewhere due to considerable internal as well as external pressures to 'catch up' on the rest of Europe. As a whole – Croatia apart, but including Slovakia – ECE also has moved well into consolidation in some respects but with some cross-national variation in progress apparent: Hungary and Poland may be said to be somewhat in advance of the other countries. But how much is such a conclusion supported by theories of regime change? There are basically four groups of theories, and these will be discussed in turn: the functionalist; the transnational; the genetic; and, the interactive.[5] These emphasise or concentrate respectively on socio-economic structural conditions, international influences and trends, political elite strategy and decisions, and lastly the dynamic relationship between the political and socio-economic structural conditions. The first and third have commonly been regarded as in succession the prominent schools of thinking in transition theory, while the other two describe different forms of approach to democrat-isation more broadly.

Functionalist theories

These have in the past stressed the requisite economic, social and cultural pre-conditions for democracy, and have drawn lessons from modernisation theory with its twin focal points of economic development and social mobilisation. Their guiding observation was that some societies were not as ready for democracy as others, leading to the view that the chances of achieving democ-racy depended crucially on the level of socio-economic development. Thus, modernisation was seen as producing value change which favoured democrat-isation. From this developed a political–cultural version of functionalist theory. According to this, some political cultures are conducive to the estab-lishment of democracy, while others are not, for certain mass orientations must be present before embarking on democracy.[6]

These theories were invariably criticised for being deterministic, for espous-ing a linear view of political development and for paying too much attention to material factors. One major reaction was to emphasise the crucial role played by political choice, but others have continued to find validity in the link between economic development and democracy.[7] Such a link has to some degree been rehabilitated in work on democratisation in the past few years, owing to the global shift to democracy in the 1990s. There are many more empirical cases and, it is claimed, the correlation between economic develop-ment and democracy has strengthened compared with the late 1950s, when Lipset wrote his original article.[8] In the case of ECE as well as Central and Eastern Europe generally, the combined transformation at both economic and political levels has obviously highlighted this link and forced transitologists to take more note of what Rustow called 'the deeper layer' of socio-economic conditions[9] and to consider interactions with political democratisation. While all this happened, the original claims of the modernisation theories have been scaled down from causality (economic development as a cause for the emergence of democracy) to environment (economic development as providing a milieu favourable to democracy). This modification connects with the view that economic development may not be a necessary prerequisite for democratic transition, but it correlates well with the sustainability of democracy, hence with the consolidation process.

Transnational theories

These offer a broad-sweep or semi-historical approach in common with functionalist theory, having developed from the latter towards a more complex array of factors, both internal and external. For instance, structural explanations based on socio-economic conditions have come to be seen as strengthened through diffusion tendencies.[10] These theories have the virtue of drawing attention in an imprecise way to the importance of international factors and their influence on domestic change.

Samuel Huntington has sought to explain the transition to democratic regimes in terms of a variety of factors – economic, social, cultural and external – and developed the thesis of 'waves' of democratisation.[11] He defines a 'wave' as 'a group of transitions from non-democratic to democratic regimes that occur within a specified period of time and that significantly outnumber transitions in the opposite direction during that period of time'.[12] A 'snowball' effect occurs as a function of transnational influences or interactions and of geographical proximity. Particularly important in the recent wave has been the expansion of global communications. References to the collapse of Communist regimes in Central and Eastern Europe as a 'media revolution' – because of the effects of transmitting news about the one case on another – is convincing, although obviously not to the exclusion of other factors. But, this approach lacks a viable framework for estimating cause and effect. What, for instance, are the exact conditions that allow diffusion to be successful?

Genetic theories

Such theories differ fairly radically from the functionalist and, to some extent also, the transnational theories, both in their actual focus on the process of regime change and emphasis on political choice and the actions of elites as well as in their belief in the intrinsic uncertainty of transition. It is the way transition pans out that determines regime outcomes. Structural preconditions, if treated, tend to be regarded primarily as background factors. The main contribution of genetic thinking to the democratisation literature is that it has usefully centred attention on the dynamics of the process, although – and this is not always admitted – its concern has been essentially the transition to, rather than the consolidation of, liberal democracy.

Various approaches have been developed including those of pactism, political crafting, path-dependent analysis and contingency. 'Pactism' makes a

number of assumptions, especially that it is the leaders of groups who determine strategic calculations and engage in pragmatic choices. Work on 'elite
settlements' and 'transition by transaction' are very much in the spirit of this
concept. Closely related, too, is the idea of 'political crafting' which draws
attention to the style and means whereby elite settlements are carried out, and
understandably it places an onus on the quality of leadership. Genetic theories have become increasingly criticised on several grounds – above all, for
being too elitist and over-voluntaristic, and for disconnecting political action
from socio-economic factors. In other words, there is a tendency to assume too
much freedom on the part of transition actors, notwithstanding the fluidity
and uncertainty of that process. There is a decided need to counter this by
placing the study of transition within a framework of structural–historical
constraints.[13] By focusing largely on the matter of political choice, genetic
thinking has been limited in its ability to grasp the interactions between the
different transformations.

Interactive theories

Similar to genetic theories in inspiration, these develop a broader and more
dynamic framework for the democratisation process as a whole and not just
simply the transition stage. In fact, interactive thinking has been present in
some form or other in regime theory from the beginning; but it did not
advance much until multiple transformation in the 1990s required that much
greater consideration is given to this kind of approach.

   Kirchheimer's theory of 'confining conditions and revolutionary breakthroughs' was in fact the first serious attempt to develop an interactive
approach to the problem of regime change.[14] In his 1965 article, he explained
'confining conditions' as 'the particular social and intellectual conditions
present at the births of these regimes' and sought to answer the question: to
what extent do circumstances attendant at the emergence of a new regime
determine its subsequent actions? What matters 'is the inter-relation between
socio-economic conditioning and the discretionary element left to the decision
of the regime'.[15]

   In short, the last decade confirms the relevance of modified functionalist
approaches because the relationship between democratisation and economic
transformation is vital to appreciating the prospects for democratic consolidation. The worst effects of economic restructuring are seemingly over,
although one is reminded of some cross-national variation, with Slovakia
somewhat behind the other Visegrad countries. Transnational theories help to
describe the events of 1989–90, although the long-term effects of globalisation on these countries have yet to be seen. Genetic approaches assist in understanding the management of early transition, especially in those cases like
Hungary and Poland where there was an element of pactism. Also, they
provide some insight into why the elitist though hardly consensual handling

of the tortuous division of Czechoslovakia remained peaceful. But, as a whole, genetic approaches do not sit easily with the significant mass-level or bottom–up pressures that helped to instigate and carry along transition in several of these countries. It is, however, the interactive approaches that provide the most effective means for understanding the dynamics of democratic consolidation.

Realising that the overall democratisation process is rather complex and multi-dimensional encourages a broader and more open-minded approach to regime-change theory. It is the changes in Central and Eastern Europe that have urged fresh thinking because of the compelling relationship between economic and political transformation in terms of relative priority but also of mutual interdependence. Interactive thinking offers the best scope for accommodating the growing diversity and complexity of such dynamics in regime change and, above all, for responding to these multiple transformations. Furthermore, interactive approaches have a dynamic potential that is particularly attractive as it allows us to bring into play historical determinants and explore how legacies from the past impact on the present as well as obtain a grasp on the interplay between top–down dictates and bottom–up pressures.

As noted above, democratisation in East-Central Europe has differed from earlier experience in Europe mainly through multiple transformation where political regime change is but part of this process. For instance, the question of nationalism in parts of East-Central Europe, and especially the Balkans, forces us to confront its importance in relation to democratisation as a potentially basic threat. Yet, so far, there has been little dialogue between democratisation studies and the interdisciplinary field of nationalism studies, which have paid some attention to this relationship.[16] But a decade of change in ECE has pointed up additional considerations for explaining post-Communist change.

Matters relating to culture raise linked and often contentious issues that make the regime change in ECE especially complex. The relationship between state and society involves the nature of conflict between the two, and to what, if any, extent the former is rooted in the latter. Furthermore, an aspect much underplayed in comparative work on democratisation is the societal. Popular mobilisation has been neglected in the democratisation literature, with its focus rather on elites and implicit if not explicit assumption that this could be dangerous to the fragile exercise of constructing elite agreements to keep the transition on course.[17] Nevertheless, civil society has emerged as significant in the transitions in East-Central Europe, drawing attention to an obvious, and in retrospect surprising, area of neglect in democratisation theory.[18] The role of the party-state as a means for the dominance of society in the Communist regimes furthermore underlines the importance in democratisation theory, to some degree also in empirical work, of the need to think through more carefully the implications and consequences of the prior-regime type. This is one dimension where the difference between authoritarian regimes in Southern

Europe and Latin America and Communist regimes in Central and Eastern Europe needs highlighting.

One principal difficulty facing the application of standing democratisation theory to East-Central Europe is, therefore, that several of its main assumptions or 'givens' have been called into question. Studies of democratisation in the former Communist states have continued to dispute the relevance of paradigms in the transitions literature, 'just as some economists have challenged the applicability of models drawn from non-Communist societies to the dilemmas of economic reform in post-Communist states'.[19] A frequent, indeed obvious, stricture of regime-change theory has been that it has essentially been posited on countries having a capitalist framework and that claims like 'no market – no democracy' are simply non-applicable.[20]

It is evident from this survey that future work on democratisation needs to devote more attention to certain broad concerns; and these enhance our ability to interpret developments in the post-Communist world including East-Central Europe. There is a need to

- take into account an historical dimension as not merely passive background but as an active component of regime change;
- embrace the democratisation process as a whole from pre-transition liberalisation under authoritarian regimes through transition and then consolidation out to regime outcome;
- embrace the multiple transformation (whether dual or triple) that is perhaps the greatest particular challenge; and,
- above all, accommodate different levels of this process while focusing on its dynamic qualities, including bottom–up as well as top–down pressures.

On this basis, one may construct a multilevel framework for exploring in interactive fashion the dynamics of democratic consolidation. The following levels or dimensions are pertinent to democratic consolidation and also encompass transition, given possible overlap between both processes. They are successive in that they suggest a gathering momentum of regime change leading through to its conclusion. The way these dimensions interconnect backwards as well as forwards allows us to combine, where necessary, elements of democratic transition and consolidation. Inevitably, some of them focus rather more on one or the other – the first ones, and especially those concerned with the formal transition and with actors and linkages, with transition; and later ones particularly with consolidation, such as economic transformation, civil society and stateness and national identity. However, effects both ways between transition and consolidation may be identified.

1 *historical determinants*: change and continuity factors, inheritances from the previous authoritarian regime as well as longer-term historical influences, opportunities for 'overcoming the past' and also difficulties confronting this; finally, patterns creating or reinforcing democratic traditions;

2 *authoritarian breakdown and collapse*: growing pressures on the previous regime, tendencies of its liberalisation and eventual authoritarian collapse

leading to the shift to democratisation, with implications for the nature of transition and prospects for consolidation;

3 *formal regime transition and institutional design*: the establishment and importance of institutions in buttressing new democracies and their introduction of the rule of law, with the likely positive or negative effects of rules and procedures on a new democracy's performance;

4 *the political dimension – actors and linkages*: political but also non-political elite groups, and relationships between them during regime change, their own adaptation to this change, and their accommodation and role in legitimating new democracies.

5 *economic transformation and democratisation (dual transformation)*: interactions between these two parallel developments, and how these contribute to or detract from regime-change dynamics, as well as how government decisions in the economic policy area affect new regime credibility and legitimacy;

6 *civil society, political culture and top–down/bottom–up dynamics in democratisation*: the impact of elite behaviour on society, influences from the latter on the former and the development of democratic values, and how change and problems here help or hinder democratic consolidation;

7 *stateness, national identity and democratisation (the third transformation)*: how stateness and its different forms interact with the democratisation process and therefore affects the prospects for democratic consolidation;

8 *international dimensions of regime change*: the importance of external influences, events and developments and their impact on the process of regime change, as well as the ways in which domestic developments encourage such change.

This multilevel framework will be applied in the next section to the countries of East-Central Europe and their first decade of systemic change in an effort to assess their progress and the problems encountered on the path towards democratic consolidation.

East-Central Europe in the 1990s: patterns and problems

One may start by asking the 'why not' question – why have the democratisations in this region not failed? This question was not unrealistic as of the early 1990s, despite post-1989 euphoria, not merely because of the high uncertainty often characteristic of early transitions to democracy. This question was justified in view of the sheer magnitude of the task ahead and, in particular, the prospect of economic dislocation impacting powerfully on the chances for these then-fragile new democracies to consolidate themselves. The economic recession in the early 1990s helped to dispel the euphoria and added to the speculation as to whether ECE countries would make it through transition to consolidation. Then, in neighbouring Yugoslavia systemic change took a violent turn, leading to sustained bloodshed. Rather by contrast, the one case in ECE of state disintegration – that of Czechsolavakia – occurred without this pattern of events – 'velvet' indeed, albeit acerbic at times, and not very consensual.

Democratisation in ECE has not failed for a combination of reasons which are difficult to isolate individually in terms of causal impact. Firstly, a sustained commitment to making the new democratic politics work has been evident at both elite and public levels to a degree not found in the other post-Communist regions, as shown consistently by opinion research trends (see chapter 5, this volume). This is despite the hard experience of economic change; hence, the more dire predictions, that such change would undermine these new democracies, have not been upheld.

Secondly, the severe economic recession through which these countries moved – and which deepened the 'valley effect' of their transitions – turned out to be more of a difficult phase rather than a semi-permanent structural condition inhibiting consolidation.

Moreover, and thirdly, their starting points for socio-economic modernisation were rather better than other post-Communist regions, in particular because the distorting effects of their Communist regimes were less strong than elsewhere.[21] Almost by contrast, the Communist regimes in the Balkans in many cases reinforced historical legacy problems relating to the dominance of the state over society and patrimonialist traditions deriving from Ottoman rule.[22]

Fourthly, civil society is present and to a limited degree vibrant in ECE countries, a factor which tends to mark them off from countries in the Balkans – notwithstanding differences between Romania and Bulgaria and, say, Albania – and also those from the former USSR, again with the exception of the Baltic states and occasional evidence of civil concerns, even in Russia.

Fifthly, state-and nation-building have been far more of a necessity in these two other regions than in ECE, although this cannot in fact be an absolute distinction. In ECE, the main cases have been the same Baltic states as well as Slovakia and Slovenia. The Czech Republic was able to resolve matters by benefiting from the former Czechoslovak institutional infrastructure in Prague and from the absence of strong minorities. Despite complications over large Russian minorities in the Baltic republics, and official antagonism towards the Hungarian minority in Slovakia in the mid-1990s, these problems were not comparable with the – at times – overwhelming difficulties of state development and ethnicity in many of the Balkan countries.

Finally, while the same European or international organisations have been available for the other regions, East-Central Europe has benefited more from close contact for a number of reasons. These include political approximation (greater ease in satisfying the demands of democratic conditionality, more transnational conformity of political parties with those in Western Europe) and more dynamic economic change; but – not to be underrated – is a sense of historical–cultural mission behind the 'return to Europe'. In the Balkans, by virtual contrast, motivation towards Europe has been more negatively inspired by a wish to 'escape from the Balkans', with the weight of its traditional and still current problems. Geographical proximity of ECE to the European heartland may be a factor too, but this should not be over-emphasised in the age of the new technology.

For these reasons, East-Central Europe comes across, by and large, as a distinctive region in the post-Communist age. Some of the reasons are conjunctural, and relative than absolute compared with other regions; but, also, some of them have historical roots within ECE countries. This goes for socio-economic modernisation and state and nation building and, to some extent, also for civil society and the international dimension. While ECE may be differentiated in comparison to other areas of Europe (less developed than Western Europe, but more advanced than the Balkans), it has enjoyed at the same time a sense of its own identity. This has been highlighted by the idea of 'Central Europe', or *Mitteleuropa*, which has a long historical lineage and has been revived as a point of discussion since the fall of Communism.[23]

The above points of distinction, while having a continuing relevance for future trends, are nevertheless somewhat *static* in their explanatory value as background factors. We turn now, therefore, to examine the different levels of democratic consolidation presented above. Applying these to the countries of ECE should provide us with two advantages. It should help us to assess more exactly how far ECE countries have moved down the road to achieving consolidation (while elaborating on various points above); but also this approach allows us a better means for appreciating the positive dynamics of regime change in the region. These levels will be discussed in order, before we consider what they indicate concerning the present state of democratisation in the region.[24]

Historical determinants

These may comprise both negative elements (the difficult weight of the past) and positive elements (usable democratic legacy), but it is how they are utilised and handled that matters in transition. In this sense, ECE countries have mixed patterns, with both democratic and authoritarian experiences and traditions prior to the Communist period. Their interwar democracies did not last due to a combination of varying domestic circumstances and adverse international trends, both economic and political. In some cases, these fragile democracies were replaced by authoritarian solutions before the end of this period. It was mainly in Czechoslovakia that positive recall of this experience was harnessed during the founding democratic years after 1989.

Rather stronger was the reaction to the Communist era, and here some cross-national variation was evident in the way those involved in the previous regime were dealt with, as over the issue of 'lustration'. But, as a whole, there was a

basic difference between ECE countries and those in the Balkans, where authoritarian practices developed either because hardly reconstructed ex-Communists
remained in or returned to power (as in Romania until 1996) or because new
rulers followed similar practices which did not conflict with long traditions in
their countries (as in Albania). By contrast, almost, former ruling parties
in ECE countries converted into centre–Left ones (the one exception being that
in the Czech Republic), and this undoubtedly helped these countries to 'overcome' the past. Not insignificant, too, was a marked (and revived) sense of
belonging by tradition by cultural Europe; and this, at the level of elite mentalities and educated circles, contributed towards ECE moving on to the future – one
which drew inspiration from the past. Of course, the international environment
was far more favourable for the chances of new democracies from 1989 than it
had been after 1918 and 1945. There was, for instance, no world war to recover
from, there were no potentially dangerous neighbours, the West was more willing
to help with reconstruction and, finally, the existence of the European Union
offered a form of integrated framework that was unprecedented.[25]

Authoritarian breakdown and collapse

Unlike the countries of the Balkans, those in ECE went through reform cycles
during the Communist period and these tended to end in strong protest
against Soviet rule, as occurred in Hungary in 1956, Czechoslovakia in 1968
and Poland in 1980–81. There developed a protracted crisis in Communist
regimes – specifically, and most openly, in Poland, which became a trend-setter
for eventual transition, while in Czechoslovakia, almost by contrast, the failed
push for reform in 1968 was followed by two decades of 'normalisation' or re-
imposed Stalinisation. All these developments nevertheless were significant in
that they pointed towards the possibility of systemic change at some undeter-
mined date, dependent on wider circumstances changing – which turned out
to come from Moscow's change of strategy under Gorbachev. In short, these
countries experienced, to varying degrees, forms of liberalisation, albeit brief
in several cases, and these facilitated the move to democratisation when it
came. Such experiences left an imprint on inchoate civil society (which itself
became a debating point with special reference to East-Central Europe in the
final decade of Communism); and they became a reference point for the new
democratic politics after 1989. Needless to say, the various transitions, when
they came, turned out to be markedly peaceful in ECE, with less violence (only
really briefly, with war in Slovenia, but more seriously so in Croatia) and distinctly less disruption than in other post-Communist regions.

Formal regime transition and institutional design

These countries were not exceptional in modifying former Communist constitutions, but there was a clearer movement here than in the Balkans and coun-

tries from the former Soviet Union towards executive accountability rather than the concentration of executive powers, evident in the preference for parliamentary over presidential government. In some cases, this preference prevailed after phases of uncertainty as in Poland under Walesa and Slovakia under Mečiar. In several Balkan countries, and notably in Russia, variations of presidential rule have persisted or dominated. In ECE, where hybrid regimes have been the exception (as in Croatia) rather than the rule, this cross-national option for parliamentarism has had various effects (including reinforcing a tendency for elitism in these new democracies); but, most importantly, it has opened the way for democratic institutionalisation. Institutional guarantees (constitutional provisions and restrictions on constitutional revision) and the establishment of judicial review illustrate this. But there remains an absence of legal culture, and there are problems of creating constitutional legitimacy, something which at this relatively early stage is still fairly dependent on functional requisites, namely government performance. While support in ECE countries is high for democratic institutions, there is low support or approval for their performance.[26] Nevertheless, on balance, the consequences of institutional design are rather more hopeful than otherwise as an indicator of progress towards democratic consolidation.

The political dimension – actors and linkages

Various developments have been surprisingly positive, given transition difficulties envisaged at the outset, although some of these have persisted. In particular, ECE countries have a healthy record of regular alternation in power, more than in the postwar and Southern European democratisations. This is usually taken as an indicator of a new democracy working, although in Poland's case it also reflected party system instability. Such alternation cannot be taken as steadfast evidence of regime consolidation as such, but the fact that it continues to be uncontested is a sign of progress. In ECE countries, this success owes something to the democratic conversion of former Communist regime parties, admittedly in part for opportunistic reasons, thus making it easier for them to be accepted as elected parties of government – in stark contrast, for instance, with postwar Italy where the Communist Party remained in opposition for decades. Even in Slovakia, where the Mečiar experiment leaned towards authoritarian practices, alternation has taken place and, most notably, in 1998 with Mečiar's defeat by a more united multi-party opposition. In Balkan countries, alternation has more commonly had systemic implications, as in Romania and Bulgaria during 1996–97 when ex-Communist forces were voted out of power. On other counts, ECE is less distinguished in not developing effective and cohesive oppositions and overcoming party system fragmentation, except in Hungary. Nevertheless, parties have come to dominate the new democratic politics, in line with Western European parliamentary patterns, while they have remained weak in articulating links with society.

This clear control by political elites is underlined by the relatively easy establishment of civilian control over the military.

Economic transformation and democratisation

Economic experience has not been easy in ECE countries, as indeed elsewhere in the post-Communist world, because it has been a matter of economic system change rather than merely adjustment and modernisation – which is, simply put, what occurred in previous European democratisations from 1945. But, by and large, ECE countries have recovered from the most difficult phase of this change by regaining the pre-1989 level of GDP from the mid-1990s, although in some cases (like Slovakia) unemployment has remained at a high level. This pattern is in some contrast with Balkan countries where economic renewal has been much more difficult and thus poses more of an obstacle to democratic consolidation. Economic transformation in ECE has not as such threatened the chances of new democracies in the region, because of underlying elite and mass commitment to democracy, although there is a case for arguing that it has perhaps slowed progress to democratic consolidation. But that is to be expected, for multiple transformation makes for more difficult – and, in reality, lengthier – democratisation, at least in comparison with Southern Europe two decades earlier. Having said that, it should be noted, there were marked cross-national variations in economic strategy across ECE. These ranged between shock therapy in Poland and to a degree also in Czechslovakia/the Czech Republic and, on the other hand, gradualism in Hungary and a more chequered pursuit of economic policy in Slovakia. It is difficult to draw firm conclusions as to whether the one strategy or the other facilitated democratic consolidation the more, but undoubtedly political factors intervened in all cases such as through the division in Czechoslovakia and short-term pressures in Poland's push for radical economic change. Interactions between economic transformation and democratisation are, of course, complex and are not exclusive of other influences, such as civil society developments and trends in public attitudes.

Civil society and democratisation

The record at this level is mixed, but this is not really surprising given the deeper effects of the Communist legacy and the fact that this level of democratisation simply takes time to develop. This is only qualified where pre-transition liberalisation allows for some early start (as in Hungary) or where a civil consciousness has remained despite the totalitarian experience and draws on previous democratic politics (as in the Czech Republic). Slovakia benefited less from association with the interwar democracy than did the Czech Republic, but then civil society certainly emerged in the course of the 1990s, stimulated by, among other things, aversion to Mečiar's authoritarian leanings. But, various problems remain and are easily identified: parties have had persistent difficulties in establishing meaningful links with the publics (in part because of the very elitism of transition in these countries); there is accordingly a low trust in parties and in public authorities, which is in part a consequence of Communism (significantly, this is less of a problem in Hungary, which underwent liberalisation under the former regime); and, again, associational development has been hampered by this previous regime legacy. It could, then, be said that changes at this level, albeit limited, are basically a hopeful sign for eventual consolidation; but that, in view of the remaining problems, achieving consolidation at this level is likely to take the best part of a generation as from 1989. There will almost certainly be some cross-national variation here. Countries with strong ethnic cleavages are likely to take longer, and this problem tends to demarcate ECE from the Balkans, where they are much more common. Meanwhile, one positive factor is that education levels in ECE are relatively high, precisely as a result of the priority given to education under the previous regimes. Ironically, this positive Communist legacy has made the spread of democratic values easier. Altogether, therefore, the prospects for fostering democratic traditions in these countries are fairly good in the long run.

Stateness, national identity and democratisation

There have been serious difficulties in bridging ethnic divides across Central and Eastern Europe, and even political parties have had problems in this respect. However, ECE has for historical–cultural reasons less of such a burden to face in its democratisation processes than is the case with the Balkans. The issue of the Russian minorities in the Baltic states has not been easy to resolve, but it has been facilitated by economic development while EU pressure on behalf of their status has been influential. In Slovakia, where difficulties did arise they were more for political than societal reasons because of intransigence towards the Hungarian minority on the part of the Mečiar Government. The different political atmosphere since the 1998 election has alleviated matters, not least because the Hungarian party has been included in the Coalition Government. There was, admittedly, the high tension between both parts of the former Czechoslovakia in the early 1990s, which for a time detracted from transition tasks, but it was resolved through the split in the country, which has probably been beneficial to democratisation in both new states, notwithstanding complications in the Slovak case. Thus, this phenomenon has represented no serious threat to democracy, although for a time in the earlier 1990s this was not clear. Issues of national identity have occasionally arisen, but there is now a noticeable tendency for this to be related to the European framework, suggesting that identity issues are less likely to overflow into nationalism. Another positive development yet to come could be that eventual economic prosperity will help to integrate ethnic minorities better into the societies in which they live. That would again suggest a difference from the Balkans, for the reason stated above.

International dimensions of regime change

Progress during the 1990s has been considerable for most ECE countries, as shown in the extent to which they have joined various European organisations and have been moving towards membership of the European Union. They are well ahead of Balkan countries, despite some differences in this respect between ECE countries, with Slovakia and two Baltic republics behind the others; while non-Baltic republics from the USSR have much less chance of going this far in integrating into Europe. The consequences of this development are quite self-evident, all the more as the EU is insistent in its demands for accession, and these include pressure but also support for democratisation and economic transformation. This progress is likely to continue into the near future – dependent, that is, on the EU itself preparing adequately for a major enlargement.

Finally, what lessons can be drawn regarding countries in East-Central Europe and cross-national aspects of their regime change? This multi-level framework tends to fill out the picture of these countries having passed through transition and being recognisably on the road towards democratic consolidation. Poland finally agreed on a full constitution in 1997, thus satisfying the main formal requirement of transition, although it had already in several respects progressed with consolidation tasks, not least because of its decisive economic strategy. As Hungary shows, a pre-transition liberalisation phase usually helps to accomplish democratisation more speedily. Czechoslovakia and its two successor states did not benefit from such a development, although their interwar democratic experience provided a reference point of which no other ECE country could boast. Slovakia may be said to remain on the cusp between completing transition and early consolidation – as there is a remaining problem of achieving firm elite consensus on liberal democracy – although at the level of civil society it has made substantial progress.

In conclusion, therefore, noteworthy progress has been made towards achieving democratic consolidation, especially in the establishment of a full range of democratic institutions, tenacity in working through economic transformation, limited but significant evolution in civil society and some success in containing ethnic problems. It may be suggested that another decade will see many, but perhaps not all, ECE countries near or at the end of the road to consolidation. Inevitably, however, this conclusion for the whole region has to be modified on two grounds – cross-national variation and, obviously, in relation to the different levels of consolidation. While there is not likely to be a dramatic time difference between regime-change outcomes in these countries, now that Slovakia has been catching up over the past two years, clearly Croatia has still a decade of Tudjman's rule to overcome, despite the best efforts of the new democratic government there to work through transition. On all levels there are still major tasks to be achieved during democratisation in ECE. These include obtaining constitutional legitimacy, improving elite–mass linkages, much sustained effort to complete economic transformation before its beneficial effects have a deeper impact on democratisation and a fuller evolution of civil society. Altogether, then, East-Central Europe is by and large at the halfway stage in the course of its consolidation process.

Conclusion: advancing towards democratic consolidation

Given this halfway stage, it might strictly be argued that no grouping of countries could be viewed as a model of transformation since the outcome is not yet fully known. We cannot be absolutely certain that all ECE countries will see democratisation through to a final and successful conclusion, as in a few cases uncertainties remain. Slovakia has in some respects begun to consolidate its new system, but there remains a lack of firm elite consensus between government and opposition over democratic procedures, which may be resolved at the next parliamentary election. In that event, the path to democratic consolidation there is likely to become less complicated. The future of the Baltic states remains uncertain only until their international allegiances finally allow them to move away from the Soviet past, but Russia's antipathy to their joining NATO is bound to inhibit developments in the coming few years. And, there is the underlying question of whether the EU will actually find the will and capacity to accommodate extensive enlargement to the east. Any reversal of present trends towards the integration of post-Communist countries may well have some negative repercussions on their own accomplishment of democratic consolidation.

However, it is generally recognised in the democratisation literature that it is the first decade which is vital in determining regime change outcomes; and, this is now past. Thereafter, there is no guarantee of success, but one may speak of a growing probability that new democracies will become consolidated. If this volume is therefore something of an interim assessment of democratic consolidation in East-Central Europe, what is its verdict?

The international environment has been particularly important in determining the course of regime change in this region; and this is the subject of the first two chapters. Robert Bideleux provides theoretical and historical perspectives on ECE regime change, and argues that the relationship between Europeanisation and democratisation is not as mutually reinforcing as is commonly supposed. This is because the European Union has increasingly become what is termed a supranational liberal legal order, even though it applies quite strict and specific criteria of democratic conditionality to applicant states. But it is above all wider international trends, with a changing role of the state in the economy and society due to globalisation and privatisation, which accounts for this quandary whereby democratic accountability becomes more difficult. The EU does, of course, strengthen the tendency towards top–down policy processes. However, it also provides an elaborate regulatory system that is beginning to deputise for democratic control; and it offers the best mechanism there is for resolving problems of inter-communal strife. The countries of ECE are those best placed to take advantage of this opportunity, given their fairly elaborate state of international networking and their will to succeed in 'returning to Europe'. This is a very definite plus to their prospects for democratic consolidation.

Geoffrey Pridham explores the diverse ways in which international influences interweave with domestic developments. It has often been repeated that these have been more impactive on post-Communist regime change than was the case, for instance, in Southern Europe; but this phenomenon has been little analysed in terms of specific impacts. His chapter attempts this by examining and applying standing concepts in the democratisation literature but also by providing a differentiated approach to estimating external factors and their importance. From this, the complexity of interactions between the external and the domestic is conveyed within the general dynamic of regime change. It is concluded, for instance, that external factors cannot simply be relegated to a secondary influence, for it is not always true that they remain a variable dependent on domestic developments. Given that the EU is by far the most important of the external actors, its own particular influences on democratisation in ECE are tested through a five-dimensional analysis. From this, it is evident that the EU's influence has varied somewhat according to the dimension in question; but that, overall, its influence has been quite pervasive in providing a stabilising framework for new democracies in the region.

Wolfgang Merkel approaches the question of civil society from the standpoint of its classical functions in political philosophy, from which he deduces its democratic functions in post-autocratic situations and identifies cycles of civil society during the course of democratisation. This helps in our understanding of a certain decline in societal mobilisation following transition. Applying civil society's democratic functions to East-Central Europe, he then examines how far it has helped or hindered democratic consolidation in the region. Since, in his view, civil society is the last level of new democracies to be consolidated, no final assessment is possible. However, as an interim judgement, it appears that the answer depends on the definition of democracy: an elitist definition would acclaim as positive the limited development of civil society so far. However, a participatory definition of democracy would highlight deficiencies of civil society and suggest that this remains something of a burden for democratisation.

Peter Ulram and Fritz Plasser then explore the progress towards democratic political cultures in post-Communist countries, using concepts of policy, process and system culture. His evidence reveals that after a decade democratic attitudes have taken hold among a sizeable majority in ECE states and that the trend is away from idealistic and material concepts of democracy towards realistic and formal ones. This democratic political culture has evolved despite the political, economic and social tensions of post-Communist transformation. Almost by way of contrast, the situation is quite different in Russia and the Ukraine, thus confirming our argument as to inter-regional differences within the post-Communist world. However, problems remain in the field of policy and process culture due to the persistent performance difficulties of these countries in ECE, but such problems have not reverberated on new system culture.

Klaus von Beyme examines in some detail the party systems in East-Central Europe within the wider context of Central and Eastern Europe. He concludes that most ECE states have developed forms of moderate pluralism and that political parties play a prominent role in ECE democracies rather in conformity with established democracies in Western Europe. However, parties in these post-Communist democracies are not so well articulated as co-ordinative networks in state and society, and they also suffer from low party identification and membership density. While suggesting a lack of depth in their contribution towards democratic consolidation, such difficulties are also apparent in many more mature democracies.

This prominence of parties in the operation of democratic institutions is emphasised by Attila Agh in his discussion of the case of Hungary. This is a clear instance of a parliamentary democracy, but one where the consensual institutional design has yet to be completed through resolving problems of asymmetrical and fragmented institution building. This is clearly a consolidation task awaiting Hungarian democracy. On the other hand, the party system has largely been consolidated with a somewhat unique continuity and stability in party actors over the past decade. There is nevertheless a contrast between Hungary's democratic character, which includes a strong commitment to democratic procedures among elites and masses, and what Agh calls a performance legitimacy – thus confirming Ulram's conclusion for ECE as a whole. As Agh points out, the EU is both a cause of this legitimacy problem (through its consistent pressure for adapting to eventual membership) but also a solution to it by providing an added support for consensualism.

Poland is one ECE state that is commonly regarded as well advanced towards consolidating its new democracy. Paul Lewis and Frances Millard explore this theme by focusing in particular on political parties and elections as providing the most important driving force behind regime change. This is because of their link with such factors as a sense of political community and consensus, as well as the embeddedness of the rule of law. Indeed, the authors find that parties in Poland have distinctive but overlapping ideologies, with a common commitment to democratic capitalism. While the historical cleavage between the former Communist establishment and anti-regime opposition has persisted through the new party system, political parties have nonetheless moved on from old conflicts and have embraced considerable changes over the past decade. Elites responded readily to the imperatives of democratisation. On the other hand, again in line with the findings of Ulram and Agh, party actors have been less effective as agents of political participation and in terms of their policy responsiveness.

Finally, Karen Henderson compares the Czech and Slovak Republics which, until 1993, were the parts of the state of Czechsolavkia. While tendencies thereafter suggested a pattern of divergence in their transition trajectories, by the late 1990s these had turned back towards convergence, Slovakia in several respects moving towards consolidation a year or two behind the Czech Republic. Both have satisfied institutional requirements, and the operation of their new systems has, apart from the Mečiar Government in Slovakia, proceeded according to conventional liberal democracy. While the two countries do not, contrary to international images, have different political cultures, their historical experiences vary somewhat, and their socio-political environments are also different. Altogether, the Czech Republic is at this stage a slightly more secure bet for achieving democratic consolidation than is Slovakia.

Altogether, the evidence of our different contributors tends to agree that ECE countries have essentially moved from transition into the consolidation process. Transition did nevertheless absorb the energies of these countries for the best part of the first decade after Communist rule ended; although in some respects there is already progress towards consolidation. A model of post-Communist transformation? The answer depends on the perspective taken. Notwithstanding cross-national differentiation within the region of East-Central Europe, there are sufficient similarities which serve to contain differences between the countries concerned. Given, too, the perhaps surprising advances made in these countries, it is possible to refer to them in general as a model of positive development towards establishing new democracies. This sense of ECE being at the forefront of post-Communist experience is supported by the reckoning that they are the likeliest future member states to join the EU from the east. But East-Central Europe cannot easily be considered a model for other post-Communist countries to emulate, for – as we have discovered – the differences between ECE and the countries of the Balkans, not to mention those that broke away from the Soviet Union, are too strong for this to happen without considerable problems and without a marked delay.

Notes

1 This is the title of a book on the subject: G. Stokes, *The Walls Came Tumbling Down: the Collapse of Communism in Eastern Europe* (Oxford University Press, New York, 1993).
2 Of the eight cases in question in East-Central Europe, five have been undergoing the third transformation of nation-building: Slovenia, Slovakia and the three Baltic states of Latvia, Lithuania and Estonia. So is Croatia but, unlike Slovenia, it has not fully extricated itself from Balkan entanglements, and has only recently begun to move away from the hybrid version of regime that it was under Tudjman. The three Baltic republics, while in East-Central Europe for geographical and historical

reasons, are in a sub-category because of their separate experience as part of the Soviet system for half a century; and, not to forget, that the former German Democratic Republic is clearly a case apart because of its merger with the Federal Republic. Nevertheless, there are strong signs that the democratisation of its political culture will take a long time before finally overcoming the 'Wall in the Head'.

3 The 'Latin American' scenario may be described as one of recurrent socioeconomic crisis and dire poverty inhibiting democratic consolidation, together with the region in question being part of the capitalist periphery rather than of the capitalist core. Economic dependence on external actors as well as problems of corrupted privatisation do, however, invite parallels with ECE countries. But Latin America has faced a continuing threat to new democracies from military intervention, which does not apply to ECE.

4 There is some similarity here with the conventional interpretation of how political systems generally operate. Easton, for instance, sees this as involving three hierarchical levels of decision making, as follows: nation building, or decisions on identity, citizenship and the territorial as well as social and cultural boundaries of the nation state (who 'we' are, relating to passion); constitution making, or decisions on rules, procedures and rights (relating to reason); and the politics of allocation and distribution, or decisions (within these parameters) on 'who gets what, when and how' (relating to interest). See D. Easton, *A Systems Analysis of Political Life* (Wiley, New York, 1965), chapters 10–13. This framework is used by Offe in his discussion of the triple transformation: see C. Offe, *Varieties of Transition* (Cambridge, Policy Press, 1996), pp. 32–5.

5 For a more detailed discussion of these groups of theories, see G. Pridham, *The Dynamics of Democratization: a Comparative Approach* (Continuum, London, 2000), chapter 1.

6 G. Almond and S. Verba, *The Civic Culture: Political Attitudes and Democracy in Five Nations* (Princeton University Press, Princeton, NJ: 1963).

7 For example, see K. Bollen, 'Political democracy and the timing of development', *American Sociological Review*, 1979, pp. 572–87; E. Muller, 'Democracy, economic development and income inequality', *American Sociological Review*, 1988, pp. 50–68; L. Diamond, 'Economic development and democracy reconsidered', *American Behavioral Scientist*, March/June 1992, pp. 450–99. See also S. Lipset, 'The social requisites of democracy revisited', *American Sociological Review*, February 1994, pp. 1–22.

8 See S. Lipset, S. Kyoung-Ryung and J. Torres, 'A comparative analysis of the social requisites of democracy', *International Social Science Journal*, 1993, pp. 155–75. Cf. also D. Rueschemeyer, E. Stephens and J. Stephens, *Capitalist Development and Democracy* (University of Chicago Press, Chicago, 1992). Lipset's original article was 'Some social requisites of democracy: economic development and political legitimacy', *American Political Science Review*, March 1959, pp. 69–105.

9 D. Rustow, 'Transitions to democracy: toward a dynamic model', *Comparative Politics*, April 1970, p. 343.

10 See e.g. J. Londregan and K. Poole, 'Does high income promote democracy?', *World Politics* 1, 1996, pp. 1–30, for the argument that the democratising effect of growing incomes is significantly increased by external influences.

11 S. Huntington, *The Third Wave: Democratisation in the Late Twentieth Century* (University of Oklahoma Press, Norman, 1991).

12 *Ibid.*, p. 15.
13 Cf. T. Karl and P. Schmitter, 'Modes of transition in Latin America, Southern and Eastern Europe', *International Social Science Journal*, 1991, p. 271.
14 O. Kirchheimer, 'Confining conditions and revolutionary breakthroughs', *American Political Science Review*, 1965, pp. 964–74.
15 *Ibid.*, pp. 964, 965.
16 P. Kopecký and C. Mudde, 'What has Eastern Europe taught us about the democratisation literature (and vice versa)?', *European Journal of Political Research* 37:4, 2000, p. 529.
17 See N. Bermeo, 'Myths of moderation: confrontation and conflict during democratic transitions', *Comparative Politics*, April 1997, pp. 305–22.
18 See G. Ekiert, 'Democratisation processes in East Central Europe: a theoretical reconsideration', *British Journal of Political Science* 21, 1991, pp. 298–300.
19 B. Parrott, 'Perspectives on postcommunist democratisation', in K. Dawisha and B. Parrott (eds), *The Consolidation of Democracy in East-Central Europe* (Cambridge University Press, Cambridge, 1997), p. 2.
20 See review of theories on transition and their bearing on Eastern Europe in D. McSweeney and C. Tempest, 'The political science of democratic transition in Eastern Europe', *Political Studies*, September 1993, pp. 408–19. See also Kopecký and Mudde, 'What has Eastern Europe taught us about the democratisation literature?', pp. 517–39.
21 This is supported by the evidence provided on twenty post-Communist countries in Ole Norgaard, *Economic Institutions and Democratic Reform: the Comparative Analysis of Post-Communist Countries* (Edward Elgar, Cheltenham, 2000).
22 On these problems in the Balkans, see G. Pridham, 'Democratization in the Balkan countries: from theory to practice', chapter 1 in G. Pridham and T. Gallagher (eds), *Experimenting with Democracy: Regime Change in the Balkans* (Routledge, London, 2000), esp. pp. 9–18.
23 See A. Ágh, *The Politics of Central Europe* (Sage, London, 1998), pp. 4–5; and A. Hyde-Price, *The International Politics of East Central Europe* (Manchester University Press, Manchester, 1996), pp. 51–2.
24 The following discussion of the different levels, where no acknowledgement is made, draws on the results for East-Central Europe in Pridham, *The Dynamics of Democratization* (2000).
25 R. Bideleux and I. Jeffries, *A History of Eastern Europe: Crisis and Change* (Routledge, London, 1998), p. 606.
26 See e.g. D. Fuchs and E. Roller, 'Cultural conditions of transition to liberal democracy in Central and Eastern Europe', in S. Barnes and J. Simon (eds), *The Postcommunist Citizen* (Erasmus Foundation and Hungarian Academy of Sciences, Budapest, 1998), esp. p. 63.

'Europeanisation' and the limits to democratisation in East-Central Europe

Introduction

The burgeoning literature on transitions to democracy has been described as 'the outstanding recent achievement of comparative political research'.[1] However, while this literature has had considerable heuristic value and has yielded many important findings and insights, some of its implicit assumptions are questionable. This chapter primarily offers a critique of a few of the most basic (and taken for granted) assumptions informing the growing literature on democratic transition and consolidation in East-Central Europe. Many theorists of democratic transition and consolidation, as well as some of the current East-Central and South-East European candidates for membership of the EU, seem to be working to outmoded 'nationally contained' models or specifications of liberal democracy which no longer apply within the EU. Moreover, it is widely assumed that the steadily advancing 'Europeanisation' of the East-Central European countries is marching hand-in-hand with the consolidation of the transition to liberal democracy in this region, or even that these are two sides of the same coin, and that further democratisation is therefore one of the essential requirements and corollaries of EU membership for the current 'eastern' candidates for EU membership. This chapter contends that 'Europeanisation' and 'democratisation' are not as mutually reinforcing as is generally supposed. In important respects these tendencies are pulling in different directions, and this has significant implications for the ways in which transitions to – and consolidations of – liberal democracy should be conceptualised. Taken together, the percolation of power from the legislative to the executive branches of government in advanced capitalist democracies, the seemingly inexorable erosion of the capacity of states to determine what occurs or does not occur within their formal spheres of territorial jurisdiction, and what Klaus von Beyme has described as 'the colonisation of the state and society by political parties',[2] are steadily restricting the scope for democratic control, scrutiny and accountability. Therefore, the terms 'democratic transition' and 'democratic consolidation' are to a large extent misnomers for the processes which are actually taking place. The sooner and the more fully this is understood and acknowledged by European elites and public opinion, the smaller and the less dangerous will be the eventual popular disillusionment with the current rhetoric of democratisation, and the more smoothly and securely the eastward enlargement of the European Union and the restructuring of east-central and South-East European countries will proceed.

One of the great paradoxes of the current epoch is the fact that the outward forms of liberal democracy are spreading more widely than ever before, and yet liberal democracy is everywhere becoming more and more compromised, eroded and vulnerable – not only in the relatively fragile 'new democracies' of East-Central and South-Eastern Europe, the former Soviet republics, Latin America, and parts of Africa and Asia (where democracy is often more illiberal than liberal), but even in its longstanding heartlands in Western Europe, North America and Australasia. The democratic–capitalist triumphalism of the West since the collapse of Europe's Communist regimes at the end of the 1980s has encouraged massive (and some would say dangerous) complacency concerning the health and resilience of liberal democracy, not least within its traditional bastions.

The growing emasculation of the specifically *democratic* components of liberal democracy in Western Europe would provide stronger grounds for alarm were it not for the fact that it has been accompanied by countervailing steps to strengthen and extend the essentially *liberal* components – namely limited government, the rule of law, and the autonomy of the legal order (especially supranational EU law). The latter provide strengthened and extended legal and constitutional safeguards of fundamental rights and liberties, which are in large measure having to compensate or even substitute for the seemingly inexorable erosion of democracy as such in advanced capitalist countries. Inasmuch as the East-Central European countries are striving to become ever more deeply enveloped in the laws, rules, structures, procedures and norms of an expanding European Union (not least because they currently have 'nowhere else to go'), it would be more accurate and more helpful to characterise the process which is having to take place in East-Central Europe in terms of the strengthening and extension of limited government, the rule of law, and legal safeguards of fundamental rights and liberties, rather than in terms of 'democratic transition' and 'democratic consolidation'. In other words, the trajectory which they are having to follow might be more aptly described as *liberalisation* rather than *democratisation*, because the democratisation underway in East-Central Europe is likely to be very circumscribed.

Of course, the scope for democratic control and accountability in East-Central Europe initially increased as a result of the collapse and/or dismantling of the Communist regimes and Soviet domination. Nevertheless, as these former Communist countries become more integrated into the European Union, they will find themselves increasingly regulated and 'boxed in' by rules, regulations, laws, decisions, procedures and policies which are formulated in Brussels (as the headquarters of the EU) and in Luxembourg (as the seat of the EC Court of Justice[3]), rather than domestically and democratically. This occurs partly as a result of the important supranational functions and prerogatives of the EU Commission and the Court of Justice, but also because the Council of Ministers and European Councils operate as a 'cartel of governments', further enhancing the power and influence of the executive branches of the state at the expense of elected national parliaments.

> Community and Union governance pervert the balance between executive and legislative organs of government . . . The member state executive branch, government ministers, are reconstituted in the Community as the principal legislative organ with . . . an ever-widening jurisdiction over increasing areas of public policy. The volume, complexity and timing of the Community decisional process makes national parliamentary control . . . more an illusion than a reality.[4]

Indeed, national elites are 'in an especially strong position to shift issues around from one arena to another, particularly in order to shield an issue from public scrutiny'.[5]

Since the 1980s, moreover, the nature of liberal democracy has been transformed by the changing role of the state in the economy and in society. Extensive privatisation and economic liberalisation, together with the proliferation of semi-autonomous regulatory bodies, have changed the nature of governance in ways that have further reduced the controlling and monitoring functions and capabilities of democratically elected institutions, even though state expenditure has not decreased significantly as a percentage of GDP in most of the advanced capitalist economies and societies. National, regional and local government can still play crucially important roles, but the principal function of government at all levels is now essentially a *reactive* one – to *position* countries, regions and localities to maximum advantage in the global market economy, with the main emphasis falling on micro-economic supply-side measures to enhance the constituent community's competiveness, rather than to endeavour *proactively* to manage and restructure economic activity to meet or conform to preordained macro-economic targets.[6] States can still facilitate the creation of conditions favourable to business, but they can no longer control these conditions as much as they did from the First World War until the 1970s (an era dominated by various forms of neo-mercantilism, corporatism and etatism). As a consequence, there have been reductions not only of national sovereignty but even of the degrees of democratic control and accountability which are possible at this level. At the same time, the regulatory functions and autonomy of the executive branches of government have greatly expanded[7] and executives have also come to exercise greatly increased control over national legislatures, with the result that parliaments have become less and less effective as restraints on and as counterweights to the power of the executive.[8] National parliaments are increasingly marginal to the processes of government, and only a small fraction of the huge volume of government business is scrutinised by elected parliaments in most Western liberal democracies. Indeed, 'Democracy does not exist in practice. At best we have what the ancients would have called elective oligarchies.'[9]

If the East-Central European states wish to be fully 'Europeanised' or fully accepted and assimilated into the European Union and its prevailing political and economic precepts (and this seems to be their only serious option at present), it is inherently implausible to assume that they can miraculously escape or be shielded against the forces and practices which have already greatly limited the scope for democracy – at the national even more than at the supranational level – within the European Union. This is what makes it most inappropriate to use the terms 'democratisation' and 'democratic consolidation' to characterise the changes that are currently taking place in East-Central Europe.

Paradoxically, it remains the case that only liberal democracies are considered eligible for membership of the European Union. The admission criteria laid down by the European Council in Copenhagen in June 1993 stipulated that the candidate country will have had to achieve

> stability of institutions guaranteeing democracy, rule of law, human rights and respect for and protection of minorities, the existence of a functioning market economy as well as the capacity to cope with competitive pressure and market forces within the Union. Membership presupposes the candidate's ability to take on the obligations of membership including adherence to the aims of political, economic and monetary union.[10]

The established members of the EU do not see these stipulations as merely a matter of choice or preference. They are rightly regarded as indispensable to the long-term viability of the EU, which ultimately rests upon the fairly uniform acceptance and application of a common system of rules, laws, policies and legally binding treaty provisions. These requirements have indeed provided powerful leverage and incentives for the political leaders of the applicant countries in East-Central Europe to consolidate the transitions to liberal democracy initiated since the end of Communist rule. European states which do not uphold liberal democracy, basic individual rights and liberties, market principles and the rule of law in effect *exclude themselves* from potential membership of the EU, because of their resulting incapacity to discharge in full its essential requirements.

Nevertheless, it ought to be regarded as very odd for Westerners to judge the 'political performance' of Europe's post-Communist states and their future suitability for EU membership primarily by the criterion of how much progress they have made towards a Utopian model of representative liberal democracy in which it is presumed that a freely elected 'national' parliament has the sovereign authority to approve, reject or rescind all the major laws and to sanction and control most of what is done or not done within its 'national' territorial jurisdiction, when in fact the current members of the EU are moving ever further from such a model. Realistic assessments of 'Europeanisation' and 'democratisation' within East-Central Europe have to determine what kinds of polity the EU and its current member states represent. One cannot assess the likely implications and requirements of 'Europeanisation' and eventual EU membership for the candidate countries and the criteria by which they should be judged without also having coherent perceptions of the directions in which the EU and its current members are moving. The view put forward here and elsewhere[11] is that the EU is in essence a supranational liberal legal order rather than a democratic project or democratic polity. It is characterised by *the rule of law*, by *limited (and increasingly regulatory) governance and* by *the strongly consensual mutual accommodation of elites*, rather than formal majoritarian democracy, democratic accountability and mobilisation of popular support. Indeed, most EU negotiations continue for however long it takes to reach outcomes with which all the parties to these negotiations feel they can live. EU methods and procedures are slow and cumbersome, but their outcomes may be more durable than those imposed by temporary majorities on dissenting or discontented minorities.

During the 1950s and 1960s, admittedly, it was still possible for the creation of the European Coal and Steel Community and the European Economic Community to contribute strongly to the extension and consolidation of democracy in post-Fascist Italy, post-Vichy France and post-Nazi Germany, just as in the 1970s and 1980s it was still possible for the European Community to provide powerful leverage and incentives for democratic transitions and consolidations in Greece, Portugal and Spain.[12] Up to the mid-1980s, the EC remained essentially an inter-governmental organisation which retained considerable scope for national autonomy and sovereignty and hence for a modicum of parliamentary scrutiny and control of national governments and the major inter-governmental association of states over which governments still exercised paramount control, as emphasised by the major inter-governmental interpretations of the emergence of the EC.[13] Admittedly, up to the mid-1980s there was also a supranational dynamic of integration running in parallel with the inter-governmental one, but the former remained firmly subordinate to the latter and the governments of the member states remained firmly in the driving seat.

Now, however, Europe is faced with a very different situation – one on which inter-governmentalist interpretations of West European integration have much less purchase. During the 1980s the supranational dynamic of integration crossed a threshold which allowed it to escape inter-governmental control and take on a life of its own. Since then, Western Europe's 'sorcerers apprentices' have in effect lost control of their miraculous 'broom'. The combined effects of the Single European Act (1986), the Single Market programme, the dynamism of the EU Commission under Jaques Delors (1985–94), the growing importance of 'the social dimensions' of European integration, the major increases in the EU Structural Funds (1988, 1993), the provisions of the Treaty on European Union (1992), the project of Economic and Monetary Union, and (above all) the somewhat earlier accomplishments of the EC Court of Justice in 'constitutionalising' the EC treaties have been to extend, proliferate and strengthen the supranational functions, powers and prerogatives of the European Union,[14] at the very same time that the combined effects of globalisation, privatisation and economic liberalisation have been steadily diminishing the capacity of states and, especially, of national parliaments to control whatever occurs or does not occur within their own formal jurisdictions.

As a consequence, most Europhobes and many democrats have tended to decry the European Union's so-called 'democratic deficit' and to make the EU a convenient scapegoat for the major erosions of democracy which have undoubtedly taken place, but they have largely been barking up the wrong tree. Although the EU has itself contributed to the constriction of democracy in some ways, for example by making it easier for national governments to evade domestic mechanisms of democratic accountability,[15] its major and absolutely invaluable role has been to *mitigate* the large reductions in the scope for democracy (which have come about mainly for reasons that have *nothing* to do with the European Union as such). It has done this primarily by constructing a unique supranational legal order which is capable of maintaining a modicum of European control over what happens in Europe and of entrenching and protecting fundamental rights and liberties.[16] This has major implications for the manner in which its member states are governed and for the ways in which liberal democracy is conceived, as is further explained in the final two main sections (pp. 37–49).

This chapter has no quarrel with the oft-repeated claims that the East-Central European states have made remarkable headway with so-called 'democratic consolidation' since the early 1990s. They deserve all the credit for these achievements, since they have actually received precious little assistance from the West. My prime concerns here are to emphasise the changing and increasingly circumscribed nature of the liberal democracy which is being consolidated as these countries move closer to membership of the EU, and to highlight ways in which eastward extension of the European Union's supranational legal order could help to defuse ethnic and religious minority problems and inter-communal tensions or conflicts.

Rival criteria of 'Europeanisation'

The term 'Europeanisation' has been used in various different ways. The most colloquial usage refers to the assimilation of Western values, attitudes, ways of doing things and lifestyles. However, this usage is slightly misleading, in that much of what is being referred to as 'Europeanisation' could be more accurately described as 'Westernisation', 'Americanisation' or even 'globalisation', since the former Communist states are being (re)integrated into a capitalist, media and communications world system in which American-led practices and orientations currently predominate.

Nevertheless, the term 'Europeanisation' also has more specific meanings and connotations in the east-central and South-East European contexts. At its simplest it is a synonym for the so-called 'return to Europe', referring to the need to re-absorb a dozen or more former Communist states into the mainstream of European politics and development after forty years of 'de-Europeanisation' by Marxist–Leninist dictatorships. In this perspective, the challenge of Europeanisation in East-Central Europe has many facets, including the democratisation of political institutions in post-Communist states, the privatisation and marketisation of post-Communist economies, and the creation of a new civic political culture.[17] According to Danica Fink-Hafner, it is primarily 'a matter of performing specific tasks according to EU standards for particular products, services or even ways of managing particular domains of public life'.[18]

The breadth and depth of the systems of regulation engendered by the Single Market programme, the Single European Act and the Treaties of Maastricht and Amsterdam, together with the concurrent extensions of the policy remit of the EU, have also resulted in a pervasive 'Europeanisation' of most spheres of public policy and policy making, which have increasingly visible 'European' dimensions and/or inputs. The establishment of EU regulatory frameworks has induced widespread restructuring of political and economic contexts, galvanising hitherto passive political and economic actors into new informal networks and ties between the grassroots and Brussels, often channelled through but increasingly by-passing the central institutions of the nation-state.[19] Analogous changes can be expected to take place in the East-Central European states as they move closer to full membership of the EU.

It is useful to distinguish between at least four aspects of 'Europeanisation':

- the restoration of the region's European traditions and institutions 'after the decades of de-Europeanization';
- 'the concrete process of joining the EC, and the emergence of structural compatibility with EC institutions and its system of legislation–jurisdiction';
- the promotion of East-Central European integration (e.g. through the Central European Free Trade Area, alias CEFTA) as part of the larger pan-European integration process; and
- 'Europeanization as the fundamental transformation of civil society, political culture and patterns of behaviour – 'i.e. the establishment of democratic traditions' in the large masses of the ECE population'.

Attila Ágh recognises that 'Europeanisation' and 'democratisation' have been 'closely interwoven', but also that each has its 'own special character and logic'.[20] 'Europeanization' entails not only the eventual incorporation of many thousands of pages of EU legislation and regulations into East-Central European legal systems, but a gradual convergence towards West European parliamentary practices, party systems, political and commercial lobbying networks, the slow and costly upgrading of physical and telecommunications infrastructures and environmental regulations to West European standards, the gradual adoption of West European health, safety and product standards, the promotion of EU-compatible financial and taxation systems, and the organisation, representation and consultation of entrepreneurs/employers and trade unions (the 'social partners') and interest groups, and the linking of these to their West European counterparts.[21]

Progress towards democratic consolidation in East-Central Europe

By most of the criteria currently in use, Poland, Hungary, the Czech Republic, Slovakia, Slovenia and the Baltic states have already travelled a long way down the difficult road to 'consolidated democracy'. Their elections have become as free and fair as those in Western European states. Their newspapers have remained free as well. Electoral registers have been well maintained and election turnouts have remained fairly high (partly a legacy of the previous Communist regimes, which took voting very seriously despite the lack of real electoral choice!). The resolving of political and economic choices through the free ballot has become a settled habit. All the major political parties accept the rules of the democratic game. Elections focus on policy choices and personalities, as in the West, rather than on choice of regime. Unlike certain Balkan states, the East-Central European states now exist within settled boundaries which are not seriously in dispute, thus minimising the scope for de-stabilising irredentism. With the partial exceptions of Estonia, Latvia and Slovakia, each of the new democracies has a quite clearly defined *demos* whose members are accorded full rights of 'belonging' and political participation.

Conversely, the political performance and prospects of states such as Serbia, Croatia, Albania, Romania and Bulgaria are being impaired not so much by a lack of tolerably free and fair elections (they actually have executives and legislatures which have been duly elected under universal suffrage), as by insufficient respect for minorities and for the rule of law, by inadequate constraints on the power of the state, by the weakness or shallow roots of liberal sentiment, and by the contested nature and territorial extent of these states. What has placed countries such as Hungary, the Czech Republic and Poland at the front of the queue for membership of the EU is not a greater commitment to free and fair elections, but stronger commitment to the rule of law, greater respect for the liberties of individuals, stronger constraints on the power of the state (including independent judicial review), and deeper understanding of the requirements of liberal governance. These same qualities also explain the greater successes of their transitions to market economies.

As a consequence, the EU Commission recommended in July 1997 that it would be safe to open membership negotiations with Hungary, Poland, the Czech Republic and Slovenia (along with Cyprus and Estonia) in 1998, and this was approved by the European Council on 13 December 1997. However, in its July 1997 recommendations the Commission deemed that 'Slovakia does not fulfil in a satisfying manner the political conditions set by the European Council in Copenhagen because of the instability of Slovakia's institutions, their lack of rootedness in political life and the shortcomings in the functioning of democracy'. Nevertheless, after the rejection of Vladimir Mečiar and his authoritarian nationalist proclivities in the elections of September 1998, Slovakia took large strides towards democratic consolidation and economic liberalisation. In October 1999 the EU Commission complimented Slovakia on its rapid political and economic progress, and recommended that it be allowed to commence EU membership negotiations in 2000, and this recommendation was approved by the European Council on 10 December 1999.

This is not to suggest that there are no longer any problems. On the contrary, the Czech Republic has been repeatedly rocked by economic difficulties and financial scandals with roots in the half-hearted ways in which privatisation and economic liberalisation were carried out during the first half of the 1990s. In October 1999 the EU Commission criticised the Czech Republic for its faltering economic progress. There have been nasty reminders of the heritage of intolerant Catholic nationalism in Poland and Hungary, with occasional hints of latent antisemitism. Relations between Hungarians and Slovaks have remained tense in Slovakia, despite the signing of an agreement between Hungary and Slovakia in March 1995 which pledged respect for their minorities and the inviolability of the existing borders between them. Gypsies have remained *persona non grata*, especially in the Czech Republic, and this too has elicited criticism from the EU. And a recent survey of East-Central European elites refers to rampant and debilitating corruption in post-Communist Hungary, Slovakia, the Czech Republic and Croatia.[22]

Nevertheless, the mid-1990s witnessed the start of a 'virtuous circle between socio-economic and political consolidation, with the emergence of a new professional elite in the ECE countries having a firm commitment to Europeanization'. Civil society, which was partially demobilised by a combination of severe economic recession and a conservative–nationalist backlash during the early 1990s, has revived somewhat since then. Moreover, the excessively fragmented party-systems which emerged in the early 1990s (other than in Hungary) have given way to more stable, consolidated and 'Europeanised' party systems geared to interest representation and aggregation, as most of the numerous small parties have either merged or gone to the wall since the

Table 1   *1998 Satisfaction ratings for the current regime among East-Central and South-East European EU membership candidates*

	Regime satisfaction ratings (% approving)		Corruption in 1998 relative to 1980s (% of replies)		
	Current	*Communist*	*Higher*	*Same*	*Lower*
Poland	66	30	51	37	12
Hungary	53	58	77	20	3
Czech Republic	56	31	70	24	5
Slovakia	50	46	81	15	4
Slovenia	51	42	59	28	14
Bulgaria	58	43	71	26	3
Romania	56	33	84	13	3
Russia	36	72	73	23	4
Belarus	48	60	70	25	5
Ukraine	22	82	87	11	2

Source: R. Rose, 'Two cheers for democracy', *The World Today* 54: 10 (1998), pp. 253–5.

mid-1990s.[23] Poland led the way to economic recovery, being the first post-Communist state to move into positive growth of GDP (in 1992) and the first to regain its 1989 levels of output (in 1996). In per capita terms, Hungary, Slovenia, the Czech Republic and Poland have been most successful at attracting foreign direct investment.

In 1998, according to Eurobarometer opinion survey evidence presented by Richard Rose, more people were more satisfied with the current regime than with its Communist predecessor in each of the east-central and South-East European candidates for EU membership except Hungary, whose relatively mild Communist regime (under János Kádár) still enjoyed a high approval rating. The reverse was the case in Russia, Belarus and Ukraine. However, most people in all nine countries stated that their living standards had fallen and that corruption had increased since 1989 (see Table 1).

The limits to democratisation in East-Central Europe

Juan Linz and Alfred Stepan have warned that (as in Latin America) the dichotomous 'civil society versus the state' discourse constructed in East-Central Europe has been inimical to the consolidation of liberal democracy. The leading players in civil society should endeavour to achieve complementarity with, rather than antagonism towards, the post-Communist and political parties. Unfortunately, the experience of Communist party states has bequeathed popular legacies of deep suspicion and sullen mistrust towards political parties and towards the state as an institution which are not easy to overcome.[24] Moreover, prominent figures in Polish and Czechoslovak civil society have tended to be scathing towards compromise, give-and-take, party politicking and internal dissent.[25] 'In fact, most of the values and language of ethical civil society that were so functional to the tasks of opposition are dysfunctional for a political society in a consolidated democracy.'[26] The 'core attitudes of ethical civil society' in East-Central Europe may not be authoritarian, but they are 'fundamentally different from a Lockean concept of liberal democracy' and are more communitarian than cosmopolitan–liberal.[27] Indeed, genuinely liberal democracy involves a general acceptance that one can disagree with someone without feeling that one has utterly to discredit, defeat or demolish the other person's stance and/or integrity.

Nevertheless, the degree of consolidation of liberal democracy in East-Central Europe is much higher than in either the CIS or the Balkans, largely as a consequence of the more securely established infrastructural and regulatory capacities and rule of law in East-Central Europe, which contrasts with the more stunted authority and weaker infrastructural capabilities of the less law-abiding and outwardly 'fiercer' states of the CIS and the Balkans.[28] Moreover, the coming to power of coalitions led by 'reformed' Communists in Lithuania in 1992, in Poland in 1993 and in Hungary in 1994, together with the ample evidence that these reconstructed Communists 'accepted the democratic rules of the game in how they contested the election and later in how they ruled', demonstrated that victors and losers alike had recognised that 'democracy was becoming the only game in town'.[29] Indeed, those same Communist-led coalitions later returned with good grace to the opposition benches when subsequent elections transferred power to their rivals.

Thus there are very substantial grounds for optimism. Poland, Hungary, the Czech Republic, Slovenia and, belatedly, Slovakia have clearly travelled much further and faster down the paths of 'democratic transition and consolidation' than the pessimists dared hope in the early 1990s, when East-Central European democratisation seemed to be threatened by a combination of severe economic recession, resurgent nationalism, fears of a Communist comeback and the apparent reluctance of the EU states either to open up their markets to the main exports of Europe's former Communist states or to offer them much in the way of economic and technical assistance. This does not mean that East-Central European 'democratisation' failed to derive *any* benefits from the existence of the EU, but such benefits as there were emanated mainly from the incentives and leverage for modernising reforms embedded in aspirations to and preparations for EU membership rather than from positive EU concessions and assistance. One can only hope that the EU will provide more support in the future than it has done so far.[30]

Nevertheless, liberal democracy cannot be made really secure anywhere in a short space of time. It gradually *accumulates* strength by weathering various crises and adversities and becoming rooted in public consciousness, not merely by achieving economic prosperity or receiving economic assistance. In the words of Sir Reginald Hibbert:

> When a country which has suffered a long dictatorship tries to evolve into a pass-able democracy, strict adherence to legality, to the newly defined constitutional processes, and to the careful implementation of correct electoral procedures is more important than the outcome in terms of winners and losers. What such a country needs above all is habituation to the possibility of change . . . until a form of democracy becomes a settled habit.[31]

Moreover, it should not simply be taken for granted that liberal democracy is Europe's *natural* political order, towards which it has inexorably evolved in modern times.

> Though we may like to think that democracy's victory in the Cold War proves its deep roots in Europe's soil, history tells us otherwise. Triumphant in 1918, it was virtually extinct twenty years on . . . By the 1930s the signs were that most Europeans no longer wished to fight for it; there were dynamic non-democratic alternatives to meet the challenges of modernity. Europe found other, authori-tarian, forms of political order no more foreign to its traditions, and no less effi-cient.[32]

This was especially true of Southern, Central and Eastern Europe.

The maintenance of the impressive degrees of 'democratic consolidation' achieved in East-Central Europe since the early 1990s remains heavily depen-dent upon continued export-led economic recovery, which in turn remains very vulnerably dependent upon the health of the much larger and stronger Western economies and increased access to Western markets. Renewed prob-lems in the East Asian economies, or a compression of demand for industrial products among the crisis-stricken primary export economies, or (worst of all) a collapse of the exceptionally long-running boom which has been taking place on Western stock markets since the early 1990s, could easily plunge Western Europe and the USA into severe economic recessions, which would in turn wreak havoc upon the very vulnerable economic revivals underway in East-Central Europe. The 1930s' experience demonstrated just how quickly European electorates can transfer their allegiances from liberal democratic parties to illiberal nationalist, Marxist and Fascist movements when liberal democrats appear to be incapable of overcoming economic collapse and the resultant exacerbation of inter-communal conflicts.

Optimists point out that the Federal Republic of Germany and post-Francoist Spain were being held up as models of consolidated liberal democ-racy less than twenty years after the deaths of Hitler and Franco. Yet it would be rash to assume that such happy outcomes as these are inevitable, or that they can be guaranteed by 'modernisation', 'elite pacts' and membership of the European Union. The results of the consciously engineered 'top–down' strategies of democratisation that are being pursued in East-Central and South-Eastern Europe, often in quite recently established states with relatively modest experience of constitutional government, liberal capitalism and the rule of law, are inherently likely to remain quite different from the outcomes of the protracted and largely accidental emergence of liberal and social democracy in West European societies that have had the good fortune to pass through a long 'apprenticeship' of law-based constitutional government and liberal capitalism during the nineteenth and early twentieth centuries – when most of their 'eastern cousins' remained in the grips of either imperial abso-lutism or illiberal successor states engaged in strenuous and often strident nation building.

Beyond national democracy: incorporation into a supranational legal order

The progressive deepening and widening of the EU is changing the *nature*, *scope* and *context* of East-Central European democratisation. Attila Agh has drawn attention to the potentially troublesome fact that the states of East-Central Europe will not long have recovered their full national autonomy and sovereignty before they will be expected to start surrendering it again as the price of admission to the EU.[33] The new entrants 'have to accept all the pre-vious contracts of the EC and fit them into the framework of their own legal system. This involves a substantial reduction of national sovereignty. This . . . could be a serious difficulty for the ECE countries, since they have to renounce some parts of their newly regained national sovereignty.'[34] The likely difficulties will be compounded by the presumption that the 'eastern' candidates must simply accede to the requirements of membership of the EU as presently constituted, instead of being allowed to exert some influence on the future development of its structure and policies, even though the needs and capabilities of the east-central and south-east European states may prove to be very different from those of the current EU membership. This incipient surrender of their newly regained sovereignty is the point at which the dynam-ics and exigencies of 'Europeanisation' start pulling away from those of 'democratisation'.

The growing ambivalence of East-Central European attitudes towards these tensions between 'Europeanisation' and 'democratisation' was thrown into sharp relief in February 2000 by the initial East-Central European reac-tions to the decision of EU governments to cold shoulder the Austrian Government led by Wolfgang Schüssel, due to its inclusion of members of Jörg Haider's Freedom Party. Václav Klaus, the Speaker of the Czech Parliament and a former prime minister, declared: 'It seems very strange to me. Austrian voters elected someone, and somebody from outside wants to dictate to them who will be in their government.' Viktor Orbán and János Martonyi, respectively Hungary's prime minister and foreign minister, were disinclined to join the EU in isolating Austria diplomatically. Some East-Central European politicians compared the treatment of Austria by Brussels to the treatment of East-Central Europe's former Communist states by Moscow, and/or saw the treatment meted out to Austria as a portent of what might lie in store for themselves at some future date.[35] Such misgivings could dampen East-Central European enthusiasm for EU membership. Parties on the nationalist right intimated that 'the boycott signifies a new 'Brussels doctrine' which empowers the EU to intervene at will in the internal affairs of member states. There is confusion in much of Central Europe about the difference between involuntary servitude to Moscow and voluntary association with Brussels.'[36]

In Western Europe, interest groups have increasingly recognised 'the reality of a federal Europe. Whatever term we may use to describe the EC – whether it be federal, neo-federal, would-be state . . . the reality for interests is that much of the regulatory framework under which their own policy areas are governed is now affected by EC intervention'.[37] Indeed, 'the EU level is now the level at which a high proportion (possibly 60 per cent) of what used to be regarded as purely domestic policy-making takes place. The locus of decision – and therefore power – has shifted'.[38] In the case of Germany 'fifty per cent of the matters which the *Bundestag* discusses have already been decided in Brussels. Thus these discussions concern only the 'domestication' of these measures.'[39] Indeed, member states can find themselves in a situation of having to enact norms 'adopted wholly or partially against their will'. Even Commission rulings and regulations have supremacy over national law on EC matters. As a result of the inexorable extension of EC jurisdiction into new areas and the breaking down of walls between EC and member state spheres of jurisdiction during the 1970s and 1980s, 'no core of sovereign state power was left beyond the reach of the Community'.[40] 'There simply is no nucleus of sovereignty that the Member States can invoke, as such, against the Community.'[41] If it therefore makes little sense to continue to treat the national parliamentary–democratic arena as the main locus of power, politics and policy making, it makes even less sense to suppose that 'Europeanisation' necessarily advances 'democratisation'.

The European Union is a liberal project much more than a democratic one. It embodies a supranational system of rules, regulations and laws fostered by judicial and quasi-judicial processes as well as by highly consensual negotiation between liberal democratic states, involving the mutual accommodation of European elites. It rests upon indirect functional legitimation (its capacity to 'deliver the goods', however these are defined), and on minimal popular and parliamentary acquiescence in what this achieves, rather than on more direct and active forms of democratic legitimation at a supranational all-Union level. There have been no great surges of popular support *for* a united Europe – certainly none that are even remotely comparable to the periodic populist backlashes *against* the idea. Structurally, authority in the EU is de-centred and diffuse, lines of political accountability and administrative responsibility are blurred, and there is no supranational EU 'government' which voters can vote out of office in EU elections. There are no major 'Union-wide' political parties fighting EU elections on transnational 'European' platforms and issues. Elections to the European Parliament are characterised by low and declining turnouts and by minimal public engagement with 'European' as distinct from 'national' programmes, policies and issues. There is little in the way of a transnational EU 'public sphere' and public opinion. And, despite being directly elected, the European Parliament is not really a conventional democratic parliament – not least because it is not the main legislature and there is no European *demos* for it to represent.

This introduces the arguments that there can be no democracy without a *demos*, that there is no European *demos* standing above the separate *demoi* of Europe's individual states, and that the widely acknowledged desirability of – and official commitment to – preserving and protecting Europe's rich diversity of peoples and cultures may help to prevent the emergence of a European *demos* in the future.[42] Certainly, the oft-repeated goal of the European Community remains 'ever closer union' – not fusion – 'of the peoples of Europe', with care always being taken to refer to 'peoples' rather than 'people'. However, it must be stressed that a European *demos* need not (and probably should not) take an organic ethno-cultural form, analogous to the *demoi* of many nation-states. A political community can be constituted through the pursuit of a common project such as the creation of a common market, especially if that project entails the creation of a grouping with clearly defined membership requirements and a legal order of its own. It need not be conditional upon either the prior existence or the subsequent creation of a coterminous ethno-cultural community or 'people'.

Nevertheless, while denying the need for a political community to be based upon *demos* conceived in organic ethno-cultural terms, one must also ruefully conclude that the European Community/Union still lacks a fully-fledged *demos* in the sense of a shared supranational public sphere, a supranational public opinion and supranational political parties capable of generating the kind of 'constitutional patriotism' (allegiance to a common set of values and political practices) that fully integrates – and sustains liberal democracy in – such multicultural and non-unitary political communities as the USA and Switzerland. The latter examples

> demonstrate that a political culture in the seedbed of which constitutional principles are rooted by no means has to be based on all citizens sharing the same language or the same ethnic and cultural origins. Rather, the political culture must serve as the common denominator of a constitutional patriotism which simultaneously sharpens an awareness of the multiplicity and integrity of the different forms of life which coexist in a multicultural society.[43]

Weiler argues that a supranational, civic, EU *demos* of this sort could fruitfully co-exist with a multiplicity of ethno-cultural *demoi* located in the member states, with each EU citizen 'belonging simultaneously to two *demoï*.[44] While it is quite conceivable that such an EU *demos* and an analo-gous 'constitutional patriotism' might emerge and make democracy possible in the European Union in due course, they are not yet in sight.

However, the elitism of the European integration process has been not a weakness, as its critics often proclaim, but one of its strengths. If it had been necessary to wait for its peoples to voice *demands* for 'ever closer union', Western European integration would not have advanced nearly so far as it has done in just half a century. The crucial point is that European states would have had to devise ways of co-existing more peacefully and harmoniously, no matter what the subjective preferences, prejudices, bugbears or grievances of their citizens, in order to avert any potential return to the destructive inter- and intra-state conflicts and the beggar-my-neighbour protectionism of 1914–45. Popular approval of, or at least acquiescence in, what has been achieved has been a bonus rather than a precondition for the success and the legitimacy of the project. The member states of the European Union accept that the deci-sions reached, the policies adopted and the laws passed by the EU collectively (and for the most part consensually) are legitimate and binding, not because the European Union is a form of democracy, but because these states have explicitly decided, in accepting and ratifying EU membership in accordance with their own internal liberal democratic procedures, to vest the European Union with the authority to reach binding decisions, adopt binding policies and pass binding laws on their behalf.

The EU is widely criticised both for its own so-called 'democratic deficit' and for its alleged 'perversion' of liberal democracy within its member states. In fact, it is the development of mighty global market forces and global infor-mation and communications networks, rather than the increasingly federal and supranational character of the EU, that poses the major threats to 'sov-ereignty' and democratic accountability/control – not only at the national but even at the EU level. Globalisation and the diminishing capacity of either national or EU parliamentary and executive institutions to control and hold to account the forces of global capitalism and global information and com-munications networks have created 'democratic deficits' at all levels, and there-fore these should not be simplistically or demagogically 'blamed' upon the EU. The latter, far from being the intrinsic *source* of Western Europe's 'democratic deficits', is one of the most promising means of *mitigating* the potential neg-ative effects of the 'democratic deficits' caused by the expansion of transna-tional capitalism, communications networks, bureaucratic 'big government' and transnational military bureaucracies beyond democratic control. The existence of the EU does at least afford its citizens some *mechanisms of indi-rect political and legal monitoring, regulation and control* of the forces that increasingly govern their lives. The citizens of small and medium-sized states in other parts of the world do not even have that.[45]

The strong frameworks of EU law and regulation which increasingly govern the Single Market, environmental policies, health and safety provisions, the terms and conditions of employment, and the movement of goods, services, capital and labour have transformed the EU into a multi-tiered 'regulatory federation' which increasingly defines and upholds the rights, freedoms and obligations of its citizens.[46] Political and civil rights and liberties are being ever more deeply embedded in a strong quasi-constitutional and supranational legal order. This helps to safeguard rights and liberties against potential violation by various powerful actors at the national level, including the governments of member states which still control national armed forces, police forces, law-courts, nationwide bureaucracies and other 'legitimate' instruments of coercion and enforcement at that level. Contrary to the fears of the Europhobes, the EU does not itself control or possess any such forces with which it could conceivably coerce those citizens, companies and member states who occasionally violate its rules and laws, although it has generated ever-growing political and economic incentives for compliance as well as penalties for non-compliance.

The fact that the European Union's budget has not been allowed to exceed 1.27 per cent of the combined GDP of its member states has forced it to remain an essentially regulatory 'civil association' (best defined as one in which 'governing is recognized as a specific and limited activity; not the management of an enterprise, but the rule of those engaged in a great diversity of self-chosen enterprises'[47]), even though some observers consider that it harbours (in my view unrealisable) ambitions to become more *dirigiste* and prescriptive in certain sectors. The Single Market programme, the EU's growing social and environmental regulatory functions, its regulation of the EU's external economic relations, and the project for Economic and Monetary Union should all be seen as major extensions of the law-governed *regulatory federation* and *civil association* characteristics of the EU, rather than as leaps toward the creation of 'big government' at the supranational level. The EU is obliged to eschew big spending programmes (the vaunted Structural Funds are restricted to 0.46 per cent of the EU's combined GDP), the Union is administered by a few thousand Commission officials (smaller than the municipalities of most big cities), and the Single Currency is run by a small committee of bankers and economists.

These are the means by which the EU has accommodated a diversity of states and peoples and has helped them to pursue their diverse purposes within a framework which maximises peace and prosperity while minimising friction and the scope for conflict. This involves mainly the rule of law, consensual negotiation of mutually acceptable rules and laws, the negotiated accommodation of differences, and judicious interpretation of rules and laws by the EC Court of Justice, with peripheral roles for democratically elected parliaments. A major implication of all this is that the East-Central European applicants for EU membership need not expect (nor need they be expected) to undergo major extensions of democracy as such, since their parliaments and governments are already as freely elected as their Western European counterparts.

Rather, what they will have to accept and adjust to is working within a political and economic environment which is increasingly regulated by supranational rules, regulations and laws most of which are determined either by non-elected Commission officials and judges or by highly consensual negotiations between the relevant ministries of the member states, with minimal parliamentary scrutiny or involvement.

The East-Central European candidates for EU membership need to be prepared for significantly altered relationships between the judiciary and other branches of government, between individual citizens and the state, and between litigation and other means of redress. The 'constitutionalisation' of the EC treaties and the establishment of the 'direct effect' and 'supremacy' of EC law during the 1960s, followed by the massive extension of the scope of EC competences and jurisdiction during the 1970s and 1980s, resulted in 'an overall strengthening of the judicial branch *vis-à-vis* the other branches of government'. This benefited 'courts at all levels in all member states' as well as the EC Court of Justice.[48] The increasing role of EC and national courts, the direct effect of EC law, and the willingness of the EC Court of Justice to invoke the human rights provisions in member state constitutions and in the international conventions to which they are signatories have significantly empowered individual citizens *vis-à-vis* the governments and other public institutions of member states – the more so as litigants have a steadily diminishing need for recourse to (weaker) international law and (more remote and expensive) international courts, and growing opportunities to pursue their claims in their own national courts system on the basis of directly effective EC laws. Indeed, individual citizens have become 'the principal 'guardians' of the legal integrity of Community law . . . similar to the ways that individuals in the United States have been the principal actors in ensuring the vindication of the Bill of Rights and other federal law'.[49] The upshot is more litigious societies, again increasingly resembling the USA. Moreover, it has become an implicit prerequisite for new entrants into the EU to have constitutional courts whose rulings even elected parliaments, governments and presidents are obliged to obey, not only to ensure the constitutionality of government measures and parliamentary legislation but to uphold and enforce the direct effect and supremacy of EC law *vis-à-vis* national law. This need not pose problems for the East-Central European states, because they already have such courts and generally abide by their rulings; but it could place obstacles along the path to EC entry for some other post-Communist states in the more distant future, unless they 'mend their ways'. Overall, since there are strong arguments that EU membership has also contributed to the growing empowerment of the executive branch of government, albeit 'over a shrinking public policy domain',[50] the major losers must be the elected parliaments.

Academic demands for increased democratic control, whether national, supranational or 'cosmopolitan', are mainly pie-in-the-sky. Not one of the leading advocates of supranational 'cosmopolitan democracy'[51] has convincingly explained how such a nebulous concept could be operationalised. Nor do the advocates of more radical, republican, participatory and deliberative conceptions of democracy convincingly explain why elites should wish either to relinquish the almost exclusive control over policy and decision making which they currently enjoy or to increase popular and parliamentary access to important (as distinct from trivial or cosmetic) information, power and resources, even though the technology now exists to make such changes more feasible. Taken together, globalisation, economic liberalisation, the growing privatisation of power and wealth, and the ever-diminishing scope for parliamentary control over what occurs within formal national jurisdictions have heavily tipped the scales of political and economic power against labour and in favour of capital and are making it ever more difficult to unite and mobilise underprivileged sections of the population either to enforce greater democratic accountability or to wrest power and control from the hands of the ascendant political and economic elites. In an increasingly 'globalised', 'regionalised' and privatised world, with its ever-increasing inequalities of power and wealth, it is far more realistic to suppose that laws, rules, legal orders and regulatory regimes will increasingly be called upon to deputise or substitute for the ever-diminishing scope for democratic control and accountability as the (supposedly) standard means of safeguarding fundamental rights and liberties and economic prosperity.

The accommodation of difference: the virtues of a 'cosmopolitan legal order'

Supranational European Union law has particular advantages over the 'democratic' laws of liberal democratic states with multicultural or multi-ethnic populations – nowadays, virtually every state can be so described. No matter how democratic a liberal democracy might become, its laws are still likely to be seen as embodying the interests and preferences of the dominant ethnic, religious or racial group, and as placing various minority groups in relatively disadvantageous positions.

Will Kymlicka, in his influential *Multicultural Citizenship: A Liberal Theory of Minority Rights*, contends that the most appropriate liberal solution to this problem is to give secure legal recognition to the 'group-differentiated' or 'group-specific' rights of national, religious or racial minorities. He persuasively argues that group-specific rights *need not* take the form of (illiberal) collective rights and that liberals ought to endorse various means of legally entrenching those minority group rights and liberties which can *supplement*, rather than restrict universal individual rights and liberties.[52] However, while his prescriptions might conceivably be effective in a strongly liberal political culture such as Canada (Kymlicka's 'homeland'), such *pandering* to nationalism, ethnicity and identity politics could prove quite catastrophic in countries with strong traditions of religious bigotry, nationalist intolerance, inter-communal conflict, racial or ethnic segregation, and oppression of ethnic and religious minorities. After all, as Kymlicka himself initially acknowledges[53] – but then subsequently seems to forget – one of the major reasons for the UN emphasis on promotion of universal human rights after the Second World War was that the system of minority protection treaties which the victorious Western Allies and the League of Nations had tried to impose on East-Central and South-Eastern Europe after the First World War was a disastrous failure and had been one of the contributory causes of the Second World War. These treaties were difficult to enforce and to apply consistently, stoked up resentment among the dominant ethnic/religious group in each state, institutionalised and heightened the political salience of group differences, inflamed and perpetuated inter-ethnic tensions, exacerbated the region's political and economic instability, and encouraged countries such as Germany, Hungary, Bulgaria and Italy unilaterally to violate the sovereignty of other states in the region on the pretext that these were failing to respect the internationally recognised group rights of their German, Hungarian, Bulgarian and Italian minorities. Thus the system all but invited irredentism and was profoundly destabilising, politically, economically and territorially.[54] The eminent American liberal legal theorist Ronald Dworkin has, with good reason, declared that 'self-determination is the most potent – and the most dangerous – political ideal of our time'.[55] When applied to nations and ethnic groups, it puts all states and boundaries perpetually in question.

Of course, it is not Kymlicka's intention, as a self-avowed cosmopolitan liberal individualist, that his writings should be invoked in defence of nationalist intolerance, religious bigotry and ethnic collectivism. However, his cosmopolitan liberal individualism must be barely comprehensible to peoples wedded to strongly embattled and collectivist conceptions of the nation, ethnicity and religion and to essentially communitarian conceptions of political community. Like Woodrow Wilson's principle of national self-determination, which was never intended to give the green light to 'ethnic collectivism' and inter-ethnic conflict, Kymlicka's carefully qualified and nuanced championship of group-specific rights is liable to be misused by ethnic collectivists and religious bigots for their own nefarious purposes. Kymlicka's fine distinctions will be completely lost on such people, who will merely seize upon the fact that a well-known liberal cosmopolitan philosopher appears to be endorsing the group-specific rights of minorities such as the Serbs of Croatia, Bosnia and Kosovo or the Romanians of northern Transylvania, who have their own ways of asserting these rights and little understanding or regard for Kymlicka's liberal cosmopolitan stipulations and sensibilities. He is inadvertently giving a hint of respectability to thugs and ethnic cleansers. More generally, Kymlicka's prescriptions can only help to accelerate what Roland Robertson has aptly called 'the universalization of particularism and the particularization of universalism',[56] further eroding and compromising the liberal cosmopolitanism and universalism which he claims to hold dear. Championing group rights greatly increases the dangers that people will come to be considered and catered for primarily on the basis of their collective rather than their individual identities. 'In that way individual political and civil rights may come to be undermined and barriers may be erected where none previously existed.'[57] Kymlicka has usefully clarified a few important issues and has drawn some fine distinctions which might receive the careful and detached consideration which they deserve in areas where such problems are not (and are not regarded as) life-and-death issues. He is playing with fire. It is dangerous to approach such matters simply under the guidance of political theorists with formally restricted horizons, limited engagement with the real world and confused or overly schematic readings of history.

Unfortunately, Kymlicka seems to have persuaded such eminent 'transition theorists' as Juan Linz and Alfred Stepan that the democratisation of east-central and South-Eastern Europe can only be consummated if it is accompanied by legal recognition and protection of the group rights of ethnic minorities.[58] There has been strident agitation for recognition and protection of ethnic, racial, religious, homosexual, lesbian and other group rights in North America, Europe and Australasia since the 1960s, and, as the cause became increasingly fashionable, so more and more politicians, academics, media pundits and international organisations have jumped on the bandwagon. Group rights were taken up by the CSCE (later OSCE) and the Council of Europe in the later 1980s. Since 1991 the EU has made respect for minority rights a key criterion for the recognition of newly independent states, beginning with those that emerged out of the former Yugoslav Federation. Since 1993 such respect has also become a formal criterion for admission of new members into the EU and an official 'litmus test ' of the degree of 'democratisation' attained in formerly authoritarian states.[59] Attila Agh has interpreted the June 1993 Copenhagen criteria stipulating 'respect for and protection of minorities' as requiring the current 'eastern' candidates for EU membership to adopt consociational democracy and formal recognition of 'collective minority rights'.[60] If he is correct, this would suggest that the EU is both ignoring the 'lessons' of the interwar era and attempting to impose on prospective members a form of polity which is certainly not required of the current member states. However, this stipulation may simply – and more justifiably – require the prospective members to respect and uphold the equal *individual* rights of their ethnic and religious minorities and to endeavour to settle the various inter-communal conflicts and disputes which have flared within and between the applicant states before they can be admitted to the EU, on the grounds that the EU cannot afford to import many more inter-communal conflicts of the sort that have bedevilled the Basque Country, Northern Ireland and Belgium.

The fact that such problems already exist among its current members should also put the EU on guard against charges of double standards, and should not be allowed to obscure the great advantages of EC law as a close approximation to a system of *cosmopolitan law* that could gradually draw some of the poison out of such conflicts. The building of a legal order on the basis of cosmopolitan law, rather than on Utopian (and potentially dangerous) conceptions of 'cosmopolitan democracy' and the legal recognition/protection of group rights, is the way forward for the EU, and is the basis on which it could help to defuse some (though by no means all) of Europe's most explosive inter-communal problems. By 'cosmopolitan law' I mean law which does not express and embody the aspirations, interests and beliefs of a single dominant ethnic, racial or religious group and which does not blatantly discriminate between ethnic, racial or religious groups in potentially divisive and inflammatory ways. Pure 'cosmopolitan law' is of course an unattainable ideal, but the more closely and comprehensively EC law can approximate that ideal, the better the prospects for inter-communal harmony within an expanding European Union. Attempts to resolve such problems within the framework of nation–states are unlikely to succeed, because such states nearly always contain a dominant group and subordinate minority groups, with at least some conflicting priorities, interests and aspirations. However, expanding the framework to the point where no single group can dominate and every group is a small minority presents far greater scope for devising, adopting and elaborating institutions, policies and laws which approximate to impartiality. That is the great beauty of European Union.

The resurgence of potentially destabilising ethnic nationalism and inter-ethnic tension in parts of East-Central and South-Eastern Europe has been treated mainly as a *security* issue. Without denying that inter-ethnic tensions have been and could yet again become major sources of political instability and violent conflict in the region's multi-ethnic states, it needs to be emphasised that the problems posed by the prevalence of (mainly collectivist) ethno-cultural conceptions of national identity and citizenship extend much *wider* and *deeper* than the current focus on 'security hot spots' suggests. Ethnic collectivism seriously impedes the full fruition and realisation of liberal conceptions of democracy and individual rights, even in the absence of significant ethnic minorities and/or inter-ethnic tensions. The EU implicitly rests upon the belief that societies should primarily be based upon and held together by impersonal law, interests and contractual relations of a Lockean kind, rather than by 'primordial' ties of religion, race, ethnicity and kinship. Religious, ethnic and racial collectivism are fundamentally at odds with the cosmopolitan supranational legal order which is being constructed by the European Union. To allow societies which continue to be based upon and held together by such ties and mentalities to become members of the EU could place the EU project in jeopardy. The EU therefore has to consider whether such societies should be expected to change in this respect, as a condition of admission. On the other hand, such changes are very difficult to effect, and may be more palatable and slightly easier to achieve after they have been admitted.

Article 7 of the Treaty of Rome states that '[W]ithin the scope of this Treaty

. . . any discrimination on grounds of nationality shall be prohibited'. While Western European states not infrequently depart or lapse from this civic norm, and while the increasing 'ethnicisation' and 'racialisation' of West European identities and identity politics during the 1980s and 1990s should caution West European analysts against the danger of complacency regarding the extent to which their own house is in order, these lapses and deficiencies pale by comparison with the challenges posed by the potential admission of states which are in many cases regarded as being in the sole possession of particular ethnic groups, or whose very legitimacy and *raison d'être* have rested on ethnic nationalism and exclusivity.

In most of the east-central and South-Eastern European candidates for membership of the EU, ethnic discrimination and the preferential status of numerically dominant ethnic groups are not just unfortunate and regrettable lapses or aberrations: they have been made the very basis of the state, democratic representation, public employment and many social, political and economic rights and entitlements. It is this, rather than the often overstated contrast between 'Eastern' and 'Western' forms of nationalism, that still divides Western from east-central and South-Eastern Europe.[61] States in the latter regions have tended to uphold the perceived *collective rights and interests* of particular ethnic and religious groups, rather than the rights and interests of individuals and of *society as a whole*. Most are 'ethnocracies', treating the state as the exclusive property of a particular ethnic group, to degrees not currently found in Western Europe. (The concept of 'ethnocracy' was elaborated by the Romanian nationalist Nichifor Crainic in 1938.[62]) Unfortunately, when embodied in nations and states conceived in exclusive 'ethnic' rather than more inclusive 'civic' terms, democracy has had strong inherent tendencies to degenerate into ethnocracy, especially when the going gets rough; and from there it has been but a short step to 'ethnic cleansing' and 'ethnocide'. The scope for such evils is still far from exhausted, and in such contexts democracy is part of the problem rather than the solution. The main hope of durable solutions to such problems lies in changing the context and the framework, as Jean Monnet tirelessly pointed out.

Contrary to claims that narrowly ethnic conceptions of citizenship and national identity pose no real problem in countries such as Poland and Hungary, which have 'achieved' high levels of ethnic homogeneity, it should be recognised that exclusive ethnic collectivism and the illiberal values and mentalities associated with it (especially antisemitism) can still persist – and will then be less subject to healthy scrutiny and challenge – even *after* the almost complete elimination of ethnic minorities (which has been accomplished almost invariably at appalling human cost). In the case of Poland, it is the Roman Catholic Church which champions the *collective rights* of Polish Catholics by claiming to speak for 95 per cent of Poland's population, as if all Polish Catholics were of one mind. The Polish Catholic Church still assumes the right to lay down the law on moral and spiritual matters, such as abortion and religious instruction in schools, and expects its teachings, its moral agenda and its claims to a monopoly of religious broadcasting and religious instruction in schools to be incorporated into the laws of the land and made binding upon all citizens. As stated by Bishop Pieronek on behalf the Polish Episcopate in 1995: 'Do you expect 95 per cent of the nation . . . to keep quiet because 5 per cent want to have their constitution? Don't we have rights? We are guided by the concern for our common good. If we say that the Church is the community of the faithful, then it totals 95 per cent of the nation.'[63] Such confessional collectivism and a communitarian conception of the political community have helped the Polish Catholic Church to get its own way on some legislative matters 'against the expressed wishes of most Poles'.[64] Continuing manifestations of latent antisemitism, and the disputes in the late 1990s over the erection of Catholic crucifixes at Auschswitz, suggested that the 'leopards' of illiberal Polish Catholic nationalism had not yet changed their spots, even if they had changed their eating habits.

In the long term multi-ethnic societies with a greater diversity of spiritual and cultural resources are more likely to adapt successfully to the incipient multiculturalism and (strained) 'civic ideals' of the EU (especially if they can work out stable internal accommodations between ethnic groups) than are societies which pride themselves on having supposedly attained ethno-cultural homogeneity. The continuing idealization of ethnic and/or religious homogeneity will have to be exorcised from the East-Central European states if they are fully to assimilate the cosmopolitan precepts of the EU. This is not to demand the impossible. In the sixteenth century, after all, the Polish–Lithuanian Commonwealth and the then-Hungarian principality of Transylvania were justifiably proud of their cosmopolitanism and their religious tolerance.

These issues are of immense importance because Europe is still made up of bounded political communities. The rights, obligations and welfare entitlements of Europeans are conferred by membership of groups (usually nations), although these groups vary greatly in their degrees of inclusiveness and exclusiveness. Europe currently knows only *national* democracies; a successful supranational democracy has yet to be constructed. It is conceivable that the energies and passions aroused and engaged by nationalism and nation building could play constructive roles in the promotion of democratic power structures and consensual sources of social cohesion and political legitimacy. Maurice Keens-Soper has argued that 'liberal democracy has almost everywhere been parasitic on nationalism. Democracy possesses no theory or force of its own capable of either generating or explaining the very ties of attachment upon which its workings in practice depend'. Nevertheless, 'nationalism does not guarantee democracy'. Most democracies are national, yet 'few of the world's nationalisms sustain democracy'.[65] This points to a crucial dilemma facing the transitions to democracy in the post-Communist states. It may well be that stable democracies have normally required an under-girding of nationalism and an implicit or explicit belief that they are coterminous with relatively homogeneous national communities and national territories. Yet any thoroughgoing attempt to make national identities and attachments the basis of state loyalties, public duties and citizens' rights and allegiances in the troubled ethnic patchwork of east-central and South-Eastern Europe is bound to be dangerously divisive and a recipe for endemic instability and conflict. I am not suggesting that the current candidates for EU membership can or should become ethnically impartial states – such a state is probably impossible anywhere. The minimum requirements are that these states must be capable of accommodating internal cultural diversity and even learning to welcome and appreciate its advantages, instead of seeking and extolling homogeneity and encouraging cultural differences to harden into unbridgeable chasms and antagonisms.

President Václav Havel has rightly emphasised that in Central and Eastern Europe the paramount task must be 'to free human beings from the bondage of ethnic collectivism – that source of all strife and enslaver of human individuality'.[66] EU membership has crucial roles to play in this regard, because (as intimated above) EU policies, regulations and laws neither reflect nor embody the interests, beliefs and aspirations of any dominant national, ethnic or religious group. Indeed, it is arithmetically impossible for any such group to dominate the law making and governance of the European Union. The Germans, the largest single nation/ethnic group, make up no more than one-quarter of the population and, in common with the French, the British and the Italians, are greatly under-represented in the EU Commission, the Council of Ministers and the European Parliament due to the significant weighting in favour of smaller nations. Roman Catholicism, the largest single religious denomination in the EU, receives even less in the way of special consideration. EU law making and governance are in no way directed against national, ethnic and religious minorities 'native' to Western Europe, even though few (if any) of the member states can wholly escape charges of racism and/or religious intolerance towards certain categories of immigrants of non-EU origin.

Conclusion

The EU has often been likened to the Austro-Hungarian Empire, which was similarly held together by a supranational rule of law and in which no single ethnic group held an absolute majority – i.e. every group was a minority group. Nevertheless, the cosmopolitan universalism of the EU is a vast improvement on the ethnic particularism, the parochial narrow-mindedness and the widespread religious bigotry and segregation which many East-Central Europeans have acknowledged as major characteristics of the Habsburg monarchy, which did indeed have dominant (albeit non-majoritarian) ethnic groups and a dominant collectivist religion. EC law, which has 'direct effect' and 'supremacy' in the member states, is the only extant legal framework in the world within which 'cosmopolitan law-enforcement' can be rendered fully operational.[67]

There is a further sense in which the term 'Europeanisation' has been used, and which could be quite helpful by way of conclusion. Thomas Mann famously argued the case for the 'Europeanisation' of Germany as a safeguard against the 'Germanisation' of Europe, and this aphorism was at the heart of German policy from Adenauer to Kohl. It has clearly involved the enmeshing and embedding of Germany in larger 'European' political and economic structures, in order to save itself and Europe from any resurgence of the 'old demons' of German nationalism and racial supremacism. By the same token, the most valuable form of 'Europeanisation' of East-Central Europe will be to enmesh and embed the current candidates for EU membership in larger European political and economic structures which will help to keep their own 'old demons' at bay. The resultant shift of emphasis, from unfettered sovereignty and democracy to a supranational liberal legal order that drastically curtails national sovereignty and democracy, far from signifying some huge 'sacrifice' or 'retrograde step' (as many Europhobes and the more blinkered democrats would have us believe), is actually the greatest gift that Western Europeans can bestow on their eastern 'cousins'. The alternatives foregone are only illusions (or delusions) of national sovereignty, mere fig leaves which barely conceal the reality of inescapable 'democratic deficits' at all levels, as the region gradually falls to the hammers of global capitalism, global information and communications networks, and an expanding transnational security community.

Notes

1 R. Hague, M. Harrop and S. Breslin, *Comparative Government and Politics: An Introduction*, 4th edition, Basingstoke: Macmillan, 1998, p. xiii.
2 K. von Beyme, *La clase política en el Estado de partidos*, Madrid: Alianza Editorial, 1995, pp. 41, 60–99.
3 The terms EC Court of Justice, EC law, and the like, are rightly still in use (especially in legal analyses of the European Union) because they pertain to the European Community, which still survives as the 'first pillar' of the European Union.
4 J. Weiler, *The Constitution of Europe*, Cambridge: Cambridge University Press, 1999, p. 266.
5 D. Wincott, 'Does the European Union Pervert Democracy? Questions of Democracy in New Constitutionalist Thought on the Future of Europe', in Z. Bankowski and A. Scott (eds), *The European Union and Its Order*, Oxford: Blackwell, 2000, p. 123.
6 P. Cerny, 'Paradoxes of the Competition State: The Dynamics of Political Globalization', in *Government and Opposition*, Vol 32, 1997, pp. 258–72.
7 G. Majone, 'The Rise of the Regulatory State in Europe', *West European Politics*, 17: 3, 1994, pp. 77–101; and *Regulating Europe*, London: Routledge, 1996, Chs. 1–4, 12–13.
8 F. Hayek, *Law, Legislation and Liberty*, London: Routledge, 1973, vol. 3, Ch. 13.

9 J. Burnheim, *Is Democracy Possible?*, Cambridge: Polity Press, 1985, p. 1.

10 R. Baldwin, *Towards an Integrated Europe*, London: ECPR, 1994, p. 155.

11 This view is expounded more fully in R. Bideleux, 'Civil Association: The European Union as a Supranational Liberal Legal Order', in M. Evans (ed.), *The Edinburgh Companion to Contemporary Liberalism*, Edinbugh: Edinburgh University Press, 2001.

12 R. Bideleux, 'The Southern Enlargement of the EC: Greece, Portugal and Spain', in R. Bideleux and R. Taylor (eds), *European Integration and Disintegration: East and West*, London: Routledge, 1996, pp. 127–53; R. Bideleux, 'La Grèce: Ni intérêts nationaux, ni idéaux fédéralistes', in A. Landuyt (ed.), *Europe: Fédération ou nations*, Paris: Editions SEDES, 1999, pp. 217–27ff.; and G. Pridham (ed.), *The International Context of Regime Transition in Southern Europe*, London: Leicester University Press, 1991, *passim*.

13 A. Moravcsik, 'Negotiating the Single European Act: National Interests and A. Conventional Statecraft in the European Community', *International Organization* 45: 1, 1991, pp. 19–56; 'Preferences and Power in the European Community: A Liberal Intergovernmental Approach to the EC', *Journal Of Common Market Studies* 31: 4, 1993, pp. 473–524; and *The Choice for Europe*, London: UCL Press, 1998; A. Milward, *The Reconstruction of Western Europe, 1945–51*, London: Routledge, 1984, Chs. 12–14; *The European Rescue of the Nation–State*, London, Routledge, 1992, especially Chs. 1, 2 and Conclusion; S. Hoffmann *The European Sisyphus. Essays on Europe, 1964–1994*, Boulder CO: Westview Press, 1995.

14 A.-M. Burley and W. Mattli, 'Europe Before the Court: A Political Theory of Legal Integration', *International Organization* 47: 1, 1993, pp. 41–76; J. Weiler, *The Constitution of Europe* (Cambridge: Cambridge University Press, 1999), Chs. 2, 5 and 6; J. Richardson (ed.), *European Union: Power and Policy-Making*, London: Routledge, 1996, Chs. 1, 9 and 15; L. Tsoukalis, *The New European Economy*, 3rd edition, Oxford: Oxford University Press, 1997; D. Dinan, *Ever-Closer Union*, Basingstoke: Macmillan, 1999, Chs. 5–7, 13, 15 and 16.

15 J. Weiler, *The Constitution of Europe*, p. 266, and D. Wincott, 'Does the European Union Pervert Democracy?', pp. 114, 123, 125, 127, 130.

16 Weiler, *The Constitution of Europe*, pp. 24, 102–28.

17 K. Jasiewicz, 'Political Consequences of Electoral Laws: The Case of Poland, 1989–93', in M. Szabo (ed.), *The Challenge of Europeanization in the Region: East Central Europe*, Budapest: Hungarian Political Science Association and the Institute for Political Sciences of the Hungarian Academy of Sciences, 1996, p. 207.

18 D. Fink-Hafner, 'The Challenges of Europeanization of Sectoral Policy-Making: The Case of Agriculture in Slovenia', in M. Szabo (ed.), *The Challenge of Europeanization in the Region*, p. 135.

19 B. Laffan, R. O'Donell and M. Smith, *Europe's Experimental Union*, London: Routledge, 1999, Ch.1.

20 A. Ágh, 'The Europeanization of ECE Polities and the Emergence of the New ECE Democratic Parliaments', in A. Ágh (ed.), *The Emergence of East Central European Parliaments: The First Steps*, Budapest: Hungarian Centre of Democracy Studies, 1994, pp. 9–10.

21 *Ibid.*, pp. 16–19.

22 J. Higley and G. Lengyel (eds), *Elites After State Socialism*, Lanham, MD: Rowman and Littlefield, 2000, pp. 9, 41, 58–9, 78–80 and 149–50.

23 A. Ágh, *The Politics of Central Europe*, London: Sage, 1998, pp. 44, 59, 68–9, 123, 148–58, 161.

24 J. Linz and A. Stepan, *Problems of Democratic Transition and Consolidation: Southern Europe, South America and Post-Communist Europe*, Baltimore, MD: Johns Hopkins University Press, 1996, pp. 8–9, 247, 270–5.

25 *Ibid.*, pp. 10, 271, 273, 331.

26 *Ibid.*, p. 272.

27 *Ibid.*

28 *Ibid.*, p. 13.

29 *Ibid.*, pp. 454, 456.

30 For critical accounts of the EU record from 1989 to 1997, see R. Bideleux, 'Bringing the East Back In', and 'In Lieu of a Conclusion: East Meets West?', in R. Bideleux and R. Taylor, (eds), *European Integration and Disintegration: East and West*, London: Routledge, 1996, pp. 225–51 and 281–95; and R. Bideleux and I. Jeffries, *A History of Eastern Europe*, London: Routledge, 1998, pp. 596–641.

31 R. Hibbert, 'Albania: Aftermath of the Elections', *Albanian Life* 60, Autumn 1996, p. 11; and L. Namier, *1848: The Revolution of the Intellectuals*, Cambridge: Cambridge University Press, 1946, p. 31.

32 M. Mazower, *Dark Continent: Europe's Twentieth Century*, London: Allen Lane, 1998, pp. 3–4.

33 A. Ágh, *The Politics of Central Europe*, London: Sage, 1998, p. 81.

34 Ágh, 'The Europeanization of ECE Polities', p. 16.

35 P. Green, 'Central Europeans React Hesitantly over Haider', *International Herald Tribune*, 4 February 2000, pp. 1 and 4.

36 C. Gati, 'For Wary Central Europe, Brussels Isn't Moscow', *International Herald Tribune*, 22 February 2000, p. 6.

37 S. Mazey and J. Richardson (eds), *Lobbying in the European Community*, Oxford: OUP, 1993, p. 255.

38 J. Richardson (ed.) (1996), *European Union: Power and Policy-Making*, London, Routledge, 1996, p. 3. Cf. N. Nugent, 'Sovereignty and Britain's Membership of the European Union', *Public Policy and Administration* 11:2, 1996, p. 8.

39 A. Ágh, 'The Europeanization of ECE Polities', p. 16.

40 Weiler, *The Constitution of Europe*, pp. 73, 20 and 43.

41 K. Lenaerts, 'Constitutionalism and the Many Faces of Federalism', *American Journal of Comparative Law* 38, 1990, p. 220.

42 Weiler, *The Constitution of Europe*, pp. 337, 344–5.

43 J. Habermas, 'Citizens and National Identity: Some Reflections on the Future of Europe', *Praxis International* 12:1, 1992, p. 7.

44 Weiler, *The Constitution of Europe*, pp. 344–6.

45 This is a major reason why other regional blocs, most notably in Latin America, are seeking to emulate the EU's success.

46 G. Magone, 'Regulatory Federalism in the European Community', *Government and Policy*, 10, 1992, pp. 77–101.

47 M. Oakeshott, *Rationalism in Politics and Other Essays*, London: Methuen, 1962, p. 189.

48 Weiler, *The Constitution of Europe*, pp. 33, 42–3.

49 *Ibid*, p. 20.

50 *Ibid*, pp. 59, 97 and 348; Wincott, 'Does the European Union pervert democracy?', pp. 114, 123;

51 D. Archibugi and D. Held (eds), *Cosmopolitan Democracy: An Agenda for a New World Order*, Cambridge: Polity Press, 1995.

52 W. Kymlicka, *Multicultural Citizenship: A Liberal Theory of Minority Rights*, Oxford: Oxford University Press, 1995, pp. 7, 41, 45–8, 109, 126, 153, 204.

53 *Ibid.*, pp. 2–3, 57–8.

54 R. Bideleux, 'In Lieu of a Conclusion: East Meets West?', pp. 288–90; and in more detail in R. Bideleux and I. Jeffries, *A History of Eastern Europe*, pp. 407–34, 460–6.

55 R. Dworkin, *Freedom's Law*, Cambridge, MA: Harvard University Press, 1996, p. 21–2.

56 R. Robertson, *Globalization*, London: Sage, 1992, p. 100.

57 C. Gilligan, 'Citizenship, Ethnicity and Democratization after the Collapse of Left and Right', in K. Cordell (ed.), *Ethnicity and Democratization in the New Europe*, London: Routledge, 1999, p. 47.

58 J. Linz and A. Stepan, *Problems of Democratic Transition and Consolidation*, pp. 33–4.

59 A. Burgess, 'Critical Reflections on the Return of Minority Rights Regulation to East/West European Affairs', in K. Cordell (ed.), *Ethnicity and Democratization*, pp. 49–53. In the same volume Martin Kovats emphasises that national self-interest can play a part in the championing of minority group rights: 'Minority rights is a good issue for Hungarian governments to promote because it helps protect Magyar minorities abroad, demonstrates the country's commitment to 'democracy', shows up its neighbours and provides long-term security for the Magyar language and culture' (p. 147).

60 A. Ágh, *Processes of Democratization in the Central European and Balkan States: Sovereignty-Led Conflicts in the Context of Democratization*, Budapest Papers on Democratic Transition, No. 229, Budapest: Hungarian Centre for Democracy Studies, 1998, p. 18.

61 Argued more fully in R. Bideleux, 'The Problems of Building a Pan-European Identity', in G. Timmins and M. Smith (eds), *Unsettled Europe*, London: Routledge, 2001.

62 N. Crainic, 'Programul Statului Etnocratic', in his *Ortodoxie si etnocratie*, Bucharest: Cugetarea, 1938, pp. 283–4, reissued 1987. See excerpts (translated into English by J. Niessen) from 'Romanian Nationalism', in P. Sugar (ed.), *East European Nationalism in the Twentieth Century*, Washington DC: American University Press, 1995, pp. 274–5.

63 S. Ramet, *Whose Democracy? Nationalism, Religion and the Doctrine of Collective Rights in Post-1989 Eastern Europe*, Lanham, MD: Rowman and Littlefield, 1997, pp. 98, 105, 172.

64 *Ibid.*, p. 109.

65 M. Keens-Soper, 'The Liberal State and Nationalism in Post-Cold War Europe', *History of European Ideas* 10, 1989, pp. 694–5.

66 V. Havel, 'The Hope for Europe', *New York Review of Books*, 20 June 1996, p. 40.

67 This phrase is used in a more military and inter-governmental sense by Mary Kaldor: *New and Old Wars*, Cambridge: Polity Press, 1999, pp. 124–31.

Rethinking regime change theory and the international dimension of democratisation: ten years after in East-Central Europe

Introduction: highlighting the international dimension

The collapse of Communist rule in Central and Eastern Europe in 1989 instigated a process of regime change and transformation that has challenged many standing assumptions and concerns in the study of democratisation. In particular, interactions between concurrent transformations – economic and state building as well as political – are a major consideration that requires some rethinking of conventional approaches to democratic transition and consolidation. And, not least, the role of external factors is one further aspect of post-Communist experience that conflicts with the previously held view – that they were essentially secondary to domestic processes of regime change.

International factors were highly visible in regime change in Central and Eastern Europe (CEE) when the Communist regimes collapsed. The pace of change in that autumn of 1989 created transnational effects, with Poland enticing other countries, Hungary opening the way for pressures to emerge in the former East Germany and Berlin impacting powerfully on Prague. The most common determinant of regime change then was Gorbachev's liberalisation policy – abandoning the Brezhnev doctrine of limited national sovereignty – and this strategic departure eventually moved the earth under regimes for which Moscow had been a vital support factor. In the past decade, external developments have in many different ways helped to mould the course of regime change in the post-Communist world.

At the same time, there has in the post-Cold War period been far more uncertainty about the future of the international system than in the previous two sets of democratisations in postwar and, later, Southern Europe. The sheer magnitude of these regime changes in the 1990s – occurring in some two dozen new and old countries – was an international event of the first order. It led rapidly to the dissolution of the Warsaw Pact and eventually the withdrawal of Soviet forces from the countries concerned. In three cases, the state system broke apart – in Czechoslovakia, Yugoslavia and the Soviet Union itself. Overall, these developments made for instability in the international environment, with predictable repercussions on domestic politics; but there were also general developments in the 1990s which have affected regime change:

- the simultaneous restructuring of the international system following the end of the Cold War and close linkages here with problems of regime change;
- the occurrence of war in the former Yugoslavia in both furthering demo-cratisation through national independence (Slovenia) but more commonly in delaying democratisation, if not reinforcing authoritarian tendencies in other republics during the 1990s (Croatia and Serbia);
- the much more decided effects of European integration on democratisation compared with the regime changes in Southern Europe a decade-and-a-half earlier;
- the greater attention on the part of both financial and political interna-tional organisations to political conditionality and in particular questions of human rights;
- the international consequences of both economic transformation and state and nation building on democratisation itself;
- the various influences deriving from globalisation and the new technology on socio-economic and political attitudes and behaviour insofar as these directly or indirectly have affected democratisation's prospects.

Such powerful international impacts on regime change as well as the diverse forms in which they have interwoven with domestic developments argue for a reconsideration of the role of external forces in democratisation. While the influence of international factors in post-Communist Europe is now widely recognised, this has not really been explored adequately at either the theoret-ical level or in terms of specific impacts on regime change.

This chapter argues for differentiation in estimating external factors and in particular for looking at how they actually interact with domestic develop-ments in the context of democratisation. Attention will first be given to regime change theory and its usefulness for discussing external influences on post-Communist states. Then, the relevance of the multilateral international system in which post-Communist states have found themselves in the past decade will be discussed, concentrating on the regime changes in East-Central Europe (ECE) but drawing, where appropriate, comparisons or contrasts with other areas of the post-Communist world. This sets the scene for the main section, which will examine external influences in this region and their different impacts on countries, seeking admission to the European Union, before moving to an assessment of how these have contributed to the prospects of achieving democratic consolidation in East-Central Europe. Conclusions will then be drawn about the real impact of European integration on democratisa-tion and the prospects for the future.

Regime change theory and international–domestic interactions

It is not merely a question of international factors being greater in post-Communist CEE than previously, for they were in any case underplayed in comparative and theoretical work with respect to earlier democratisations. The distorting impacts of the Cold War on transitions to democracy in Europe from the later 1940s emphasised their prominence; as did, in a different way, the intervention of the USA in Latin America on matters relating to types of regime. Nevertheless, regime change theory long proceeded on the implicit and sometimes stated notion that the dynamic focus of transition from authoritarian rule remained the domestic arena, international factors being seen as of secondary importance, although occasionally decisive. Accordingly, an emphasis on national specificity tended to hinder generalisation, although this is more true of the European than of the Latin American environment. Treatment of international factors was rather broad and imprecise, given the habit of seeking basic explanations of a within-state category. This trend of thinking fitted well with conventional approaches in comparative politics, which consider the international arena as a backdrop to what 'really' matters, which is governance domestically defined.

Genetic theories, emphasising the unpredictability of the transition process, have been somewhat in this spirit. While, conceivably, this approach should be open to considering international influences, in practice however its concern for 'political crafting', the role of elite pacts and path-dependent analysis have dwelt – sometimes exclusively – on domestic trajectories of change. Nevertheless, empirical work inspired by genetic thinking has, where appropriate, given due attention to external factors; but this has not really risen above the case-study approach. On the other hand, functionalist theories, which looked to socio-economic development as enhancing democracy's chances, suggested an avenue for exploring the international context, although this was not as such advanced to any particular degree. Przeworski has however drawn attention to the process of modernisation through internationalisation with respect to post-Communist states and their adopting of forms of organisation (democracy, market economies and consumption-oriented culture) already existing elsewhere in the advanced capitalist world.[1] Here, the countries of East-Central Europe have advanced further than others in the post-Communist world.

More recently, the globalisation literature has drawn attention to internationalising effects in productive processes and capital markets, and in the liberalisation of trade barriers. It has also emphasised the decline in state authority, the consequent increase in political opportunities for international organisations and the expansion in transnational forces – all of which raise important issues about how these might impact on domestic change. Nevertheless, it is erroneous to interpret democratisation as essentially the outcome of common patterns involving greater interdependence – what Held calls 'growing global interconnectedness' – between states.[2] For that ignores national diversities and oversimplifies the complexities of regime change. Rather, the impact of such developments should be viewed in terms of two-way interactions between domestic and external variables. It suggests a view-point opposite to those standard theories which have claimed political choice and the actions of domestic elites as the key to transition outcomes. But glo-balisation accounts have in fact received little attention in the democratisation literature, even though there is growing evidence that globalisation trends are straining democracies and the societies they govern. It goes without saying they have far more bearing on regime change in post-Communist states than in previous democratisations in Europe since 1945.

Transnational theories have in a different way acknowledged the impor-tance of the international context by virtue of identifying 'waves' of demo-cratisation, where clearly room is allowed for individual transitions in the same period and geographical area to impact on each other.[3] They undoubt-edly appeal in explaining the events of 1989, although much less so the subse-quent process towards consolidation. This approach has generated different concepts along similar lines, like 'demonstration effect' (setting an example or precedent for successful transition), 'contagion' (a non-coercive form of this), 'control' (promotion of democracy by one country in another through direct means) and 'consent' (the generation through international processes of new democratic norms), but also – elaborating on the 'wave' syndrome – 'diffusion' and 'emulation'.[4] However, difficulty lies in applying them as a means for esti-mating cause and effect; and, also, they tend to suggest one-way effects rather than interactive forms of influence.

Rather different, however, are the concepts of 'convergence' and 'condi-tionality'. While *convergence* entails gradual movement in system conformity with a grouping of established democratic states with the power and institu-tional mechanisms to attract transiting countries and to help secure their dem-ocratic outcomes, *conditionality* refers to deliberate efforts to determine from outside the course and outcome of regime change. These two concepts point more than the others towards regime consolidation, and they also provide a means for exploring interactions between external effects and domestic devel-opments. Furthermore, they highlight the need to focus on the regional context, which is now increasingly recognised as the most effective interna-tional context in which external impacts and influences may be identified and measured.[5] In other words, we need to explore closely the effects on regime change of institutionalised mechanisms of multilateral cooperation, in partic-ular those of the European Union.

Altogether, the argument is compelling for embracing different interna-tional dimensions at the theoretical level and for integrating them with com-parative approaches to democratisation. Already, some critical accounts of standard approaches to democratisation have in recent years noted this need.[6] Moreover, the process of multiple transformation in Central and Eastern

Europe requires closer consideration of the way in which international factors combine and interweave with the process of change in different countries undergoing transition there. Problems of economic transformation and state or nation building inevitably involve the international environment in a fairly basic and central way. It becomes obvious, then, that the boundaries between a set of factors called 'domestic' and another called 'international' are difficult if not impossible to maintain, as had been assumed in previous regime change theory.

It is for this reason that interactive theoretical approaches offer the best means for exploring the complexity of international politics and its linkages with domestic arenas. These combine, essentially, political choice and structural factors, but in a way that captures the dynamics of democratisation by focusing on interactions between different levels of the regime-change process. This may be taken forward in a number of ways, notably by thinking in terms of two-way effects and by accepting the need for differentiation among international factors in democratisation.

Firstly, it has usually been claimed that external factors are a variable dependent on openings and opportunities in the domestic arena for impacting on regime change. On the other hand, the external environment can in its different forms impose a set of confining conditions for internal regime change. These confining conditions may derive from either multilateral linkages (membership in international or regional organisations) or bilateral linkages with other states, be they contiguous, regional or superpower (where the linkages may vary in quality between one of client or subordinate status and one of partnership based on common membership of multilateral organisations). The state of the regional or international political economy or common systemic trends, which may be said to 'spill over' national boundaries, can also influence internal political developments. The prevalence of liberal democratic norms in a region like Western Europe, for instance, can reinforce the democratic option in new regimes, thus contributing positively to democratic consolidation. Undoubtedly, therefore, external causes of democratisation have to be examined in terms of two-way effects and the degree to which interactions develop and affect regime-change dynamics.

Secondly, it is, in fact, debatable whether one can at all speak of an 'international dimension' as such, as simply one level alongside others like democratic institutionalisation and the emergence of civil society. It is a collective term for highly diverse external factors and influences and a wide array of actors that happen to be located, or which originate, outside a country's borders. Given this diversity and the differential impact of external influences, not to mention that external actors often do not act in unison, it is even misleading to emphasise the international dimension as if it were some unitary experience.

While external factors may originate as geographically separate from domestic developments in a country undergoing regime change, in other ways

– especially political, cultural and attitudinal – it is unrealistic to view them as absolutely separate from these in our interdependent world. It is one rather more interdependent than when Southern Europe abandoned authoritarian rule, and certainly very much more so than when Fascism was defeated and replaced by new or restored democracies. For this reason, it is all the more necessary to disaggregate the 'international dimension' and focus on particular forms of external influence, and on how these push forward or inhibit the course of democratisation.

Since there is undoubtedly some complexity in interactions between the external and the domestic in regime change, it is important to approach this in a way that helps to integrate the national-specific with the general. One may start with recognising the diversity of international factors and therefore the need for some form of differentiation in evaluating their role in the process of democratisation. A number of *comparative hypotheses* are offered and explored which also cast light on two-way effects. These are discussed with reference to previous democratisations in Europe since 1945 to throw comparative light on those still taking place in post-Communist Europe.

In the first place, *certain types of transition may be more likely to open up to external influences than others*. Transitions that derive from defeat in war are one special type, since war is a first-order international event with usually radical effects on domestic systems. In the case of the postwar transitions, external actors had a powerful and direct influence in the two post-Fascist states but also in Austria, all the more in view of strong impacts from the early Cold War. In West Germany, for instance, the occupation authorities had a direct role in the introduction of democratic rule. In the mid-1970s, it was the corrosive effects of disastrous colonial wars that proved the decisive force in the collapse of the Estado Novo in Portugal, although one has to measure this against internal problems in the regime by that time. In Greece, external influences were significant in the transition but these were due not merely to the Turkish invasion of Cyprus, which brought down the Colonels' regime, but also to factors in Greek political culture such as a sensitivity to outside influences based on long memories of external interference in that country's affairs.

War therefore features as a prominent causal factor, in one way or another, in the two earlier sets of transitions in Europe. This is somewhat in contrast to the transitions in CEE but also those in the former USSR. In the latter case, persistent strains from Moscow's policy choice of increasing expenditure in the arms race, and perhaps, too, the domestic impacts of the war in Afghanistan, are contributory factors. But they are not equivalent to external events having a direct link with transition as in postwar and Southern Europe. By further contrast, however, armed conflict has been a central and lethal factor in regime change in the former Yugoslavia, for which there is no precedent in the late 1940s and early 1950s and the years from the mid-1970s. In the light of all these examples, transitions in ECE stand out as the most peaceful either because they were evolutionary (Poland and Hungary) or because the division of the Czechoslovak state avoided a resort to violence or may even have been the reason for that not occurring.

It is easy to conclude that disruptive or contested transitions automatically engage external actors who may take sides with the contestants. Italy's early transition occurred at a time of febrile international relations, with the coming of the Cold War. Both superpowers developed an intense interest in that country's fortunes, not least because of its crucial strategic location in the Mediterranean. Portugal's fragile transition nearly led, in the dangerous year of 1975, to external intervention by NATO had suspicions of Soviet interference been strengthened and warnings to Moscow been without effect.[7]

The equivalent to this in CEE was outside intervention in Bosnia and, later, in the Federal Republic of Yugoslavia (FRY) over Kosovo, primarily for reasons other than determining the course of regime change; i.e. to prevent ethnic cleansing, to maintain regional security interests and stability – even though President Clinton subsequently appended 'transition to democracy' in Serbia as an additional war aim over Kosovo.[8] In 1991, the EU did under German pressure 'intervene' controversially in recognising Slovenia and Croatia. But this was to buttress national independence, even though in Slovenia's case this helped secure a fairly smooth transition to democracy. Among East-Central European countries, it was Slovakia that aroused the most European concern because the policies of the Mečiar Governments moved that country along authoritarian lines and nourished the suspicion that Bratislava's allegiance might not be so firmly to the West. But, as a whole, transitions in ECE have proved less controversial and less of a threat to international security interests than those in the Balkans and parts of the former Soviet Union.

Secondly, *authoritarian collapse and the shift to democratic transition usually brings a reconsideration of external policy allegiances, and this engages the concern of interested foreign powers.* As a fairly dramatic example, in 1974 Portugal abruptly abandoned her colonies in a matter of months, a decision strongly linked to democratisation because it was the colonial wars that had contributed so much to the fall of the dictator Caetano. This produced some international concern about destabilising effects in Africa in particular. In looking at interim governments during democratic transition, quite some cross-national variation has been found in the extent to which external policy direction broke or broke soon with that under authoritarian rule, using examples from the regime changes in Southern Europe and CEE. The nature of the transition in question, including the existence or not of power-sharing arrangements and the independent role of the military, accounted for this variation. All the same, the conclusion was drawn that improved relations with other democracies, and especially the embedding of a young democracy in a web of new international commitments that established democracies have already founded, create additional incentives for holding steady to the democratisation course and are conducive to eventual democratic consolidation.[9]

The postwar transitions were notable for the post-Fascist states embracing European integration as the mechanism for gaining a new international acceptability. At this time, the democracy requirement was subsumed within Cold War rhetoric. By the time of the Southern European transitions this requirement was more prominent, and in Spain's case 'Europe' and 'democracy' were virtually synonymous in elite thinking and to some extent at the public level. The idea that EC accession would help to guarantee liberal democracy was more overtly voiced than after the Second World War, when European integration was in its infancy and less embracing of domestic politics. Since then, the EC/EU has gained gradually in political weight, and this is all the more evident when comparing the transitions in CEE with those in Southern Europe. The motive of a 'return to Europe' is most pronounced with ECE states for cultural, historical and geographical reasons; whereas countries in South-East Europe see this in part as a means for escaping from the difficult legacy of the Balkans.

Thirdly, rather than viewing external impacts as *ad hoc* events relating to individual national circumstances, an alternative is to see them as part of *the structure and conditions of international relations surrounding transitions*. This provides a framework that encompasses events but also actors in a way that relates and compares their different roles. Thus, in looking at the transitions in postwar Europe, it may be noted that the emerging Cold War poignantly coloured political attitudes in the transition countries, contributed to domestic polarisation (notably in Italy) and provided an urgency in setting up the new Federal Republic in Germany. Similarly, the different international climate surrounding the Southern Europe's transitions provided a more relaxed setting – one that included the debate about 'Euro-communist' parties and their role in liberal democracies, although not one that excluded geostrategic schemes in the area on the part of the Soviet Union.

The post-Cold War situation in which transitions in the many CEE countries have occurred is again different, including a fundamental change in the structure of international relations with the passing of bipolar confrontation and the consequent need to redefine international allegiances. The Cold War had provided a convenient mental frame in which to promote the cause of liberal democracy, although one marked strongly by the insecurities of the time.[10] By comparison, the post-Cold War situation – initially, and somewhat naively, viewed as a 'new dawn' in international relations – has turned out to be one of greater regional uncertainties and proneness to actual armed conflict than that surrounding the previous two sets of transitions. There is a potential danger from the instability of some new regimes, most prominently the Russian. And the possibility of some regimes ending up as non-democratic – Belarus being a first pointer to this – of course raises the question of their external policy orientations. Such instability explains the fairly strong security motive for NATO and EU entry on the part of various ECE states, notably the Baltic republics.

As seen, new democracies may, following authoritarian rule, redirect external policy in a way that reinforces their legitimacy. It may in this respect be hypothesised, fourthly, that *multilateral allegiances usually prove more benign for democratisation than do bilateral ones.* This is because the former are more likely to accord a high priority to democracy promotion as an external policy objective. Bilateral allegiances run the risk of developing a patron–client status with a dominant external sponsor that may distort the dynamics of regime change.

Thus, both postwar Italy and post-civil war Greece became 'penetrated systems' of the USA to a disproportionate extent, involving direct political but also covert interference in the fortunes of domestic actors to the disadvantage of the Left. It is clear that Washington prioritised security concerns over democratisation. What emerged was a somewhat restricted version of parliamentary democracy in the Greek case; while in Italy democratic exclusivism buttressed long-term Christian Democratic rule, obstructed alternation in power to the Left and for some time acerbated polarisation between government and opposition. The link with Italy's much delayed democratic consolidation is obvious. Greece underwent a brutal authoritarian interlude in 1967–74 very much with American connivance. But the depth of such bilateral allegiances is enhanced by the climate of international relations at the time. The USA's pattern of geostrategic interference in Latin America, favouring dictatorships over democracies when security interests so dictated, has in the past decade been replaced by a more relaxed approach to regimes to the south (save Cuba), involving support for democratic consolidation through economic means.[11] The prospects for democracies in Latin America now look brighter than at any time since the Second World War; and the end of the Cold War is one major factor explaining this.

In the Southern European transitions, security interests were less predominant, despite a growing Soviet naval presence in the eastern Mediterranean. This was shown in the readiness of the USA to allow these countries a margin for maneouvre in their regime changes.[12] At the same time, the EC had emerged as the most important external actor, offering multilateral links that were supportive of the new democracies.[13] For the EC and its member states, security interests were obviously not absent, but democracy promotion was more to the fore, not least as this was a firm precondition for accession. Significantly, countries like Greece and to some degree Spain were thus able to disengage from the American embrace – in Greece's case rather polemically because of US involvement with the discredited Colonels – and this opened the way for a multilateral relationship with the EC, which helped to foster democratic rule.

With the transitions in the CEE countries in the 1990s, the EU has been even more central and influential an external actor and the USA even more in the background. This new multilateral link has replaced the bilateral relationship with the USSR, which was a classic case of collective subjugation to an outside power. During the 1990s, the EU and its member states have come to develop an extensive portfolio of support mechanisms for the new democracies to the East, while articulating a more precise and insistent form of democratic conditionality. The EU's capacity for democracy building is far more extensive and influential than was the case with the Southern European new democracies only two decades ago. Thus, while the USA was content with versions of formal democracy, the EU has emerged as an advocate of substantive democracy for its eventual entrants. This engagement with democracy building is particularly true of East-Central Europe and some Balkan countries, such as Bulgaria and Romania. Somewhat by contrast, a prominent American role with overriding security interests has been present in other parts of the Balkans, notably the ex-Yugoslav republics involved in ethnic conflict. For example, Western support for the increasingly authoritarian rule of Sali Berisha in Albania in the mid-1990s was explained by a concern for stability in an effort to contain war in the Balkan region.

Democratisation obviously takes time, and this reminds us of one fifth and final point of differentiation – that *external impacts may vary between phases of the democratisation process*. Since early transition is likely to be disruptive, there is potential here for external influences to intrude, depending on how much early transition actually causes concern by affecting interests (security, political, economic) in the region and thus what foreign actors choose to do in response. Once transition moves into the constituent phase – regime choice is clear, transition actors become absorbed in the business of working out their governance – then, supposedly, the need to look to external actors for support lessens. It is notionally at a later stage that important decisions on key external matters are taken. For instance, the two Iberian states applied for EC membership in 1977 once their constituent processes were virtually completed. Subsequently, the interweaving between external developments and democratic consolidation will probably occur in a more evolutionary way, given especially the relatively slow pace of procedures in Brussels over accession to the EU. In reality, however, such phases – presented here in schematic form – admittedly do not evolve so neatly; and this is particularly so when the pace of change is high, as in Central and Eastern Europe. For instance, many countries in that region showed a strong interest in EU links already in their early transitions. This had to do with their regime changes being much more demanding, and as a consequence their need to look outwards for support was the greater. The pace of change has been particularly marked in the ECE countries, which have the best prospects for EU entry and are already, in three cases, member states of NATO.

The above points of differentiation with historical comparisons provide us with three lessons. Firstly, it is obvious that external factors cannot simply be relegated to second-order importance in explaining the dynamics of regime change. Any such assumption plays havoc with the diversity and complexity with which international influences interact with domestic developments. It is, furthermore, not always true that these influences remain a dependent variable in this respect. The structure and conditions of international relations may in a particular time context have a powerful effect on internal change, somewhat irrespective of national particularities. But the type of influence, and especially the emphasis on democracy promotion, depends on the form of linkage with external actors. Thus, obviously, there is room for national specificity but it is counterbalanced by structural factors in international relations. In this way, approaches to transition emphasising political choice have to be modified by confining conditions. Even though new democratic elites have the opportunity to reframe their country's external relations, there are different pressures and constraints even here relating to past regime inheritances and current concerns of outside actors about where their transition is leading.

Secondly, one cannot baldly conclude that there is an overall diachronic and perhaps incremental progression in international impacts on democratisation when comparing successive sets of transitions. Comparisons with the postwar transitions suggest that international factors were no less prominent then; indeed, in some ways they had more direct 'bite' through the coincidence of the Cold War and the mechanisms of control by outside actors, such as occupation and patron–client status. On the other hand, in the 1990s, it is clear that international factors have a far more pervasive, diverse and also institutionalised impact. It is therefore the general type of international context that seems to matter most.

At the same time, particular trends are evident, such as, notably, the continuous growth in European integration evident when comparing the transitions in the CEE countries with those in Southern Europe. Furthermore, there is the increasing internationalisation of human rights as an issue. Introduced after the Second World War (Declaration of Human Rights 1948, European Convention on Human Rights 1950), this featured modestly in the Southern European transitions, except in the Greek case.[14] At the same time, human rights began to be promoted by the Helsinki Accords of 1975, and more and more networks of human rights activists emerged while the new policies of the Carter and Reagan administrations with respect to Latin America contributed to this trend.[15] It is in the 1990s that human rights issues have come really to the fore in European politics, in conjunction with democratisation in the CEE countries, primarily because of major problems involving ethnic minorities in many cases – though more so in the Balkans than ECE. One might also add that informal international networks have much intensified in the intervening period. And, then, there are various developments arising from the new technology and its growth in global connections. These are much more evident in the 1990s than during previous democratisations in Europe.

Thirdly, it is clear in different ways that regime changes in CEE differ from previous sets of transitions not merely because the international order has simultaneously been open to reshaping, but as the magnitude of change there has had wider international consequences. Undoubtedly, the EU's eastward enlargement is a more difficult process than its previous southward enlargement, with the multiple transformation taking place in that region. It follows, then, that international factors have to be considered in a new light. Problems of economic transformation and state and nation building – especially when there are implications for national boundaries and national minorities – inevitably raise special problems for international relations.

Multilateral cooperation, the European Union and democratisation

It is evident the international context has, over the past decade, been far more embracing of the democratisation process than ever before, notwithstanding the strong impacts on domestic politics in the early Cold War period. This was for three reasons: international organisations have become more interventionist while engaging in democracy promotion or building; the international order has itself been restructured with predictable consequences for domestic politics; and, the extent of transformation in post-Communist Europe is so much greater than in previous-regime change and this has engaged international attention and efforts more than ever before. As we have seen with East-Central European countries, international motives have often been overriding as shown in their compulsive strategy focused on European integration and, with it, security enhancement. Accordingly, the pace of change deriving from this strategy has become increasingly frenetic just as the process of accession has impacted more and more on domestic concerns usually with a direct or indirect relevance to regime change. At the same time, regime change in ECE has been distinctly less controversial than in the Balkans since it has been more straightforwardly directed towards liberal democracy, with the interim or partial exception of Slovakia. Thus, in most cases, ECE states are seen as on course for democratic consolidation.

Given this importance of the European international environment for democratisation, discussion will now concentrate on ways in which the one may impact on the other and in particular on how the EU – the most influential by far of the regional organisations – has chosen to determine regime change in post-Communist states and in ECE in particular. The prospects for this are then assessed with some attention to cross-national variation. In the next section, attention will turn to specific areas in which regime change and other forms of transformation are affected by outside influences and how they respond to these. In this way, two-way effects are taken into account while differentiation between levels of regime change, phases of that process and, of course, countries is possible.

Broadly speaking, the European environment has been much more supportive of new democracies' chances than they were in the interwar period, when conflicts over national minorities and especially the rise of Nazi Germany complicated their fortunes. By virtual contrast with post-1919, the post-1989 situation has been markedly different not least as mechanisms for multilateral cooperation were already well-established when the transitions began, while Germany was already a stable liberal democracy and one committed to promoting both democracy and security in ECE especially. Unlike in the more unstable Balkan environment, there are also no serious regional conflicts or minority problems; or, where these may exist, as in Slovakia and the Baltic republics, international and especially EU pressure has helped to ameliorate conditions.[16] All this helped to counteract the worst effects of the uncertainty of a radically changed international context, although admittedly the economic and political instabilities in Russia remained a source of anxiety.

Post-Communist states have been undergoing democratisation at a time when the political weight of European organisations (above all, the EU) and transnational networks are more developed than ever before. Furthermore, these organisations' capacity for democracy building is far more extensive and influential than was the case with the Southern European new democracies only two decades ago. On the other hand, the task of system building (political, economic and in many cases also national) is immense and on a scale unprecedented. And there are time pressures from Brussels on applicant states to push ahead determinedly with their economic restructuring and modernisation; and that can in turn create strains and pressures which are not always easily accommodated by still-fragile democracies.

The post-Fascist states confronted considerable problems of reconstruction, both political and economic, and they also faced difficulties of national identity, especially in the German case, but the overall task was relatively less daunting than that in CEE. Moreover, they benefited from the Marshall Aid Programme which offered support to a degree way beyond the capacity and will of the EU in the 1990s. References back to this programme as a model have reflected some disillusionment on the part of ECE ruling circles over support from Brussels. That expectations of the EU relationship are high in ECE is no surprise, given the sense of historical mission impelling them towards Brussels, but it does mean governments there sometimes let their impatience override their sense of reality concerning current EU business and its almost impossibly overloaded agenda.

The prospect of delay in EU accession has at times caused concern, such as some few years ago prompting the then Hungarian Prime Minister Gyula Horn to remind Brussels that European integration means 'hope for the strengthening of Hungarian democracy, the guarantee of national independence and our international security'.[17] Such statements, recalling similar ones by Southern European leaders in the later 1970s about the EC's role as democratic guarantor, can sometimes contain an element of moral blackmail – the implication being that less than speedy support runs the risk of failed consolidation. This particular mentality is met rather more often in Balkan states where there is sometimes a desperate reliance on outside help to extricate given countries from the monumental problems of the Balkans. In early 1997, the newly elected Bulgarian President Petar Stoyanov warned the European Commission in his appeal for help that his country faced financial ruin. The sense that the EU might be somehow morally responsible for Bulgaria's plight produced the sensible but hardly exciting response from Jacques Santer, president of the Commission, that help would be forthcoming so long as Bulgaria formed a stable government to overcome the crisis.[18]

While the political criteria (in effect, democratic conditionality) are essential preconditions for EU entry – and they remain a reference point in pre-accession years as a matter for confirmation – during actual negotiations attention shifts to a vast range of micro-political and economic concerns. It is unusual for high politics to intrude directly save at moments of crisis (when issues are referred to the top) and of course when the grand act of treaty signature takes place. However, in the case of the CEE countries, the political criteria have been and are likely to remain more to the fore compared with the Southern European negotiations. This is because in the former case the Commission's official pronouncement (*avis*) on suitability for membership has been followed by the Accession Partnerships and the Commission's annual progress reports on applicant countries.[19]

So far, it appears that the relationship between European integration and democratisation is more complex than is often supposed, for there are pressures and counter-pressures. Democracy building cannot neatly be extracted from other concerns in the context of everyday activity, for these intermix; and of course democracy building has its many faces – with a variety of training programmes being just one of them – just as the EU's support for moving to a market economy may also have indirect effects on democratisation. Thus, the EU has a direct bearing on two of the transformations. As to the third, nation building, its importance is less obvious, although problems of ethnic minority rights do acquire high visibility in EU circles.

Other European organisations offer less promise, although they also exercise a democracy test to a lesser and variable extent and there has, over the 1990s, developed a growing tendency for this to happen. The Council, of Europe, for instance, is a much less ambitious organisation, but it highlights human and minority rights and membership of it has a certain prestige.[20] The Organisation for Security and Cooperation in Europe (OSCE) also defends human and minority rights and aims at building democratic institutions, while playing a monitoring role especially at election time. However, its obligations unlike those of the Council of Europe are not legally binding.[21] The defence organisations have democracy requirements either by association (the WEU with the EU) or have developed ones blandly defined, e.g. NATO's standards include civilian control over the armed forces, the resolution of outstanding ethnic disputes as well as a market economy and a constitutional state. Then there are various financial organisations like the International Monetary Fund (IMF), the World Bank and the European Bank for Reconstruction and Development (EBRD), all of which have exercised a form of political conditionality although usually written up as 'good governance' rather than specifically geared to a list of democratic criteria.

One cannot complete this picture of multilateral cooperation without some reference to regional organisations and their relatively modest contribution to multilateral cooperation. In ECE, a series of such organisations have been created including the Council of the Baltic Sea States, the Visegrad group and the Central European Free Trade Area and also the Central European Initiative. The success of some of these has at times been marred by bilateral tensions over remaining minority problems; but then the tendency in the later 1990s was for improvements in bilateral relations within ECE, including through bilateral cooperation agreements.[22] In recent times, the work of these organisations, and especially that of the Visegrad group, has been focused more directly on common problems of EU accession. Thus, regional cooperation and bilateral diplomacy have increasingly dovetailed with multilateral cooperation on the wider European level.

Given the superior importance of the EU as an external democratising agent, discussion now concentrates mainly on this organisation and the prospects for its eastward enlargment. In effect, we are talking about pre-accession relations between ECE countries and Brussels and at a still fairly early stage in some cases; and this restricts the scope, as yet, for assessing these democratisation impacts from outside. Nevertheless, it is vital to distinguish between (and not to confuse) the overall integration process and actual EU accession. While the latter has a historic and symbolic meaning and it fully integrates new members into EU institutions, it is but the highpoint of *de facto* integration that has been occurring for many years and will obviously continue once these new democracies are member states. This overall integration process may be likened to the transnational term 'convergence'.

There develops a direct temporal link between convergence and incorporation (EU membership) with the promise of the latter much underscoring the former. A progression becomes evident over a period of what is likely to be at least a decade: while convergence is less binding and routinely impactive than is incorporation, it moves through a series of stages involving policy orientation towards Brussels, leading to membership application, the formalisation of links (notably with an association agreement), various pre-negotiation consultation procedures and then, finally, negotiations for entry. Hence, convergence increasingly acquires features similar to incorporation – without the latter's guarantees and certainty – and these point towards the consolidation of new democratic regimes.[23] The most obvious way in which convergence affects prospective member states is through policy choice, content and commitment and of course economic interests; but, also telling is the impact and influence on elite mentalities in new democracies, with countries emerging from international isolation as these are likely to be. Such influence, deriving notably from ever closer contacts with political and other elites in established democracies, may well be system-reinforcing.

In summary, it may be generally said that most broad types of influence exerted by the EU on democratisation in applicant countries are applicable in the post-Communist cases. These may be seen as signposts in the process of convergence:

1 symbolic: the identification of the EU with liberal democracy;
2 the participation of political and economic elites and groups in transnational networks linked to the EU and other European organisations;
3 the prospect of eventual EU entry, with its energising effects on prospective member states and impacts on their policy direction;
4 the gradual involvement of political elites in the EU institutional framework, such as through membership negotiations and preparations for entry but also mechanisms linked to intermediary stages, such as Association;
5 pressure exerted from the application of democratic conditionality by the EU, including through economic aid programmes;
6 the binding policy commitments that come from adoption of the *acquis communautaire* and that, increasingly, impinge once applicants become member states, with a variety of possible effects – direct and indirect – on further progress towards democratic consolidation.

One may extract from this list those influences that relate most directly to democratisation, while considering the others in a broader context in the next section. This may be done by developing and applying the transnational concept of 'conditionality'.

As part of the overall process of convergence, prospective entrant countries have to satisfy some basic requirements, and of these the most political is the democracy test. Established democracies understandably have nothing to prove, but new democracies which are still likely to be in transition at the time they apply for membership have to demonstrate that they are moving in the right direction, have a potential for stability and meet a range of particular democratic criteria. These are called 'political conditions' in the language of Brussels.

The concept of *conditionality* expresses this, and of all the transnational concepts it is the most resonant of deliberate efforts to determine from outside the course and outcome of regime change. Conditionality is achieved by specifying conditions or even pre-conditions for support, involving either promise of material aid or political opportunities. It usually involves political monitoring of domestic developments in the countries under discussion. It is a method adopted increasingly by several international and European organisations, paralleling the greater international attention to minority rights since the collapse of Communism in Central and Eastern Europe. However, it is the EU that has come to be most associated with democratic conditionality since the eventual prize is no less than eventual membership for new democracies.[24]

Entry to the EU, being a lengthy process, allows for ample time to observe the practice of democratic conditions in what must be still-fragile new regimes. Any serious setback here threatens to abort or at least delay negotiations. Over time, the EU has come to be more comprehensive in detailing democratic criteria concerning the countries from Central and Eastern Europe. Increasingly, these criteria have moved from mainly procedural conditions of formal democracy (e.g. rule of law, separation of institutional powers, free elections, freedom of expression) to include also criteria of substantive democracy, such as the role of political parties as a vehicle for political participation, the pluralism of the media, the importance of local government and an involved civil society.[25]

Through conditionality, therefore, the EU may exercise more immediate pressures than is sometimes supposed by those who argue that European integration can only have long-term effects on the consolidation process. At the same time, this pressure from Brussels has been complemented – in a way analogous to the carrot-and-stick syndrome – by support mechanisms for democracy building. Of the various aid programmes, the most pertinent is the PHARE Democracy Programme administered by the Human Rights Foundation in Brussels. Its brief is to 'support the activities and efforts of non-governmental bodies promoting a stable open society and good governance', and it focuses support on 'political reform and democratic practice, where local advocacy bodies are weak and professional expertise is particularly lacking'. In doing so, it seeks to further many of the criteria of both procedural but even more substantive democracy itemised above.[26] In the last few years, however, PHARE has come to be more driven by accession requirements and the ability of applicants to meet them.

Democratic conditionality does, however, have its limitations. It is reasonable to assume that its effects are largely dependent on the responsiveness of domestic actors, their European commitment being the decisive factor. There is, nonetheless, a possible circular form of behaviour, for transnational elite socialisation – including the increasing participation of new democratic personnel in EU institutional fora – may affect attitudes, making them more disposed towards external pressures. But there are limits to this form of Europeanising dynamic, and in the case of Central and Eastern Europe that must reside most of all in nationalist tendencies. Hence, conditionality trades more on persuasion and temptation (over accession) than coercion, although an element of constraint does gradually arise once agreements are made (notably over Association), and entry negotiations start to produce decisions. But the main limitation on conditionality relates to transition paths being played out in individual countries. What if a transition trajectory is not clear or appears to be taking a different path from that of a familiar brand of liberal democracy? Does then the influence of conditionality stop at the national frontier? The problem arises in the case of what are called 'hybrid regimes' which meet only minimum standards for democracy and operate in some way contrary to normal democratic practice. It is likely that the scope, through convergence, for European influence on these regime outcomes is rather restricted.

While convergence has its gradual and mildly intensifying pressures (they may be described as intermediate ones), conditionality plays along in a more immediate way and adds a sharpness to the prospects of convergence. But conditionality has a wider meaning, for there are practical reasons why applicant countries need to gear up their democratic acts. For they are preparing to enter the EU system in which the principles of representative government are tested through participation in the Council of Ministers and the European Parliament, but also other mechanisms prior to membership.[27] Such systemic constraints, though of a milder kind, even begin to affect countries once they demonstrate a serious interest in joining the EU.

It is in the context of different forms of convergence that democratic conditionality carries influence. The impact of this basic demand by Brussels has been conditioned by these wider developments. These include the political will to enter the EU (in which case, extra efforts are made to meet conditionality requirements), the instrumental rationalities of political actors (sometimes leading them to meet the same requirements out of a calculation to please Brussels), economic interests and the growing trade links with EU countries (thus reinforcing the desire to satisfy on the level of political criteria) and also developments in civil society (which could both promote but also inhibit the impact of conditionality pressures). Significantly, it was the problems relating to ethnicity and the situation of minorities that acquired particular visibility at the European level, thus affecting evaluations there about meeting the political criteria. One may add at this point that the real prospect for EU accession in the tangible future is very likely to reinforce these wider pressures to meet conditonality demands; and, here, the countries of ECE comprise the most favoured category, certainly compared with the Balkans, although the EU has since the Helsinki Summit (December 1999) begun to differentiate among countries in the latter region.

What real or direct proof is there that conditionality works? Here, the process over satisfying political conditions for membership is a sustained one with a series of closely timed stages through which applicant countries have to move. Based on the Copenhagen criteria of 1993,[28] these have included the Commission's *avis* on accession applications (July 1997), the Accession Partnerships (1998) and the annual Commission reports on progress by candidate countries. Three sets of these reports have so far been published, in November 1998, October 1999 and October 2000. All of these exposed in some detail the achievement in each country's case of the political conditions, including the existence and stability of democratic institutions and procedures, free and fair elections, the independence of the judiciary, anti-corruption measures as well as respect for civil and political rights, the presence of economic, social and cultural rights and the protection of minority rights. It is made quite clear that satisfying political and economic criteria is an absolute precondition for eventual membership and that problems here may delay that event. Thus, a real pressure is exerted on governments in CEE negotiating entry to the EU and failure to live up to requirements, especially on the political level, may occasion unwelcome publicity, as the Czech Republic discovered in the autumn of 1999 over the situation of the Roma in the community of Usti nad Labem.

While most applicant states in ECE have progressively satisfied the political conditions, the case of Slovakia became somewhat notorious in the mid-1990s for its failure to do so. Slovakia is also symptomatic of deviant transition paths complicating accession prospects with consequent doubts being cast on the chances for democratic consolidation. Briefly, the story is as follows.[29] The Mečiar Government formed in 1994 took an ambivalent line towards the EU, for while meeting some formal or procedural requirements, it nevertheless adopted practices that flouted democratic rules and increasingly showed signs of authoritarian tendencies. Warnings from Brussels, through several *demarches*, failed to change the mind of the then Slovak Government, which sought every means to retain power, including measures to restrict the political activity of the opposition parties. However, its defeat by the now more united opposition in 1998 brought to power the Dzurinda Government which has given an overriding priority to achieving the political conditions. The difference was shown by the first two annual progress reports, of 1998 and 1999. Whereas the first, published only shortly after the 1998 change of power, was in effect a condemnation of the Mečiar years (e.g. the concentration of power in the hands of the incumbent government, the failure to protect minority rights), that of 1999 lauded the achievements of the new government and proclaimed that Slovakia now fulfilled the Copenhagen criteria although further improvements were necessary for strengthening the independence of the judiciary, securing the stability of democratic institutions, fighting corruption and protecting minority rights.[30]

Some lessons may be drawn from the Slovak case, but also one relating to the EU's democratic conditionality in general. Firstly, the actions of the Mečiar Government illustrated the close relationship between support for integration and EU entry and commitment to democratisation; but also the converse of that. They seemed to show the limits of conditionality, for when a government remains intransigent then Brussels has little real power beyond trying persistent persuasion to overcome this obstacle. However, Slovakia was interesting because on other grounds, such as economic, it was considered a reasonable bet for EU entry, and of course it was in East-Central Europe (the region almost certain to contain the first successful cases under eastward enlargement). While the Dzurinda Government has therefore proved that a newly elected leadership with the political will may turn around an unfavourable situation, the continued polarisation between government and opposition and the fragility of the democratic consensus are matters of which Brussels is very conscious. The consistent pressure from the EU to firm up the political conditions is something of which government leaders and top-ranking civil servants in Bratislava are all too aware and they tend to see this as a positive factor in domestic politics, even though the unremitting pressure to carry through the *acquis communautaire* is causing severe tensions around government business.[31] By implication, one may see, however, that in states whose prospects for EU membership are in doubt or not realisable for a long time the influence of Brussels over conditionality is likely to be accordingly less. They could be seen as lying within the outer rings of the EU's geostrategic pull and as not possessing those historical, cultural and geographical influences that help to underpin the motivation of elites in ECE to 'return to Europe'.

Secondly, Slovakia offers some evidence that a combination of 'top–down' pressures from the EU (and, for that matter, other international organisations) and 'bottom–up' pressures from civil society can indeed have some effect on intransigent governments. It is reasonable to suppose that the Mečiar Government, had it been re-elected, would have hardened its authoritarian course; but the fact is that it wasn't, and a significant part here was played by outside support for Slovakia's NGOs, many of which took a proactive role in the 1998 parliamentary election campaign, including direct efforts to promote voter turnout.[32] In other words, this kind of dual pressure from outside may help to tip the balance in favour of democratisation, although much also depends on the quality of political culture in the country concerned (the threat from Mečiar in fact had a stimulating effect on NGO development) and therefore the readiness of domestic actors to take advantage of European solidarity. A similar course of action has been developing in Croatia with European support in the recent elections for NGO activity, drawing directly from the Slovak example. While Croatia may be said to be far less ready for eventual EU membership because of a decade of much stronger authoritarian rule under Tudjman reinforced by war, it does not have Slovakia's continuing disadvantage of the former leader dominating the opposition, for Tudjman is dead and his party has begun to disintegrate. Croatia is of course another case of the European option closely relating to democratisation's prospects, as was underlined immediately by that country's new rulers in January 2000.

Thirdly, and generally, the EU's greater concern with significant areas of substantive democracy in the 1990s, compared say with its demands on the new Southern European democracies two decades ago, has brought that organisation more centrally into the debate about democratic consolidation. This tends to distinguish the EU from other international organisations like NATO as well as the Council of Europe and the OSCE, for the last two while stressing human and minority rights have much less power to promote them.

It had previously been assumed that European integration had far more relevance to longer-term processes like consolidation; but there was little attempt to measure how this happened. The EU now helps to provide the means for doing so. Some of its demands, as set out in the Copenhagen criteria and elaborated in the progress reports, demonstrate this when combined with its various support programmes. Thus, issues like human and minority rights, developing civil society and the democratic commitment of political parties all clearly fall into the basket of substantive democracy. But they are also in turn the more difficult areas of democratic life to influence from outside. Governments in applicant states may pass the necessary legislation, but firming up minority rights also depends on attitudes and behaviour at the public level. Brussels may have a direct effect on elites, as shown in the activity of transnational party activity, but its influence even with fairly pro-EU national publics in new democracies must be considered as at best somewhat attenuated. This linkage may be further complicated by domestic considerations like the state or an absence of political consensus over both democratic rules and EU accession.

In conclusion, convergence may therefore be seen as the context within which international influences prove beneficial or otherwise for the consolidation process. It should be pointed out, though, that convergence may have its negative effects. These may be twofold. Firstly, post-Communist countries have been under great pressure to adopt Western models of liberal democracy and of the market economy with as yet little input of their own in defining these models. They have accepted this situation because of the overriding desire in ECE countries to join European organisations like NATO and especially the EU. They may come to have more influence once they are actually member states, but meanwhile there is some scope for underlying cultural disaffection with the so far one-sided process of convergence. Secondly, the sheer burden of adopting the whole EU *acquis*, often under great if not impossible time pressure, is putting government administrations in ECE under increasing strain. This is having a serious impact on government-overload problems, with possible consequences for democratic performance and hence, indirectly, presenting some possible problems for regime consolidation, if only by delaying somewhat its achievement. As yet, no major political forces have exploited these problems, but the strains of accession negotiations may in the future begin to cause direct political tensions in some ECE countries.

External influences and their impacts on democratisation in East-Central Europe

In order to examine these problems systematically, it is necessary to apply the main lesson from this chapter so far, which is that external impacts are best judged in terms of particular mechanisms and actions. This is taken forward here by examining different levels of the consolidation process and how far these relate to European convergence before drawing conclusions about the effects of democratic conditionality. Since democratisation through convergence takes many forms, these will be discussed separately. They include the other two transformations and how these interact with democratisation.

The formal level of regime change

This level involves not merely the establishment of democratic institutions through a constitution, but also the securing of the rule of law and, generally, the institutionalisation of democratic procedures, leading over time to the fostering of constitutional conventions – features which relate directly to democratic consolidation. Conventionally seen as a level that is a domestic concern, there are, however, a variety of ways in which this may be influenced from outside, most notably through joining European organisations like the Council of Europe and particularly the EU. Whatever the real problems of the 'democratic deficit' in the functioning of the EU (a topic of polemical interest in some circles in ECE), applicant countries are entering a form of political system in which the rule of law is respected and the European Court of Justice asserts its authority in the legislative process.

There are some less tangible avenues for exploring external influences, for close association with established democracies may have cross-fertilising effects on a new democracy's evolution at this level. Such a phenomenon is quite analogous to the transnational concepts of *emulation* and *diffusion*. We are talking here of value systems being transmitted or at least coloured by practices and behavioural forms in neighbouring states or those in the same region. This is most likely to feature mainly at the elite level, perhaps extending to intelligentsia circles which may, for instance, inform themselves through relevant sources of expertise (e.g. law journals published in nearby established democracies). Clearly, this is an area which is difficult to measure exactly. Easier to establish, though, is external influence on constitutional mechanisms that are likely to further the rule of law. For example, Poland became a member of the Council of Europe in 1991 undertaking to observe its so-called European standards, which define a system of values and set out the aims, this at a time when the belief was becoming more widespread that these standards were the most reliable and tested measures of constitutional normalcy.[33]

The post-Communist states have in fact demonstrated a general fascination with models of more prosperous, viz. Western, states.[34] Constitution making there has been a complicated and in a few cases a lengthy process. In this context, some foreign constitutional mechanisms have been commonly adopted in ECE. Many post-Communist politicians looked to Western institutional arrangements as role models, in line with a broader 'return to Europe' in political elite thinking. It was the French semi-presidential system that provided initial inspiration for notions of executive power, more than the British and American executive structures, as it offered an intermediate solution.[35] This was notably true of Poland, where the French model was particularly influential partly due to traditional cultural and political linkages with France, as was the case in Portugal too.[36] German institutional imports were, however, much more in evidence across ECE along the same lines as in post-Franco Spain. Poland and Hungary adopted the constructive vote of no-confidence from Germany,

Hungary also being influenced here by the Spanish transition, while in a whole range of countries various electoral thresholds were set for parliamentary representation, again taking their cue from the Federal Republic – including 4 per cent in Albania, Bulgaria and Lithuania, and 5 per cent in the Czech Republic, Hungary, Slovakia and Poland (from 1993).[37] This is not to forget the considerable body of foreign experts involved in constitutional advice from Western European countries, but also especially from the United States.[38]

According to Rüb, the attraction of foreign models is twofold. They provide a manageable and tested central idea which is convenient while thereby reducing political responsibility for problem-solving. But they also provide a necessary legitimation for new institutions through association with successful democracies.[39] While their influence is likely to be greater when national historical influences from previous constitutional and political experience are not dominant, there are, however, problems in importing institutional models and transplanting them to a different even though comparable cultural, social and political environment.[40] This requires some flexibility in integrating external ideas when formulating constitutions, for the success of an institutional arrangement in one setting – and introduced elsewhere in an earlier period – does not guarantee a replication of positive experience in a further new democracy.

In short, it is indeed possible to see some specific if limited forms of external influence on democratic constitutions in ECE. However, the pressures of democratic conditionality have tended to reinforce the new procedures of judicial review. Establishing constitutional courts became a principle in the postwar democratisations, one repeated in the three Southern European cases and again – with these precedents in mind – in CEE in the early 1990s. If there is any reservation about judicial review in post-Communist states, it is that in some of them a legal culture incorporating its values has not yet developed much.[41] But with ever increasing contacts between ECE countries and EU institutions, these inchoate developments are likely to be reinforced gradually.

There are other pressures and influences already evident. Pre-accession strategies require some serious administrative adaptation in the direction of greater policy coordination and bureaucratic modernisation to conform to Brussels' requirements. The implementation by prospective EU entrants of the *acquis communautaire* has some implications for furthering the rule of law, an interesting field for investigation in itself. However, this does not enter into the more difficult area of compliance with possibly inhibiting effects from a political culture developed under the Communist systems. However, more important perhaps at this stage is the general recognition given to ECE governments as European partners by the EU and its member states – which is both a means of confidence building for new democratic elites but is also likely to promote the credibility and legitimacy of democratic institutions in these countries, assuming that national publics are broadly favourable to EU entry prospects.

Political actors and external policy orientation

What is still striking is the broad consensus in favour of EU accession among political elites in ECE countries, with the main exception of Slovakia where government and opposition parties have remained somewhat divided. This overwhelming support, yet to be tested against the hard grind of negotiation realities, is largely explained by high political motivation linked to historical symbolism ('return to Europe'), a concern for democratic stabilisation and security guarantees (NATO membership seen as complementing that of the EU) and of course economic and financial benefits.[42] Prestige in one way or another is always present; but what is salient is the dominance of political motives – and this fits broadly with the motivation of applicant states in previous enlargements of the EU. It presents a positive backdrop to the potential influence of conditionality demands on these new democracies.

Qualifications to this breadth of support are usually located in nationalist or populist circles. In Slovakia, for example, the parties of the former Mečiar Government evidenced mainly formal support while in office, but in fact remained ambivalent and revealed some hostile outlooks towards EU entry. For the parties of the Dzurinda Government – in power since October 1998 – EU and NATO entry is the major unifying policy commitment and they have aimed singlemindedly at improving Slovakia's chances of accession. There is no significant hostility or reservation towards EU entry in the other countries, outside fringe extremist forces like the (Fascist) Republican Party in the Czech Republic. The orthodox Communist Party of Bohemia and Moravia, also hostile, is however not a fringe party, with some 10 per cent of the vote in the last election and increased support in opinion polls since. In Poland, small parties on the Right adhere formally to EU membership although it is possible to identify some reservations from their positions on policy prescriptions.[43] This represents altogether a broader consensus behind the EU accession strategy than in the previous two sets of democratisations in Europe, where in some countries major parties of the Left were opposed at this equivalent stage.

Such a consensus may well come under strain in the years ahead during entry negotiations. This will probably be gradual, unlike the strong disaffection in these countries over NATO's bombing of the Federal Republic of Yugoslavia (FRY) and its impact on the NATO entry question. More likely a trend is growing party-political differentiation and perhaps divergence over policy issues during EU entry negotiations.[44] Meanwhile, there are various ways of testing the firmness and depth of support for the European option; and these should throw light on the state of convergence in the countries of ECE. In turn, there are implications here for a willingness to meet the requirements of democratic conditionality.

A more pronounced Eurocentric focus in external policy concerns should reinforce the strategy of EU accession, since policy priorities are established with respect to other major external allegiances. In postwar Europe, the post-Fascist democracies had no real alternative to European integration, given the Cold War situation. The Southern European democracies embraced the European option to varying degrees (in Greece, PASOK followed for a time a 'third-worldist' version of Euro-scepticism), while for Portugal the policy reorientation was less dramatic since that country was already, under the dictatorship, a member of NATO and EFTA. With the CEE countries, the policy reorientation is far more radical; and therefore any rearrangement of external priorities is significant. It amounted in effect to a basic reorientation in external relations from an eastward-looking to a westward-looking priority. There were, however, some national differences apparent.

For Poland, the historical motive behind the 'return to Europe' was poignant, given the country's historical problem of maintaining national sovereignty while pressed between the two powers of Germany and Russia. This was resolved, in part, in that a now democratically stable Germany, integrated in the EU, acted as sponsor for Poland's determined efforts to the join that organisation. Unlike in the past, therefore, relations with Germany promised to be a form of democratic guarantee. The fervour with which Warsaw has pursued EU accession can only be said to intensify the democratic commitment that goes with acceptance into that organisation. For the three Baltic republics, the security motive was particularly strong with regard to EU links since they had recently seceded from the Soviet Union, and relations with Moscow remained difficult given large Russian minorities in two of these states. More than Poland, they were vulnerable to the unpredictability and uncertainty of Russian politics. However, their commitment to EU entry was such that any reservations about losing national sovereignty were more than neutralised.[45]

For Hungary and the Czech Republic, the sense of 'rejoining' the European heartland was such that democratic commitment formed a fairly straightforward part of this – in Prague's case, reinforced by reference back to the interwar democracy, one brought down more by Nazi aggression than by internal difficulties. For this reason, redefining relations with Germany has been less easy compared with other ECE countries. However, the split in Czechoslovakia tended to strengthen Prague's westward orientation. Like Poland, these two countries are now members of NATO as well as of the Council of Europe, so that European linkages are significantly advanced with all the democracy-reinforcing effects this has through institutionalised networking and identification with these organisations (in NATO's case, this identification was for a time badly harmed because of the war with the FRY). After independence in 1993, Slovakia's foreign policy orientation remained unclear for a while and, despite accepting the European option, close relations with Russia and the Ukraine were cultivated also because of important trade links with those two countries.[46] Suspicions remained that Mečiar's real sympathies lay to the east. But Slovakia was really the exception that proved the rule, for there was a fairly obvious link between Mečiar's external policy inclinations and the less than convincing democratic credentials of his Government. This very same link has now been presented in quite a new light by the Dzurinda Government's commitment both to EU accession and to democratic procedures.

The systemic importance of external policy reorientation is thus quite marked. It is one highlighted in the statements of political leaders in these countries; and, it is evident from debates over the European option especially when this gets contested. This basic link between democracy building and Europeanisation may be explored further by looking at the value systems of elites in new democracies. There is, admittedly, little research on elite attitudes in the CEE countries that may conceivably buttress democratisation (work on mass attitudes is much more developed), so that comments have to be more impressionistic than empirical. To some extent, the answer derives from the European orientation of political elites in ECE. Some figures, Havel for instance, already had cultural links in Western Europe. Others had no such links, like his co-national Václav Klaus, who was buried away in an economics institute in Prague but then emerged in transition to establish close relations with certain countries, notably the UK, involving an ideological sympathy with Thatcherism. Many leaders in the new ECE democracies are fresh to politics, in some cases exceptionally young, and therefore supposedly malleable. Intensifying networking with the EU and its various member states together with the effects of all the training programmes of the EU over the 1990s have left their mark. English, increasingly the language of international affairs and business, is now more widespread among political and obviously economic elites in these countries.[47] Participation in organisations like the Council of Europe and its Parliamentary Assembly, not to mention frequent visits to Brussels, have enhanced this tendency – one more generally noticeable among the ECE countries than those of the Balkans.

Altogether, political learning from Western Europe among political elites in ECE countries has taken many forms. It has included practical skills such as parliamentary procedure and local government management, political ideas and policy concepts as well as election techniques (transmitted, for instance, via transnational party organisations), and not least policy solutions and outcomes from new partner governments in Western Europe. In some cases, old historical links have been revived, such as between former states of the Habsburg Empire (as evident in some Central European networks); and, at a less visible level, sub-national linkages have increasingly been established between countries formerly on different sides of the Iron Curtain. It is important to bear in mind these more informal networks as well as official EU relations when describing the framework within which ideas and practices favourable to democratic politics are fostered.

Economic transformation and democratisation

It has been one of the principal aims of EU policy towards the CEE countries to promote marketisation alongside pluralist democracy. To this end, the PHARE Programme and the Europe Agreements as well as the projects of the EBRD have been geared. This aim was stated in very general terms without the specifications usually attached to democratic conditionality. For example, the EBRD's statutes emphasised the importance of human rights as well as the formal criteria of liberal democracy and freedom of speech, peaceful assembly, conscience and religion and movement.[48] However, the focus of support departed from the premiss that sound monetary and fiscal policies were required and so help with devising and implementing stabilisation programmes remained the central theme. Here the IMF also contributed with loans, while the EU provided, through PHARE advice, training and information for the purpose of setting up the legislative and institutional framework for marketisation.[49]

The EU and the IMF therefore offered a welcome source of outside assistance in different ways. But perhaps more significant in terms of convergence was the regular pressure of requirements and deadlines coming from Brussels and Washington. In the EU's case, progress assessments were made in the sections on economic criteria in the *avis* of the European Commission on applicant countries (July 1997). The ECE countries were all now regarded as functioning market economies (Poland, Czech Republic, Hungary, Slovenia and Estonia) or as having made considerable progress towards marketisation (Latvia, Lithuania), with Slovakia seen as having introduced most of the reforms necessary to establish a market economy.[50] The section on capacity to take on the obligations of EU membership pronounced on these countries' detailed movement towards adopting the full *acquis* of EU legislation, including the Single Market and Economic and Monetary Union. The subsequent Accession Partnerships and the first two annual progress reports (November 1998, October 1999) updated information on how far they had met the economic criteria.

Undoubtedly, this process of convergence could hardly be without its different political consequences. The effects on policy strategy and action were obvious, although in fact marketisation approaches varied between shock therapy, notably in Poland but also the Czech Republic (especially after the split with Slovakia) and the more gradual approach of Hungary for example. Political effects obviously derived from the economic dislocation in the short and intermediate terms, while policy outcomes pointed to the gradual integration into the framework of economic liberalisation in the long run. It is widely assumed in EU circles that locking the CEE countries into this framework can only have reinforcing effects on the process of democratisation.

The short-term effects were usually dramatic. The pain caused by the shock of stabilisation and the collapse in intra-CEE trade was severe, with GDP falling sharply from the early 1990s. Transitional effects from market-oriented reforms usually involve a decline in output and consumption and a rise in unemployment deriving from the shift from economies that were protected and monopolistic (and, in the case of command economies, that over-employed). But economic reform has also distributional consequences in affecting the welfare of certain social categories, producing a transient deterioration in material conditions that could weaken or inhibit new attachments to democratic values and procedures. All this inevitably creates a quandary for political leaders with their electoral cycles and other relatively short-term political considerations, which do not easily match with the longer haul required for economic transformation. However, where economic issues have been to the fore in national elections, these have more often occasioned alternations in power between democratically committed parties rather than provided extremist forces with an opportunity to exploit successfully. For instance, socialist parties were elected to office in many countries in the mid-1990s (e.g. in Poland, Hungary and Lithuania) partly because of rising public concern over the pace of economic reform, a tendency that may be said to be democracy reinforcing, both procedurally and party-politically, and reconstructed ex-regime parties were thereby more integrated into the democratic game.

It is difficult at this point to isolate the EU factor, as it related fairly intimately with developments both economic and political, and because its effects are usually diverse. In one sense, it has contributed to the stresses of economic transformation, since Brussels provided an external pressure and one with considerable political influence because of the prospect of accession. Inevitably, a certain division occurred between ruling elites and national publics. The former were more conscious of long-term advantages accruing from growing links with the EU, but were also aware of its assistance in acquiring policy skills and policy infrastructure; while the latter were more inclined to feel the shorter-term disadvantages.[51] But there was in fact no straightforward relationship between the economic and the political when looking at the dynamics of the two processes. Factors relating to political culture and trust in political leaders and institutions were also present. In Poland, for example, the public was for a time captured by the boldness of the Balcerowicz Plan of 1990 for combining stabilisation policies with structural market reforms. Clearly, a sense of crisis and urgency was appreciated at a time when the coming of democracy was a major plus for any government trying to impose change. Paradoxically, perhaps, public support declined once signs of improvement were evident – a complex situation that could be explained in terms of a relaxation in perceptions of crisis, but in fact owed much to differential responses to present trends and future prospects.[52]

These vagaries of public opinion do not relate easily to EU accession prospects, and it is difficult to establish a close link with democratisation prospects. But nothing in these ECE countries has occurred comparable to the economic disaster that hit Bulgaria, for example, from the mid-1990s when the economic indicators of crisis (fall in the currency, dramatic price rises and a wave of strikes) were much magnified by political factors like government instability and the lack of a clear economic strategy due to divisions among the ruling socialists. Some ECE countries, i.e. Poland, Hungary and the Czech Republic but not Slovakia, have benefited considerably more than other CEE countries from foreign direct investment – a development that owes much to economic factors such as market size and success with economic transition, but also political ones relating to confidence in government policy as well as in the democratisation process itself.[53]

Undoubtedly, economic transformation and the much increasing trade relations with EU states will continue to have differential effects on economic groups in terms of losses and gains. Moreover, once negotiations really proceed, the more detailed aspects of EU accession will become better known; and this may well induce more critical attitudes towards Brussels at both economic and political levels. As projected, the easier issues have been dealt with in the first stages of accession negotiations with harder ones like farm policies, environmental standards and border controls coming later. However, the chances of this problem impacting heavily on the democratisation process cannot be seen as high, since by then the ECE countries will have moved further down the road towards regime consolidation.

Civil society and democratisation

At first sight, the link between this level and the international dimension, including European integration, must arouse caution both about real impacts but also how to assess them. The EU is notoriously viewed as distant from the national publics of its member states compared with national governments. It is therefore to be expected that its impact on the publics of applicant states is minimal. However, this problem is in part one of image, for in reality European integration may have various direct and indirect effects even among prospective member states. For example, adopting the *acquis* is in several areas likely to have a relevant influence, such as on matters like education and training, social affairs and the environment and quality of life.

In other words, various sectors of European legislation have a potential for influencing civil society in different ways. The problem is identifying these effects as particularly European ones since they intermix with domestic pressures; and their European salience often 'disappears' within domestic arenas except when they become controversial. A major exception has been that of civil and minority rights where the European Parliament and the Council of Europe have been insistent outside influences. Such rights have also featured under the political criteria as detailed in the *avis* as well as the Accession Partnerships and annual progress reports.

The most direct way in which the EU has sought to promote civil society has been through the PHARE Democracy Programme. It specifically aimed at supporting civil society with reference to 'non-state bodies, associations and organisations' with developing local government also placed under this heading. The PHARE programme has been modest in its spending capacity; however, seen in conjunction with other aid programmes of private foundations (notably Soros) the significance of this kind of activity was enhanced. PHARE projects for Hungary in operation in 1996, for instance, included those promoting trades union rights, public participation in community development through NGOs, the training of journalists and public awareness of basic democratic concepts.[54] Some of these projects have been focused on just one country, others on several, often with partner organisations in EU member states. The final report on this programme for 1992–97 came to the conclusion that it had been 'of considerable value for the development of democracy and civil society' in CEE, and in particular by contributing to the growth of the NGO sector. It was noted that the EU label had raised the credibility of these projects, offering protection against arbitrary action by authorities such as in Slovakia – the bottom–up approach adopted, in contrast with other EU programmes, meant that the projects did not have to be approved by the governments of recipient countries. As to the future, it was seen that the NGO sector in CEE would remain dependent on foreign funding because of 'the inadequacy of internally generated funding for NGOs' in those countries.[55]

But the countries of ECE have tended to present a favourable environment for this externally-sponsored activity. In the countries of the Balkans, however, political instability and weak civil society – not to mention the cataclysmic effects of war – have all made them even more dependent on outside assistance but also less able to exploit fully the opportunities arising from this. Nothing comparable faced European support programmes in the ECE countries. The problem in Slovakia was essentially one of government policy rather than cultural, for there the NGO sector had developed remarkably since 1989 while public attitudes towards NGO activity were largely positive.[56]

The lesson from the EU and other outside assistance was that there was indeed scope for influencing and promoting civil society when it was concretely focused on particular target groups. Doubt may, however, be expressed about how far external influences have impacted generally on national publics in ECE. As a whole, the EU enjoys a high prestige in these countries, but that is quite divorced from knowledge about its workings which is very low.[57] While there is usually majority support at this stage for accession, there is also a significant proportion of undecided in several cases.[58] This will probably remain so until governments in ECE start negotiating on difficult issues and the different implications of membership become more clearly spelt out. In Poland, a new ambivalence has begun to mark policy towards the EU, and this is connected with the emergence of contentious issues in talks with Brussels and some slide in public support for accession.[59] This does not as a whole have to

Geoffrey Pridham

mean there will be a dramatic decline in support in applicant countries but rather a much greater differentiation of attitudes.

More optimistically, some educational effects might ensue from any public debate on negotiations. Until that time, however, any assessment of the public impact of the EU – not to mention other external impacts from Europe – must see this as little more than superficial. For, the influence of the EU comes primarily from its influence on political and economic elites and actors and, to a lesser extent, sectoral groups in society. Certainly, European integration may help to determine the evolution of civil society in various ways, and this is indeed significant for further democratisation, but that is not widely noted by national publics in ECE.

National identity, ethnic minorities and democratisation

This level deals partly with perceptions and symbolism, which are difficult to measure, but it also broaches the often controversial issue of ethnic minorities which tends to receive much attention in European circles. Given the diverse aspects of this question, it is probably too simplistic to argue as with some that nation building may have adverse effects on the democratisation process or that the two may have 'conflicting logics'.[60] This does need questioning and testing empirically with respect to country cases.

Put schematically, a trilateral link may be made between recasting a national self-image, democratisation and redefining external relations in the wake of authoritarian collapse. It is partly symbolic, psychological and attitudinal, but also political in that abandoning a discredited dictatorship provides an exit from international isolation (as in Southern Europe) or an escape from subjugation to a more powerful ally (as in CEE). It is in both respects that the scope is automatically increased for a new democracy's autonomous role in international affairs. If the international (i.e. European) environment is one dominated by democratic systems and values, then that may well be democracy reinforcing with respect to identification and symbolism. Thus, post-Franco Spain drew on restored national pride, as was evident in the internal debates over EC entry, and this had powerful effects for transition because of the widespread association there of Europe with democracy at both elite and mass levels.[61] It replaced an artificially constructed national identity fostered by the Franco regime, one based on a mythologised version of Hispanic, viz. Castilian, values – therefore, one that was divisive in centre–periphery terms. With postwar Germany, national identity was severely affected by Nazism, and so the Federal Republic became a founding partner in European integration as a means for both guaranteeing democracy but also helping to neutralise the identity problem.

In ECE, similar though perhaps less dramatic tendencies have been evident. In Czechoslovakia, for example, the 'return to Europe' was one of the central slogans and aims of the 1989 revolution, and it was explicitly linked to democracy in a strongly symbolic way.[62] The sense of a European mission has been particularly strong in Poland, where security motives carry weight, so that entering the EU and NATO is seen not so much as an infringement of national sovereignty but rather as an expression of this, recently regained, and of freedom of choice.[63] Undoubtedly, reconciliation with Germany, Poland's historical enemy – a process already advanced through Brandt's *Ostpolitik* – played a vital part in this more confident and assertive national identity, as it were set in European colours. This clear sense of purpose did much to explain official Polish impatience to get ahead with EU accession negotiations.

However, national-identity construction was more complicated in those ECE countries still engaged in nation building. In Slovenia, EU membership is indeed the top foreign policy priority, for among other things it provides a convincing escape from the turmoil of the former Yugoslavia and with it 'the Balkans' – a syndrome now being repeated by Tudjman-free Croatia. But among elite circles in Ljubljana there are some doubts about this small country's identity being threatened inside the EU; and matters were not helped for some time by continuing tensions with Italy over Italian citizens' property rights there.[64]

Slovakia is a different case for unlike other major ECE countries, which are by and large ethnically homogeneous, it has a strong Hungarian minority (11 per cent) as well as several much smaller minorities. Tensions were caused by discriminatory regulations passed by the Mečiar Government, which included the crassly xenophobic Slovak National Party. Mečiar's own provincial form of populism mixed with a deep insecurity when confronted by (sophisticated) European elites, but his personal inclinations were countered by reasons of state, namely Slovakia's interests in moving closer to the EU. A country trying to establish its own identity anew invariably searches back into its own history, a phenomenon that often involves some form of mythologising and attention to heroic deeds. But that does not fit comfortably with 'returning to Europe', given that in the Slovak case this did not under Mečiar have the same mission appeal as in Poland and the Czech Republic. However, since the change of power in 1998 the new Dzurinda Government has made every effort to overcome Slovakia's poor image in Europe and this is – once more – related to promoting the chances of democratic consolidation through EU accession. Policy initiatives have included a new, more liberal, language law on the use of Hungarian – which was an explicit precondition for opening negotiations over EU entry.

The treatment of the Russian minorities in two of the Baltic states (Latvia and Estonia) was regarded as unsatisfactory in the Commission's *avis* of 1997, although this did not prevent the latter from being included in the first list of applicant countries. Estonia was regarded as having made much more economic progress than Latvia in establishing a functioning market economy and in being able to cope with competitive pressures inside the EU. Brussels has continued to apply sustained pressure on both Latvia and Estonia for more tolerant language laws; while the 1999 progress reports continued to highlight the problem of the Roma minority in many ECE countries. This minority lacks effective political organisation, and the main parties see no advantage, rather disadvantage, from supporting its rights, so that European pressure really fills a vacuum.[65] None of these cases in ECE were, however, comparable in any basic way to the severity of the problems relating to nationhood in the Balkans. There these problems reverted to ethnic nationalism and, tragically, recourse to arms, with damaging effects on processes both of democratisation and of rapprochement with the European mainstream.

Convergence trends and the effects of democratic conditionality

External influences and impacts on democratisation have in East-Central Europe been at work at all levels, but they have been variable in their intensity and consistency. At the formal level, influences have been both vaguely recognisable (on the rule of law) or very specific (in relation to constitutional provisions). The link with consolidation is evident in the former, while the latter established mechanisms – proven as effective abroad – for facilitating government performance, therefore involving a form of indirect influence but one that is distinctly secondary. Looking at political actors, however, reveals a number of significant ways in which external influences may impact on democratisation. These include policy reorientation and the degree of elite consensus as offering implicit if not explicit messages about democracy building. Where this reorientation is reinforced by elite attitudinal change and political learning, then there is considerable scope for external influences on democratisation, particularly when these continue to be accompanied by support mechanisms for countries undergoing change.

Economic transformation illustrates some positive ways in which outside assistance has helped while, at the same time, showing that pressures linked to eventual EU entry may acerbate tensions arising from transformation. However, the political effects are diverse – and also cross-nationally quite variable – making it difficult to quantify the relationship between political regime change and marketisation, let alone draw conclusions about the effects of the role of the EU and other relevant international organisations. A general judgement, however, suggests that the EU has been rather more of a facilitator than a burden for consolidation; and this is against the background of growing trade links between ECE and the EU. At the level of civil society, external influences are particularly difficult to both identify and measure in a general way. But it is possible to locate these in relation to certain activities, and the EU in particular has consciously addressed itself to this approach. The evidence suggests, nonetheless, that it is too soon to draw conclusions about civil society effects, not least as public opinion trends so far do not indicate a high degree of mobilisation over external policy choices as distinct from broad external objectives. Finally, national identity and especially nation building, while having obvious implications for relations with other states, is a problem area the dynamics of which are essentially located in the domestic arena. The ability of outside actors to determine the outcome of this and therefore the consequences for consolidation is rather limited in ECE, but that is precisely because national identity problems there have not descended into the chaos of the Balkans. Nevertheless, EU pressures for human rights and to resolve outstanding bilateral disputes are not by any means negligible factors.

From the foregoing discussion, it is evident that convergence takes many different forms. For this reason alone, it is not necessarily a uniform process for, as we have seen, changing patterns in ECE have varied in terms of both scope and pace under European pressures and influences. There has also been some significant variation cross-nationally with respect to both economic but also political performance. As regards the latter, the somewhat contrasting cases of Poland and Slovakia illustrate how much government commitment to EU accession makes an essential difference. The authoritarian tendencies but also ambiguous policy signals of the Mečiar Government were undoubtedly the major factors why Slovakia was excluded from the first list of applicant countries.

As the Slovak case demonstrated well, conditionality requirements were strictly enforced. Not only treatment of the Hungarian minority, but also Mečiar's blatant flouting of the rights of his political opponents, occasioned a series of official warnings from the EU in 1994–95. While *demarche* became the best-known French term around Bratislava if not in parts of rural Slovakia, these warnings produced a defensive attitude in government circles. For some time, these worsening relations between Brussels and Bratislava raised fears that Slovakia's transition path might become affected. As President Kovac remarked in autumn 1995, exclusion from European integration could aggravate domestic tendencies: 'We would find ourselves in even greater isolation from the surrounding world, we would lose the possibility of exerting a certain positive influence and a broader space would open for other than the democratic development in our country'.[66] Thus, two-way interactions risked setting off a negative dynamic. But the change of power in Slovakia in 1998 certainly opened the way for meeting conditionality requirements, at last. Shortly after the new Government came to office in late October, the Foreign Minister Kukan listed a whole range of issues requiring urgent treatment. Many of these touched on the political criteria and included new laws on minority rights and holding presidential elections. The aim, to 'clean up Slovakia's image', was clearly linked to improving the country's chances for eventual EU accession.[67] Indeed, since then, many of these and other promises have been carried through. They have also included reforms to strengthen the independence of the judiciary, efforts to check intimidation by the intelligence services and the calling to account of high figures in the Mečiar Government involved in criminal abuses of power.

The Commission's *avis* of 1997 tended to encourage greater press coverage

and increased awareness of relations with the EU and the fact that these countries in ECE were gradually moving towards actual negotiations.[68] They also
provoked some dispute in certain countries other than Slovakia where their
relegation to the second list of eventual EU entrants caused bitter disappointment. It was particularly noticeable in Latvia and Lithuania, for intra-Baltic
rivalry was provoked by Estonia alone being placed in the first list. Altogether,
therefore, conditionality pressures had their effects and could influence developments, depending on domestic situations. When, however, these proved particularly difficult on either political or economic grounds, then conditionality
pressures were accordingly constrained in their effects.

Conclusion: towards democratic consolidation in East-Central Europe?

The ten years since the fall of Communist rule certainly mark a number of
advances in the course of democratisation. Confining discussion to East-
Central Europe, it is easier to identify progress compared with other areas of
the post-Communist world, for most countries in this region have moved from
transition and settled into early consolidation, with reasonable prospects of
joining the EU, the most important international organisation, during the new
decade to come. Already these countries are members of other organisations
like the Council of Europe and, in some cases, NATO; and, they are generally
well networked with further inter-governmental and financial organisations
previously absent from the Second World.

It is, seen overall, a fundamental departure from the end of the 1980s when
these countries were still – just – part of the Soviet 'inner abroad'. The 'return
to Europe' has many different aspects – it is not solely a matter of policy choice
– and offers a rich field for examining external regional impacts on regime
change; and the discussion of ECE countries only reinforces the importance
of focusing on regional contexts in studying the consolidation process.
However, other areas of the post-Communist world occasion less confident
evaluations of regime-change outcomes, especially in new states deriving from
the former USSR, as well as some but not all countries in the Balkans. The
latter area, it should be emphasised, has demonstrated considerable diversity
of outcomes; and draws attention to one simple conclusion – Ten Years After
– namely, that cross-national variation among the many post-Communist
states is ever more apparent and is likely to increase in the future. This suggests only too readily that formulating interim conclusions about them is now
a difficult exercise. By comparison, Southern European democratisations
included a mere three countries, while postwar Europe saw two post-Fascist
states embarking on this process and a series of re-democratisations in former
occupied countries.

Without doubt, therefore, the international dimension has played a rather
visible part in the regime changes in East-Central Europe. Its importance is

evident, since restructuring international relations in Europe has proceeded simultaneously with ECE countries achieving transition and moving into consolidation during the decade that has now ended. At the same time, looking at democratic consolidation from the vantage point of external developments adds a particular form of complexity because of the multiple ways in which these interact with domestic developments in the context of regime change.

Much more than democratic transition, the consolidation process has invariably been multilevel. It requires, for instance, a degree of legitimation at both elite and mass levels and the resolution of past inheritances or present challenges that represent obstacles to the embedding of democratic values and procedures. Disaggregating the consolidation process therefore makes ample sense, all the more as progress in its achievement is likely to be variable in both comparing different levels but also when making cross-national comparisons. Doing this may not always provide an integral view of overall consolidation, but it should offer a means for measuring influences in central features of the process.

In general, it has to be said that convergence in its various forms has so far been distinctly one-way. It has primarily come from the new democracies in ECE moving towards and adopting mainstream European patterns. This is notably true in the case of democratic conditionality, where the conditions are distinctly taken from standard West European practice, although blessed by new international norms of behaviour. The EU has had up till now too many other preoccupations to adapt itself very much in terms of both policy and institutional reform to the dictates of eastward enlargement, which promises to be on a scale quite unprecedented as to numbers of entrants compared with previous enlargements. Meanwhile, three other general lessons may be drawn from this chapter.

Firstly, it is very clear that the most important outside actors are international organisations, with the EU well ahead in terms of commitment, influence and support mechanisms for struggling new democracies. Multilateral linkages are very much the dominant feature, more so than with the previous two sets of transitions in Europe. In the postwar cases, bilateral linkages came before multilateral ones (NATO and the ECSC were established some years after the transitions began); and, in Southern Europe, the two forms of linkage were more evenly balanced, with the EC eventually acquiring more influence as a consolidating agent. This balance relates to the relative weight of defending security interests as against democracy promotion on the part of outside powers. This trend towards greater multilateralism suggests a positive factor in favour of democratisation in ECE.

Secondly, there is some limited evidence that modes of transition can be relevant in explaining external influences. Those transitions that were difficult either because they were contested (Slovakia) or disruptive (initially Slovenia with a short war) certainly engaged European attention, although in the course of time this diminished. But it is not convincing to see any profound or long-term effect of these difficult transitions on the outcome of democratic consolidation. Needless to say, developments in the Balkans demonstrate a very different trend from the 'velvet' cases to the north, with persistent transition problems and recourse to violence dictating recurrent involvement by outside actors, with conceivably profound consequences for democratisation.

Thirdly, it is possible to see some meaning in discussion about phases of democratisation and the incidence of international factors. The revolutions of 1989 may still be viewed as the highpoint of external factors impacting on regime change. What has happened since suggests a more subtle process of interactions between outside influences and domestic politics, so that it is not always easy to identify clear phases in relation to external influences. Nevertheless, the onset of negotiations for EU accession does represent an important new phase, with possibly significant implications for the way in which external influences affect consolidation in the years ahead. Whether further delays in accessions from CEE allows countries there to be better prepared for membership or, alternatively, causes complications for their regime changes remains to be seen. However, it is also important to note, finally, that EU enlargement, following NATO expansion and other forms of newly defined international allegiances by the ECE countries, plays a major part in creating the new structure of international relations that should help to stabilise the still new democracies of this region.

Notes

1 A. Przeworski *et al.*, *Sustainable Democracy* (Cambridge University Press, Cambridge, 1995), p. 3.
2 D. Held, *Democracy and the Global Order* (Polity Press, Cambridge, 1995), pp. 89–90.
3 The most prominent exponent of this school is Huntington; see e.g. S. Huntington, *The Third Wave: Democratisation in the late 20th Century* (University of Oklahoma Press, Norman, 1991).
4 See L. Whitehead (ed.), *The International Dimensions of Democratisation: Europe and the Americas* (Oxford University Press, Oxford, 1996), own chapter 1 on three international dimensions of democratisation; also, P. Schmitter, 'The international context of contemporary democratisation', in G. Pridham (ed.), *Transitions to Democracy: Comparative Perspectives from Southern Europe, Latin America and Eastern Europe* (Dartmouth, Aldershot, 1995), pp. 503ff.
5 P. Schmitter, 'The influence of the international context upon the choice of national institutions and policies in neo-democracies' in Whitehead, *International Dimensions*, p. 40.
6 See, for example, K. Remmer, 'Theoretical decay and theoretical development: the resurgence of institutional analysis' *World Politics*, October 1997, p. 53, where she argues that 'just as economists have found open-economy models useful for addressing contemporary issues of stabilisation and adjustment, comparativists need to begin thinking more systematically in terms of "open-polity" models'. One

instance of this is D. Rueschemeyer, E. Stephens and J. Stephens, *Capitalist Development and Democracy* (University of Chicago Press, Chicago, 1992), which incorporates transnational forces alongside other variables, including social class, to explain the positive correlation between economic development and democracy.

7 G. Pridham, 'The politics of the European Community, transnational networks and democratic transition in Southern Europe', in G. Pridham (ed.), *Encouraging Democracy: The International Context of Regime Transition in Southern Europe* (Leicester University Press, Leicester, 1991), p. 236.

8 Interview with *The Sunday Times*, 18 April 1999: 'The region cannot be secure with a belligerent tyrant in its midst.'

9 A. Stanger, 'Democratisation and the international system: the foreign policies of interim governments', in Y. Shain and J. Linz (eds), *Between States: Interim Governments and Democratic Transitions* (Cambridge University Press, Cambridge, 1995), pp. 274–6.

10 This accounts, for example, for the concept in the Federal Republic of *wehrhafte Demokratie* (militant democracy) in the face of a threat from (predominantly left-wing) extremism. The point may be extended by noting the somewhat restricted notions of liberal democracy in government circles in postwar West Germany, particularly during the paternalistic Adenauer years. It was only in the later 1960s that notions of liberal democracy broadened under pressure from new social movements and generational change, a change due partly to the evolution of political culture but also, significantly, to a less tension-ridden international environment.

11 G. Philip, 'Theorising international influences on democracy in Latin America', paper for conference of UK Political Studies Association, Nottingham, March 1999, pp. 7–9.

12 See A. Tovias, 'US policy towards democratic transition in Southern Europe' in Pridham (ed.), *Encouraging Democracy*, pp. 175–94.

13 G. Pridham, 'The politics of the European Community', in *ibid.*, pp. 212–45.

14 Human rights abuses under the Colonels' regime were given salience in the international press; while human rights provisions are spelt out in some detail in the preamble to the new democratic constitution of 1975.

15 P. Drake, *International Factors in Democratization* (Instituto Juan March, Madrid, working paper 61, 1994), p. 23.

16 J. Rupnik, 'Eastern Europe: the international context', *Journal of Democracy*, April 2000, pp. 116–20.

17 *The European*, 30 January–5 February 1997.

18 *The Times*, 31 January 1997.

19 The comparative point might also be made that democratisation after the right-wing dictatorships in Southern Europe was somewhat less difficult than that following the more thorough and pervasive systems of Communist Europe. At least, Brussels' political criteria – admittedly less elaborate two decades ago – occasioned less controversy then. They tended to draw into the background during negotiations. However, the sense of complacency this may have induced was rudely shattered on 23 February 1981, when military personnel staged a coup in the Parliament in Madrid. While the crisis broke, Eurocrats working on Spanish accession in Brussels metaphorically gasped and put down their pens. However, when it became clear that the coup had failed, it was also plain that accession negotiations would not after all have to be stalled.

20 It has, however, stretched the rules somewhat with respect to the CEE countries, especially over the controversial acceptance in the mid-1990s of Romania, Russia and Croatia, whose systems fell far short of the Council's standards as over the rule of law and freedom of expression; see G. Pridham, 'The European Union, democratic conditionality and transnational party linkages: the case of Eastern Europe', in J. Grugel (ed.), *Democracy Without Borders: Transnationalisation and Conditionality in New Democracies* (Routledge, London, 1999), pp. 63–4.

21 *The Economist*, 8 May 1999, p. 45.

22 A. Hyde-Price, *The International Politics of East Central Europe* (Manchester University Press, Manchester, 1996), pp. 85–100 and 131–3; and, A. Cottey (ed.), *Subregional Cooperation in the New Europe* (Macmillan, Basingstoke, 1999), Part II.

23 Full membership of the EU, in Whitehead's summary, 'generates powerful, broad-based and long-term support for the establishment of democratic institutions because it is irreversible, and sets in train a cumulative process of economic and political integration that offers incentives and reassurances to a very wide array of social forces . . . it sets in motion a very complex and profound set of mutual adjustment processes, both within the incipient democracy and in its interactions with the rest of the Community, nearly all of which tend to favour democratic consolidation . . . in the long run such 'democracy by convergence' may well prove the most decisive international dimension of democratisation, but the EU has yet to prove that case fully' (L. Whitehead, *The International Dimensions of Democratisation*, p. 19.

24 See the discussion of the EU's approach to democratic conditionality in Pridham, 'The European Union', section (3).

25 Cf. discussion of these two categories in M. Kaldor and I. Vejvoda, 'Democratisation in Eastern and Central European countries', *International Affairs*, January 1997, esp. pp. 62–7. For instance, the so-called Copenhagen criteria, established at the European Council meeting in 1993, included human rights and respect for minorities as well as the rule of law and stable democratic institutions.

26 See Pridham, 'The European Union'.

27 This point is emphasised by J. Pinder, 'The European Community and democracy in Central and Eastern Europe', in G. Pridham, E. Herring and G. Sanford (eds), *Building Europe? The International Dimension of Democratisation in Eastern Europe* (Leicester University Press, London, 1997), p. 124.

28 These state: 'Membership requires that the candidate country has achieved stability of institutions guaranteeing democracy, the rule of law, human rights and respect for and protection of minorities, the existence of a functioning market economy as well as the capacity to cope with competitive pressure and market forces within the Union': Council of the European Union, *Presidency Conclusions: Copenhagen European Council* (Brussels, 1993).

29 The case of Slovakia under the Mečiar Government is dealt with in some detail in G. Pridham, 'Complying with the European Union's democratic conditionality: transnational party linkages and regime change in Slovakia, 1993–1998', *Europe-Asia Studies*, November 1999, pp. 1221–44.

30 European Commission, *1999 Regular Report on Slovakia's Progress towards Accession* (Brussels, 1999), p. 18.

31 Based on a series of elite interviews in Bratislava, May 2000, for a project on

European Union Enlargement, Democratic Conditionality and Regime Change in Post-Communist States: Slovakia in Comparative Perspective, funded by the Nuffield Foundation 2000–1.

32 See M. Bútora and P. Demeš, 'Civil society organisations in the 1998 elections', in M. Bútora, G. Mesežnikov, Z. Butorová and S. Fisher (eds), *The 1998 Parliamentary Elections and Democratic Rebirth in Slovakia* (Institute for Public Affairs, Bratislava, 1999). Also, interview with Pavol Demes, now head of the German Marshall Fund, Bratislava, May 2000.

33 W. Sokolewicz, 'The relevance of Western models for constitution-building in Poland', in J. J. Hesse and N. Johnson (eds), *Constitutional Policy and Change in Europe* (Oxford University Press, Oxford, 1995), p. 251.

34 *Ibid.*, p. 268.

35 R. Taras, 'Leaderships and executives' in S. White, J. Batt and P. Lewis (eds), *Developments in East European Politics* (Macmillan, Basingstoke, 1993), pp. 166–7.

36 A. Lijphart, 'Democratisation and constitutional choices in Czechoslovakia, Hungary and Poland, 1989–91', in I. Budge and D. McKay (eds), *Developing Democracy: Comparative Research in Honour of J.F.P. Blondel* (London, Sage, 1994), pp. 206–7

37 T. Remington (ed.), *Parliaments in Transition: The New Legislative Politics in the Former USSR and Eastern Europe* (Westview Press, Boulder, 1994), pp. 13–14.

38 J. Elster, 'Constitution-making in Eastern Europe: rebuilding the boat in the open sea', in J. J. Hesse (ed.), *Administrative Transformation in Central and Eastern Europe* (Blackwell, Oxford, 1993), p. 192.

39 F. Rüb, 'Die Herausbildung politischer Institutionen in Demokratisierungs-prozessen', in W. Merkel (ed.), *Systemwechsel 1: Theorien, Ansätze und Konzeptionen* (Leske and Budrich, Opladen, 1994), p. 125.

40 *Ibid.*, p. 126.

41 R. Grey, *Democratic Theory and Post-Communist Change* (Prentice-Hall, Upper Saddle River, 1997), p. 175.

42 H. Grabbe and K. Hughes, 'Central and East European views on EU enlargement: political debates and public opinion', in K. Henderson (ed.), *Back to Europe: Central and Eastern Europe and the European Union* (UCL Press, London, 1999), pp. 188–90.

43 F. Millard, 'Polish domestic politics and accession to the European Union', in *ibid.*, p. 211.

44 There are already some signs in the case of Slovenia, where the parties unequiv-ocally advocate EU membership but differ somewhat over the speed of accession and the likely costs; see I. Brinar, 'Slovenia: from Yugoslavia to the European Union', in *ibid.*, pp. 251–2.

45 G. Herd, 'The Baltic states and EU enlargement', in Henderson (ed.), *Back to Europe*, pp. 259–73.

46 Hyde-Price, *International Politics of East Central Europe*, pp. 27–8 and 169–70.

47 Equally, the absence of English among elites is a matter for comment. The minister responsible in the Mečiar Government for Slovakia's negotiations with the EU, Jozef Kalman, spoke Russian and not English. He came from the Association of Slovak Workers (ZRS), a party known for its suspicions of the West. Mečiar himself spoke a more or less proficient Russian, but that was his only language. By contrast, all cabinet ministers in the new Dzurinda Government speak at least one Western language.

48 EBRD, *Political Aspects of the Mandate of the EBRD* (EBRD, London, 1992).

49 Pinder, 'The European Community and democracy in Central and Eastern Europe', in Pridham, Herring and Sanford (eds), *Building Europe?*, pp. 117–21.

50 European Commission, *Agenda 2000: 3. The Opinions of the European Commission on the Applications for Accession* (Brussels, 1997).

51 As Przeworski put it, 'reform programmes are thus caught between the faith of those who foresee their ultimate effects and the scepticism of those who experience only their immediate consequences': Przeworski *et al.*, *Sustainable Democracy*, p. 68.

52 See A. Przeworski, 'Economic reforms, public opinion and political institutions: Poland in the Eastern European perspective' in L.C. Bresser Pereira, J.M. Maravall and A. Przeworski, *Economic Reforms in New Democracies: A Social Democratic Approach* (Cambridge University Press, Cambridge, 1993), pp. 159–63 and 166ff.

53 H. Grabbe and K. Hughes, *Enlarging the EU Eastwards* (Royal Institute of International Affairs, London, 1998), pp. 20–4.

54 European Commission, *The European Union's Phare and Tacis Democracy Programme: Projects in Operation 1996* (Brussels, 1996), section on Hungary, pp. 61–6.

55 ISA Consult, European Institute at Sussex University and GJK Europe, *Final Report: Evaluation of the PHARE and TACIS Democracy Programme, 1992–1997* (University of Sussex, Brighton and Hamburg, November 1997), pp. ii–iv.

56 M. Bútora, 'The present state of democracy in Slovakia' in M. Kaldor and I. Vejvoda (eds), *Democratization in Central and Eastern Europe* (Pinter, London, 1999), pp. 101–2.

57 It has recently been noted that in Hungary people are not particularly well informed about the structure and internal conflicts of the EU and are not much aware of the competing conceptions of the future of the EU: see A. Bozóki, 'Democracy in Hungary, 1990–97' in *ibid.*, p. 120.

58 H. Grabbe and K. Hughes, 'Central and East European views on EU enlargement', in Henderson (ed.), *Back to Europe*, pp. 186–8.

59 G. Blazyca and M. Kolkiewicz, 'Poland the EU: internal disputes, domestic politics and accession', in *Journal of Communist Studies and Transition Politics*, December 1999, pp. 131–43.

60 Notably, J. Linz and A. Stepan, *Problems of Democratic Transition and Consolidation* (Johns Hopkins University Press, Baltimore, 1996), chapter 2.

61 G. Pridham, 'The international context of democratic consolidation: Southern Europe in comparative perspective', in R. Gunther, N. Diamandouros and H.-J. Puhle (eds), *The Politics of Democratic Consolidation: Southern Europe in Comparative Perspective* (Johns Hopkins University Press, Baltimore, 1995), pp. 177–8.

62 Z. Kavan and M. Palous, 'Democracy in the Czech Republic', in Kaldor and Vejvoda (eds), *Democratization in Central and Eastern Europe*, p. 85. However, this euphoria has since given way to a more questioning and hard-headed approach, at least on the part of the Klaus Government; cf. Vaclav Klaus's stress on the loss of national sovereignty from EU membership: see V. Boland, 'Is the EU good enough for the Czechs?', *Financial Times*, 2 August 1995.

63 Interview with President Kwaśniewski, *Financial Times*, 23 October 1996.

64 Grabbe and Hughes, *Enlarging the EU Eastwards*, p. 74; 'Slovenia battles to join the Union', *The European*, 30 May–5 June 1996.

65 This is also true, for instance, of Hungary which is one of the most advanced ECE countries in EU negotiations. The 1999 progress report on Hungary noted that the Roma continued to 'suffer widespread prejudice and discrimination in their daily lives'. According to an official of the international secretariat of the Hungarian Socialist Party, parties will not campaign for the Roma because they would lose votes doing this. The issue had been discussed with the HSP's partners in transnational party circles, and he admitted that EU pressure produced a positive response, although this was not politically convenient. He took the view that EU pressure had helped to alleviate what was still a difficult issue (interview with Péter Havas, HSP International Secretariat, Budapest, April 2000).

66 Quoted in Bútora, 'The present state of democracy in Slovakia', in Kaldor and Vejvoda (eds), *Democratization in Central and Eastern Europe*, p. 103.

67 S. Taylor, 'EU applicants stuck in the slow lane', *European Voice* (12–18 November 1998).

68 See Grabbe and Hughes, *Enlarging the EU Eastwards*, p. 76.

Civil society and democratic consolidation in East-Central Europe

Introduction

This chapter seeks to bring together two strands of an argument that have as yet been insufficiently connected: research into consolidation of democracy and the concept(s) of *civil society*. While there has been rigorous theoretical consideration of their relationship and empirical research with respect to the demise of autocratic regimes (liberalisation, demise, collapse) as well as to mature consolidated democracies, there is a lack of theoretical and empirical studies on the impact of civil societies on new and consolidating democracies. In aiming to contribute to a better understanding of this problem I will develop my argument in five steps:

1 The four classical functions of civil society in political philosophy are identified.
2 The most important functions of civil societies in post-autocratic regimes are summarised.
3 A 'realistic' concept of civil society is developed, one that can be applied not only to mature and well-established democracies but to new, still unstable and not yet consolidated democracies.
4 The question whether there are typical cycles of mobilisation and organisation of activity in civil societies during the different phases of transition to democracy is considered.
5 Finally, the specific impact that civil society has had on democratic consolidation in East-Central Europe is analysed.

The four classical functions of civil society in political philosophy

The renaissance of the term 'civil society' coincides both chronologically and causally with the demise of Communism.[1] This applies above all to the end of the perverted Communist rule in Eastern Europe, but also to the shattering of the Marxist utopia in the West. In the Marxist–Leninist Soviet regimes the 'citizen society' was suppressed by the authority of the state, while in the Marxist Left in the West it was denounced as the ideological transfiguration of capitalist class rule.[2] For Eastern European dissidents civil society therefore simply appeared to be the liberal antithesis of Leninist tyranny. It articulated an ideal agenda for the development of 'independent forms of social life from the bottom up, which should be free of state domination'.[3] It was welcomed within the West European Left as an emancipation project that went beyond economic questions.[4] Since then, among Eastern dissidents and Western post-Marxists *the* civil society has since developed to become, as it always was in the liberal tradition, a concept central to the protection and continued development of democracy.

However, far from having emerged in the last fifteen years, the conviction that a developed civil society contributes to the strengthening of a democracy has a long tradition. It rests on significant arguments developed by the early modern political philosophers John Locke (1632–1704), Montesquieu (1689–1755) and Alexis de Tocqueville (1805–59) and, more recently, by Ralf Dahrendorf and Jürgen Habermas. The four most important arguments, which at the same time set out central democratic functions, are outlined below.

Protection from state arbitrariness: the Lockeian function

In the liberal tradition going back to John Locke[5] emphasis is placed on an independent social sphere *vis-à-vis* the State. Locke, and later to a greater extent Adam Smith, conceived of society as the genuine social sphere beyond the state. Here, armed with natural rights, people create a community in which the life of the society freely evolves. In the best-case scenario, this pre- or non-political arena can exist under the protection, but under no circumstances under the direction, of state authority.[6] From this perspective the protection of individuals' autonomy, the development of their rights, as well as the securing of their property are characterised as the central tasks of civil society. The function assigned to civil society is therefore above all one of negative liberty; i.e. citizens' freedom from state interference. Civil society is the sphere that is separated from the state. The reconciliation of these antinomic spheres does not appear in the Lockeian perspective.

The balance between state and civil society: the Montesquieu function

Montesquieu does away with the sharp contrast between state and society. In his complex model of the separation and interdependence of powers,[7] he identifies as a central theme the balance between a central political authority and a social network of 'corps intermediaries'. The strong central (monarchic) government must be limited by and embedded in both the 'rule of law' and controlling checks and balances. However, and this is one of Montesquieue's central ideas, the law loses its authority if it is not supported and invigorated by independent, yet legally protected, bodies. These 'corps intermediaires' are 'amphibious' bodies that possess 'a life' both within and outside the state,[8] thereby connecting the social and state spheres. This is because the powerful central authority must be embedded in the rule of law and interconnected with, but also limited and controlled by, a large number of civic associations if freedom is to be secured.[9] Thus, Montesquieu backs institutions and organisations and does not place his trust primarily in 'virtue', as did the philosophers of the ancient *polis* or of postmodern communitarianism.

The schools of democracy: the de Tocqueville function

De Tocqueville builds on Montesquieu and strengthens the notion of the 'free associations' being the most important guarantors of a free community.[10] Organisations in civil society are, for him, the schools of democracy, in which democratic thinking and civil behaviour are learnt and established through day-to-day practice. For citizens' associations actually to function as places of societal autonomy, they may not be disproportionately large, but there must be many of them. Moreover, they should establish themselves at all levels of the political system, for if they wither away at the local level then freedom and democracy at the national level are also endangered. Civil organisations serve to create and entrench civic virtues such as tolerance, mutual acceptance, honesty, integrity, trust and the courage to stand up for one's beliefs. They thereby accumulate social capital, without which, as the American democratic scholar Robert Putnam would put it 150 years later,[11] democracies are unable to either emerge or be consolidated in the long term. From the Tocquevilleian perspective civil society arms democracy with a normative and participatory potential that both serves to immunise against authoritarianism on the part of the state and places internal limits on the tyrannical ambitions of social majorities. In the De Tocqueville tradition the positive functions of civil society for the entire democratic community – that is, state and society – are underlined and are linked to a distinctive participatory component of 'self-government'.

It is above all Ralf Dahrendorf's concept of the 'civil society' (*Buergergesellschaft*) that stems from this philosophical tradition. According to him, the citizens' society is 'a world which offers individuals life chances, without the state having to play a role'.[12] The citizens' society is nonetheless an active society that calls for civic action: 'To act means to do something oneself in free association with others. It leads to the colourful world of voluntary groups and organisations and then further to autonomous institutions. It also leads to the civil society, which is the means to a meaningful life and the meaning of fulfilled freedom.'[13]

The public sphere and critique of the Habermas function

The concepts of civil society shaped by Critical Theory go a step further than Tocqueville and Dahrendorf.[14] They argue that civil society broadens the arena for interest articulation and aggregation through the establishment of a system of 'pre-institutional' pluralist interest mediation. Here those interests that are disadvantaged and difficult to organise have access to a public space. The political agenda should be influenced by these interests beyond what is power-driven within the political system through self-organised forms of participation, for every truly democratic process in organisations, parties and parliaments is 'dependent on the supply of informal public opinions' that only develop outside of 'the structures of a non-empowered political public'.[15] Jürgen Habermas's conception of civil society is extraordinarily demanding. It excludes not only state institutions and political parties, but also economic interest groups. Making up the core of 'his' civil society are above all spontaneously created groups, organisations and movements, which 'find, take up and condense'[16] the social problem areas of the private sphere and then carry them on to the political sphere as a kind of social amplifier. Such a civil society may be sensitive to problems, but as a rule is weak in politics.

Democratic functions of civil society in post-autocratic regimes

The four aspects of civil society presented above protect the individual from the state's arbitrary actions (Locke), support the rule of law and the balance of power (Montesquieu), educate citizens and recruit political elites (Tocqueville) and, through the public sphere, institutionalise a means of democratic self-reflection (Habermas). They can be systematised and specified in the following way as a catalogue of the potential for democratisation in civil society:

1. The first and basic function of civil society is protection against state interference in the private sphere, thereby ensuring the existence of a private as well as a social sphere. This could be considered as the Lockeian function of civil society, or the *conditio sine qua non* of all liberal democracies.
2. The second function of civil society is linked to the 'negative securing of freedom': the observation and control of state power. Depending on the strength of the civil society, the 'observation' of it might compel the state to act responsibly that is, to show responsiveness and responsibility.
3. The third function exists in the form of the democratic–participatory socialisation of citizens and the recruitment of democratic elites for decision making within the state. This is the Tocquevilleian function of 'schools of democracy', and this is important for developing a 'citizen culture' (Dahrendorf) but also a 'lasting democracy'.[17] This is related to de Tocqueville's schools of democracy, but it goes well beyond it by touching

on the question how to accumulate sufficient 'social capital' in a society which is vital for any sustainable democracy. It concerns the accumulation of mutual trust, social inclusion and civic engagement.

4 Civil society can open up effective channels for the generation, aggregation and articulation of community values and social interests outside of political parties and parliaments. This Habermasian function would seem to be particularly important for excluded or discriminated against groups such as ethnic, racial and religious minorities. The meaning is expressly extended to include the formation of community values, fairness and trust, which are consistently strained by the functional imperatives of the market economy. Civil society creates the 'public' in the Habermasian sense and provides both the forums and the actors for it.

5 Through their networks of associations, initiatives and movements, civil societies generate overlapping memberships that cut across or bridge deeply entrenched social cleavages and can thereby help to moderate social conflicts. This is a function that was emphasised time and again particularly by pluralist theorists.[18] By fulfilling these functions, civil society generates and facilitates control of power, responsibility, social inclusion, tolerance, fairness, trust, co-operation and, not infrequently, also efficiency in the implementation of accepted political programmes. It thereby not only contributes to the democratisation, pacification and self-organisation of society but facilitates the greater control, democratisation and unburdening of the state, as well as an increase in its effectiveness.

A 'realistic concept' of civil society

Given both the theoretical roots of the term 'civil society' and the catalogue of functions described above, we can conceive of various forms and configurations of actual civil societies. I therefore now refer to a general 'realistic concept' of civil society that in essence can be utilised for both mature and new democracies:

> Civil society exists in a pre-state or non-state sphere of activity and consists of numerous pluralist and voluntarily established organisations and associations. They articulate their specific material and normative interests and are autonomously organised. Civil society occupies the space between the private sphere and state. Moreover, its articulated objectives also always concern the *res publica*. Actors in civil society are involved in politics, yet without assuming state posts. Correspondingly, groups that exclusively pursue private goals (families, enterprises, etc.) are as little a part of civil society as political parties, parliaments or state administrations. Civil society is not a homogenous 'actor'. Rather, it is heterogeneously structured to the extent that it displays a pluralistic melting pot of vastly different actors, who do, however, share a

certain minimal normative consensus. This is based principally on the recognition of others (tolerance) and on the principle of fairness. The use of physical violence is excluded. However, this basic consensus does not do away with the existing internal pluralism. Instead, in case of the need to act defensively, it equips actors in the civil society to adopt collective strategic behaviour. Together with an alignment with public affairs and an orientation towards communicative action, the civil consensus creates the genuine nucleus of civil society that can also be found at the individual level in the formation of a civic spirit.[19]

Although this definition is not nearly as demanding in a normative sense as the concepts of civil society developed by the Critical Theorists,[20] it is still bound to a normative basic consensus. This immutable normative core consists of: tolerance, fairness and freedom from violence. Intolerant actors and violence against people cannot be described as civil. Of course, that it is not to say that force in the political realm is *a priori* always illegitimate. Indeed, normatively comprehensible reasons and justifications for tyrannical murder can be found in political philosophy since ancient times.[21] This understanding simply argues that as legitimate as the use of force against people in certain situations of political suppression might be, as an act of violence it can no longer be considered as belonging to the sphere of civil society. Not insisting on such a normative orientation would degrade the concept of civil society to a catch-all category that would lose considerable heuristic explanatory power and analytical strength.

The moderate normative connotations of our concept do not mean that we always and to the same extent attribute positive effects of the development and consolidation of democracy to every form of actual civil society. Rather, we can contend that, with respect to the success of democratisation, every form of new democratic regime or every phase of a transition needs a complementary kind of civil society. In what follows I concentrate on how the optimal internal structure, configuration and communication of a civil society should look in order to achieve the paramount aim of constructing, consolidating and deepening democracy.

At this point reference should be made to the distinction between civil society and civic culture or *political culture* more generally. The concept of political culture tries to measure the cognitive, affective and evaluative opinions, attitudes and values of citizens. In contrast, the civil society concept tries to incorporate the dimension of civic action and civil organisations. There is naturally a certain affinity and positive correlation between civic culture and civil society: a well-developed civic culture offers a good foundation for a vital civil society. However, the former does not determine the latter, nor are the two identical. Yet, while a strong civil society is almost unthinkable without a solid civic culture, stable representative democracies can exist without a strong civil society, though not without a sufficiently well-rooted civic culture.

Cycles of civil society in post-autocratic regimes

The systematic inclusion of the concept of civil society in theory and empirical research on democratic consolidation enhances our insight into the reasons for the success and failure of transitions to, and consolidations of, democracy. Studying civil society allows us to measure the extent to which democratic attitudes have developed at the micro-level of the individual (civic culture), but at the meso-level such attitudes also elucidate the logic of collective behaviour in civil society. That this logic does not always have to have the effect of consolidating democracy, and can instead create unintended destabilising effects, has been described as the 'dark sides of civil society'.[22]

In the process of a transition (end of an autocratic regime, institutionalisation of democracy, consolidation of democracy) there are clearly phase-dependent cycles of vitality for civil society. In almost all of the transitions to democracy of the 'Third Wave' there was a resurgence or emergence of civil society during the demise of the autocratic regimes and at the beginning of the institutionalisation of democracy.[23] Through this, the length and intensity of phases of mobilisation and self-organisation differed according to the specific forms of civil society. However, despite their different modes of transition, common to all of these transitions was that by the end of the democratisation phase a decline in civil society activities was already evident. As a rule the mobilisation of civil society declined in most of the new democracies in the early years of democratic consolidation. There were essentially three cross-regional and cross-cultural reasons for this:

- With the institutionalisation of democracy, i.e. the passing of new constitutional norms, the establishment of new democratic institutions and the founding elections, the power and institutional vacuums created by the transition became filled by traditional organized political actors. New constraints on the actions of civil society movements and associations thus emerged through formal political structures and arenas.
- New political actors (parties, parliaments and governments) emerged and became entrenched. Most had at their disposal considerable legal, administrative and economic resources.
- The disappointment (*desencanto*) evident within a new democracy concerning the actual limits to the influence of civil society led at the micro-level of the individual to the shifting involvements of citizens from the public to the private, already observed in consolidated democracies by Albert O. Hirschmann.[24] People's individual careers or safeguarding their own position very soon took priority over working for the public good or through collective interests.

Contrary therefore to the expectations of new social movements, at the beginning of democratic consolidation civil society's 'window of opportunity' very quickly closes up to a considerable extent. However, in no way does this have to be seen negatively as a decline in democracy. Indeed, with respect to the decision-making ability of representative democratic institutions, the decline in civil society's potential ability to block radical reform plans can also signify an important growth in efficiency and thus in legitimacy for the still-fragile democracies.[25] Paradoxically, the temporary weakness of civil society may even contribute to the stabilisation of new democracies. Revitalisation of civil society first becomes important for the participatory deepening of democracy in the process of further stabilisation. In an advanced phase of democratic consolidation the relatively low-risk dual strategy of complementary democratisation of state and society not only can strengthen a democracy's basis of legitimacy, but can increase the depth of intervention of state control and implementation through the co-operation of sections of society.[26] However, this succeeds only if political and civil society act co-operatively and with mutual restraint. With that we would, however, have strayed far from the reality of post-authoritarian democracies and moved towards the sphere of deliberative governance, a sphere largely underdeveloped even in mature democracies.

The impact of civil society on democratic consolidation in East-Central Europe

Of the four levels of democratic consolidation,[27] the constitutional and representative level, the integration of potential veto actors who might otherwise pursue interests outside democratic procedures (like the military or radical movements), and civic culture and civil society, it is the fourth level, the emergence of a vital civil society, that lasts the longest. This was shown by the new democracies of the 'Second Wave' of post-1945 Germany, Italy, Japan and Austria, and was confirmed by the processes in Southern Europe's post-authoritarian democracies from 1974 onwards.[28] The developments in East-Central Europe since the events of 1989 have also shown that the lack of civic culture continues[29] and that up until now only weak civil societies have emerged. However, there are noticeable differences not only between East-Central Europe and Eastern Europe, but also among the East-Central European countries. These differences will be considered in some detail here. In a comparison of the four ECE countries of Poland, the Czech Republic, Slovakia and Hungary, as well as of the contrasting case of Russia, the following two questions will be addressed:

1 Can the typical cycles of the mobilisation of civil society and the typical shifting involvements also be identified in East-Central Europe?
2 Ten years after system change, to what extent has civil society in the four ECE countries fulfilled its potential and role as an agent of democracy?

Activity cycles of civil society

A kind of 'typical cycle' for the development of civil society during the transition from autocracy to democracy has been outlined above. During the demise of an autocratic regime civil society frequently flourishes. This is especially likely where the regime change takes the form not of an abrupt collapse, nor of a process exclusively controlled from above, but rather where there is a gradual opening and liberalising of the *ancien régime*. With the establishment and routinisation of the classical institutions of representative democracy civil society has less room to move, and other political actors such as political parties move into the foreground.[30] What follows is a decline in the mobilisation and activity of civil society. In the more favourable cases this cycle of decline is followed by a gradual revitalisation of civil society during the phase of democratic consolidation, albeit with changed forms and functions.

The modes of transition were different in the three countries of Poland, Czechoslovakia and Hungary. Typologically, Poland's transition can be described as 'forced from below', Hungary's as 'controlled from above', and Czechoslovakia's as a 'collapse'.[31] Apart from the mode of transition the type of autocratic regime also plays an important role with respect to the emergence of civil society. In closed, autocratic, totalitarian regimes only small, non-mobilising, dissident groups may comprise the nucleus of civil society, whereas larger networks of civil associations are able to emerge in the relatively more open authoritarian regimes.

The character of the *ancien régime* and the mode of transition considerably influenced both the development of civil society in the three countries and the impact civil societies themselves had on the mode of transition. Until the autumn of 1989 the late-Stalinist closed regime in Czechoslovakia repressed any significant resurgence of civil society. Civil society was largely restricted to a few risk-taking intellectuals (Charta 77) primarily from the cultural milieu. It was not until 1988 that the HOS, the movement for civic rights, was formed under the umbrella of Soviet *perestroika*. This movement openly positioned itself against the regime, and its various streams later became the founding elites of the new political parties. However, in general it is true that these small dissident groups did not successfully mobilise the largely passive population on a significant scale.[32] This did not occur until after the repression of the demonstrations on 17 November 1989.

In the authoritarian regime in Poland there was a strong mobilisation of civil society during the 1980s. The more open nature of the regime did not allow it to suppress this mobilisation, which was unthinkable in the closed, autocratic regime in Czechoslovakia. The mobilisation of civil society had been organisationally stabilised by the Polish Workers Defence Committee (1976), by Solidarnosc, and the Catholic Church. Of additional significance was the mobilising ideology of Polish nationalism, which was able to label Soviet Communism as a foreign power. The mobilising force of Solidarnosc and nationally focused Catholicism, with their respectively charismatically led and hierarchical structures, made up the unique oppositional power that forced the regime to embark upon a negotiated transition. In spite of its internal ideological pluralism, Poland's civil society retained its character as a strategically unified actor which powerfully challenged the late Communist regime.

Although the authoritarian Communist regime in Hungary in the 1980s can be described as more open than Poland's Communist regime, no comparable mobilisation occurred. The most important reasons for this were:

- the development of a non-politicised silent civil society[33] in the second economy since the late 1960s;
- the regime change initiated from above by the reformers within the ruling MSZMP, and not forced from below as in Poland;
- comparable mobilising ideological forces of Catholicism and nationalism to those in Poland did not exist.

However, in particular it was the active willingness to reform of the old regime elites in Hungary that diminished the chances for concerted mobilising action against the regime within the civil society.[34] Only once the forces within civil society had begun to form themselves into political parties did they become a relevant opposition and a relevant negotiating partner at the Round Table for the old regime party, which was itself undergoing considerable reform.

The strength of the civil societies in the three ECE countries reached a peak early on in the process of the 'institutionalisation of democracy'. The by-then dysfunctional institutions of the old regimes, the old regime parties' loss of power and the not-yet established new democratic organisations and parties gave 'civil associations enormous room for manoeuvre and considerable political power. Jiří Dienstbier, the future Czechoslovak minister of foreign affairs, spoke of civil society in power', as the Civic Forum became the Communist regime's main negotiating partner at the Round Table during the Velvet Revolution.[35] Whereas Solidarnosc in Poland and the Civic Forum in Czechoslovakia negotiated at the Round Tables as civil society groups, large parts of civil society in Hungary were the quickest in transforming themselves into political parties.[36]

However, 'civil society in power' also meant the beginning of the end of a 'revolutionary civil society',[37] since with the withering away of the old regime it lost its enemy, which had to a large extent guaranteed the mobilising power and unity of civil society as a strategic actor. With the end of the Round Table negotiations and the establishment of democratic institutions the 'moral civil societies' (esp. in Poland and Czechoslovakia) became political blocs.[38] Whereas, the degree of mobilisation of civil society differed considerably during the demise of the three authoritarian regimes, the mobilisation and activity cycle converged after the founding elections and the constitutional establishment of democratic rules and institutions. After the mobilization of the moral and political resources of society against the authoritarian regimes

the organisation of functional needs of the society became more predominant. Interest groups, such as trades unions, business organisations, and professional associations emerged. Non-governmental organisations were
founded in those areas of social policy where the new democratic State and
the capitalist markets failed to fulfil the social needs and demands of society.
In addition youth, sport, academic and religious groups and charitable organisations were (re)founded.

In 1992, still early in the transition, about 85,000 registered civil society
organisations existed in the four countries of Central Europe:[39]

- Hungary   31,000
- Poland   17,000
- Czech Republic   13,500
- Slovak Republic   4,000

Of course these figures have to be interpreted with caution. Different legal regulations and statistical rules for counting civil society organisations exist in
these countries and may make up for the variations in the statistics. Numbers
cannot be simply interpreted as indicative of the strength and influence of civil
society. However, it is obvious, and appears to be remarkable, that Poland, the
most vital and influential civil society of the 1980s, has lost considerably in
organisational strength, whereas a mushrooming of civil society organisations
can be observed in Hungary. This can be traced back to the different character of the civil societies in both countries during the last decade of the
Communist regime. After 1968 civil society in Hungary was never in open and
confrontational opposition to the regime. It was more oriented to the self-
organisation of social life in niches which the regime did not control. The civic
organisations emerged as the response to the regime's moderate liberalisation
and the inadequate functioning of public services or the challenge of the environment. After the regime change began, civil society again was stimulated by
the malfunctioning of the state in certain policy areas such as education,
health care, social services, environment and community development.[40] An
estimated 12 per cent of Hungary's population are registered members of
these organisations. But due to the lack of a clear regulatory framework, business groups often register as NGOs and foundations, although they pursue
private economic interests disguised as non-profit organisations in order to
benefit from certain tax privileges.[41] Therefore the mere quantity of associations and organisations is not necessarily the sign of a strong civil society and
does not reflect as such on the consolidation of democracy.[42] This is because
comparative analyses based on simply counting the number of civic associations do not distinguish between such organisations as sport clubs and charity
organisations, and associations which organise activities related to democracy,
such as campaigning, educating, protesting and monitoring the transition to
and consolidation of democracy.[43]

In Poland the political mobilisation of civil society did not persist during
the phase of democratic consolidation. There are several reasons for this:

- The cycle of mobilisation that had lasted since 1980 had exhausted itself. The preoccupation with survival in the face of a declining economy, growing unemployment and falling incomes, but also in view of the opening up of new professional careers, led at the individual level to shifting involvements from public to private interests.
- With regime change, the functions and forms of the civil society changed: associations with particular economic interests grew in significance compared to the groups and heroes of the 'moral civil society'.
- In the realm of organised social and economic interests the old Communist organisations (especially the unions) enjoyed advantages over the new unions.
- However, the most important point was that, particularly in Poland and in Czechoslovakia and to a lesser extent in Hungary, the entire leadership of civil society took on positions in government or in public administration. Thus, a kind of collective transformation from civil to political society occurred.

From the perspective of mobilisation, civil society was punished with an enormous decline after the successful institutionalisation of democracy. In this stage the civil societies of East-Central Europe have become more alike, least with respect to their types and forms of activity.

Civil society's contribution to democratic consolidation

The impact of civil societies in the four countries (since 1993) will be assessed using the six democratic functions that I derived from the civil society concepts of Locke, Montesquieu, Tocqueville and Habermas. Not surprisingly, in general it can be asserted that none of the democratic functions has as yet been satisfactorily fulfilled by any of the four new democracies. Nevertheless, there are obvious differences among the countries with respect to these classical functions of civil society.

The *Lockeian function*: of all functions ascribed to a vital civil society, the classic Lockeian function of the negative guarantee of liberty, i.e. to protect the private sphere against state interference, was the first to be fulfilled. This was guaranteed soon after the founding election, although this has been achieved more strongly through the new democratic constitutional constraints and the rule of law than through the existence of vital associations in the civil societies. This is particularly true for Hungary, Poland and the Czech Republic. In the case of the Slovak Republic under the Mečiar Government, where the constitutional constraints were not sufficiently function and respected by the executive, a more 'politicised' civil society developed than in the other three countries. This was particularly evident in the 1998 election campaign when a 'Civic Campaign (OK) '98', an open, nonpartisan initiative, was established with the aim of ensuring open, free and fair elections. During the election campaign numerous NGOs co-ordinated to form a network in support of the democratic opposition, organised the observation of the elections and initiated a 'democratic Round Table'. This Round Table united the four opposition parties and four non-partisan actors in civil society in order to ensure the transfer of power from the Mečiar Government to the new democratic Governing coalition. Slovak civil society was prepared to defend its democratic character against the Mečiar Government, which represented a 'defective democratic' regime.[44]

The *Montesquieu function*: the classic Montesquieian function of the link between state and society and the checks and balances between the political powers has, ten years after the regime change, also been most fulfilled by civil society in Slovakia. This is true not only for the era of the Mečiar Governments but for the period since the 1998 parliamentary elections. Bútora and Bútorova[45] convincingly speak of a vibrant and efficient 'civil archipelago'', 'which[46] will be a partner that the new government will have to reckon with, both as a prospective collaborator and as a potential opponent'.[47] A comparable intermediary function of civil society cannot be found in Poland at the end of the 1990s. There are at least two reasons for this: first, the disappointment of large sections of civil society at the semi-authoritarian governing style of their once-charismatic leader Lech Walesa revived the distrust of the State that had shaped civil society during the Communist era. Second, the disappointment within civil society after 1993 over the government (and after 1995 the presidency) being taken over by the post-Communists, when the old regime elites, once again in control of political power in the State, increased a withdrawal into the private sphere. In the Czech Republic, and even more in Hungary, civil society seems to be more apathetic and indifferent with regard to the political aim of controlling government.[48]

The *Tocquevilleian function* – the school of democracies: if civil societies are to fulfil this function they must, particularly in their internal structure, associations and networks, acquire tolerance, democratic procedures and equal co-operation. But this is not well-developed in East-Central Europe. For instance, it does not appear to have been particularly the case with respect to the two paramount actors in Polish civil society under the Communist regime, Solidarnosc and the Catholic Church. In Solidarnosc an internally democratic school of democracy 'was largely sacrificed' to the strategic imperative of concerted action against the Communist regime. The movement Solidarnosc dissolved itself by founding political parties and traditional trade unions. The Catholic Church as an institution has only a marginal degree of democratic participation and it is subordinate to a dogmatic and organisational hierarchy. The nationalist–conservative Catholic Church in Poland is a particular example in case. It is in KOR (Workers' Defence Committee) that one is most likely to see a classical school of democracy that trained and socialised the elites for the democratic institutions. But KOR as such no longer exists. Only such outstanding intellectuals as Adam Michnik and Jacek Kuron became important individuals in the public sphere of Poland.

The *production of social capital*: as we know from Robert Putnam,[49] social capital, i.e. mutual trust, social inclusion, co-operation and civic engagement, cannot be produced in a short period of time. Rather, it is deeply rooted in a society's historical experiences. In this respect all four ECE societies have an ambivalent heritage. On the one hand, they have to cope with the legacy of almost fifty years of totalitarian and authoritarian Communist rule, where civil society, traditions, moral norms, the rule of law and a culture of free collective activity were greatly weakened.[50] On the other hand, there is the 'Habsburg Factor',[51] meaning that there is a tradition of the rule of law as well as of interest groups and civic associations which could not be completely destroyed by the Communist regime. That distinguishes the ECE states from the Balkan states (Ottoman Empire) or the successor states of the Soviet Union (Czarist Empire), with the partial exception of the Baltic states. Yet even East-Central Europe will need a long time to attain West European standards. However, it is possible that the capitalistic and individualistic societies of the West will resemble the ECE countries in the future, as important elements of social capital there are also undergoing a problematic erosion. It would be over-optimistic to expect a sufficient production of social capital in the new democracies of Central and Eastern Europe while this production is constantly shrinking in the West under more favourable economic conditions.[52]

Social capital is produced primarily by horizontal contacts of association between equals among a maximum number of citizens and not by intense vertical networks or religiously and ethnically closed communities. Viewed from this structuralist point of view I see the best prospects for success in the Czech Republic. This will be strengthened by the democratic and civil traditions of the country prior to 1938. In contrast to Slovakia and Hungary, the Czech Republic is ethnically a relatively homogenous society where mutual trust can be built up more easily.[53] The charismatic president Václav Havel also functioned as a moral institution for the whole of society. In addition the Czech Republic does not have to deal with a Catholic Church that has now and then tended towards religious intransigence, excessive nationalism and social exclusion as in Poland.[54] Additionally, in Poland there is a historically rooted tendency to denounce dissidents and political opponents as un-Polish'.[55] The Polish sociologist Anna Wolff-Poweska pointedly criticised this tendency, arguing that in Poland 'democracy without a democratic political culture exists'.[56] In all civil societies of the ECE countries there is a lack of co-operation and horizontal communication between different civic networks and advocacy groups and the service-providing organisations of civil society.[57] Ten years after the transition the level of trust within the societies of Central and Eastern Europe is still 'extremely low'.[58] Additionally NGOs do not enjoy high esteem among the publics. In Hungary the Central Statistical Bureau published an opinion poll where 68 per cent of the population considered NGOs to be useless rather than beneficial for society. Less than 10 per cent believed that they are useful, and only 12 per cent attributed to them an important role in consolidating democracy. The heritage of the socialist state regimes and the experience of recent *laissez-faire* capitalism has had a considerable impact on the ECE societies and may have to be considered as a major burden for developing greater mutual trust at this level.

The *Habermasian function*: this consists of creating a problem-sensitive and critical public outside of the political and economic society. Habermas's concept of civil society is extraordinarily demanding and is in no way sufficiently developed, even in long-consolidated democracies. This is even truer of new democracies. In each of the four new democracies such a critical public is rather small. Beginnings can be found among human rights groups in Slovakia, women's movements and ecological groups in Hungary, civic intellectuals in Polish media and political advocacy groups for Roma in all four countries.[59]

The *pluralist function*: Lipset and others have argued that, above all, it is the bridging of deep social cleavages by overlapping memberships in interest groups and civic associations that plays an important role in the stabilisation of peaceful democracies. In order to achieve this, a dense network of associations organised by citizens in their various roles and interests is necessary. Such a network of organisations which effectively bridges the Catholic-lay and nation-state Europe conflict, or that overcomes the cleavages of the ethnic communities, has yet to be properly developed. There is still insufficient communication and co-operation between the different segments of society and the organisations of civil society.[60] During the late 1990s only in Slovakia did an umbrella leadership organisation of the NGOs work in any way effectively. This 'Gremium of the Third Sector' co-ordinated several common campaigns against the Mečiar Government between 1996 and 1998. It was open, transparent and overlapping – this last by integrating also civic associations of the Hungarian community in the Slovak Republic.[61] But the experience of Poland, where the overlapping communication and cooperation within civil society of the 'authoritarian' 1980s could not be prolonged during the 'democratic' 1990s, could be emblematic. It has to be seen whether this politicised, pluralist, overlapping and active civil society can conserve these civic–political properties, after the common opponent and enemy Mečiar lost power in Slovakia.

Conclusion

If we consider the state of civil societies in all four countries, none of them has reached a sufficient level and quality of activity to fulfil the six classical functions for democracy. As I have described and explained above, there are variations between the four countries with respect to the individual functions. However, the differences are not substantial. Paradoxically, Slovakia seems, twelve years after the break-up of the Communist regimes, to have the most vibrant civil society. However, Slovak democracy is still the least consolidated among these new democracies in East-Central Europe. Yet Slovakia has appeared to undergo a 'second transition' during the last few years, in which civil society has played a major role.

Poland seems to have deeply ingrained political cleavages and its civic associations do not sufficiently bring about the overlapping of the 'national Catholic' and the 'European lay', the modern and traditional segments of society. The associations and interest groups seem to organise along these cleavages, thereby deepening them. The Czech Republic obviously contains a strong virtual, but not yet realised, potential for a civil society. Hungarian civil society seems to be the least politicised. On the other hand Hungary's civil society seems to be the most densely organised. By 1997 approximately 56,000 NGOs were officially registered. More than 1 million citizens, i.e. nearly 12 per cent of the country's population, were organised in civic associations. But sometimes business and political groups register as NGOs to benefit from privileged tax status. Moreover, the mere number of sports clubs, charity organisations and cultural associations says little about their impact on democratic consolidation. However, in the long run a dense network of civic organisations constitutes a bulwark against the non-legitimate interference of the state in social and private affairs.

Apart from these differences, a final question can be raised: are the civil societies in East-Central Europe an asset or a burden for democracy? The answer is: it depends above all on which concept of democracy we are referring to. If we refer to Schumpeter's elitist type of democracy, we can conclude: no, they are not a major burden, in particular not the peaceful and rather 'silent' civil societies of Hungary and the Czech Republic. The elites govern, and the people can vote for or against them. Between elections the government enjoys sufficient room for manoeuvre to take effective decisions. Meanwhile the non-political groups of civil society compensate for some failure of the state to provide adequate public services. But if we hold to a more demanding concept of a participatory and deliberative democracy, one which goes beyond Schumpeter and Dahl's polyarchy, the civil societies of Hungary, Poland and the Czech Republic turn out to be a burden still. Such a concept should not be simply labelled as utopian and too normative. It is not a question only of normative convictions and democratic quality. It is a question of democratic stability. The more vibrant a civil society is, the better it can fulfil its potential as an agent of protecting democracy against external shocks, internal crises and the danger of degenerating into 'defective democracies', which we find in the Balkans, Russia and among other new democracies in Latin America and East Asia. In East-Central Europe democracy is secured more by the citizens' acceptance of the new constitutions and central democratic institutions than by the vitality of its civil societies. Civil society is the last of four fundamental levels, and it which still has to be consolidated (as attitudinal consolidation), following institutional consolidation, representational consolidation through political parties and behavioural consolidation with the integration of veto actors.

Notes

1 E. Gellner, *Conditions of Liberty: Civil Society and its Rivals* (London: Hamish Hamilton, 1994), p. 1.
2 C. Taylor, 'Der Begriff der "bürgerlichen Gesellschaft" im politischen Denken des Westens', in M. Brumlik and H. Brunkhorst (eds), *Gemeinschaft und Gerechtigkeit* (Fischer–Taschenbuch–Verlag, Frankfurt, 1993); K. von Beyme, *Systemwechsel in Osteuropa* (Suhrkamp, Frankfurt, 1994).
3 C. Taylor, 'Der Begriff der bürgerlichen Gesellschaft', p. 118.
4 K. von Beyme, *Systemwichsel in Osteuropa*, p. 100.
5 J. Locke, *Über die Regierung* (*The Second Treatise of Government*) (Reclam, Stuttgart, 1974 [1689]), p. 59.
6 *Ibid.*, p. 67.
7 C. Montesquieu, *Vom Geist der Gesetze* (Reclam, Stuttgart, 1965 [1748]).
8 C. Taylor, 'Der Begriff der bürgerlichen Gesellschaft', p. 142.
9 C. Montesquieu, *Vom Geist der Gesetze*, pp. 249ff.
10 A. de Tocqueville, *Über die Demokratie in Amerika* (Reclam, Stuttgart, 1985 [1835]), pp. 106ff.
11 R. Putnam, Making Democracy Work (NJ: Princeton University Press, Princeton, 1993), pp. 163ff.
12 R. Dahrendorf, 'Die Zukunft der Buergergesellschaft', in B. Guggenberger and K. Hansen (eds), *Die Mitte. Vermessungen in Politik und Kultur* (Westdeutscher Verlag, Opladen, 1992), p. 80.
13 R. Dahrendorf, *Der moderne soziale Konflikt*, (Deutscher Taschenbuch Verlag, Munchen 1994), p. 495.
14 J. Keane, *Democracy and Civil Society* (Verso, London, 1988); J. Cohen and A. Arato, *Civil Society and Political Theory* (MIT Press, Cambridge, MA: 1992); J. Habermas, *Faktizität und Geltung* (Suhrkamp, Frankfurt: 1992).
15 J. Habermas, *Faktizität und Geltung*, p. 374.
16 *Ibid.*, p. 433.
17 A. Przeworski *et al.*, *Sustainable Democracy* (Cambridge University Press, Cambridge, 1995), pp. 53ff.
18 S. M. Lipset, *Political Man. The Social Bases of Politics* (Johns Hopkins University Press, Baltimore, MD, 1981), pp. 211ff.
19 W. Merkel and H.-J. Lauth, 'Systemwechsel und Zivilgesellschaft: Welche Zivilgesellschaft braucht die Demokratie?', *Aus Politik und Zeitgeschichte* 6–7, 1998, p. 7.
20 J. Cohen and A. Arato, *Civil Society and Political Theory*; J. Habermas, *Faktizität und Geltung*.
21 O. Brunner, W. Conze and R. Koselleck, *Geschichtliche Grundbegriffe*, vol. 7 (Klett-Cotta, Stuttgart, 1990), p. 633.
22 M. Foley and B. Edwards, 'The paradox of civil society', *Journal of Democracy* 3, 1996, pp 38ff.

23 G. O'Donnell and P. Schmitter, *Transitions from Authoritarian Rule: Tentative Conclusions about Uncertain Democracies* (John Hopkins University Press, Baltimore, MD, 1986).

24 A. O. Hirschman, *Exit, Voice, and Loyalty. Responses to Decline in Firms, Organizations, and States* (Harvard University Press, Cambridge, MA: 1970).

25 D. Easton, *A System Analysis of Political Life* (Prentice Hall, New York, 1965).

26 D. Held, *Democracy and the Global Order: From the Modern State to Cosmopolitan Governance* (Polity Press, Cambridge, 1989), p. 182.

27 W. Merkel, 'The Consolidation of Postautocratic Democracies: A Multi-Level Model', *Democratization* 3, 1998, p. 41.

28 L. Morlino and J. R. Montero, 'Legitimacy and Democracy in Southern Europe', in R. Gunther, N. P. Diamandouros u⁻m and H.-J. Puhle (eds), *The Politics of Democratic Consolidation* (Johns Hopkins University Press, Baltimore MD, 1995), pp. 231ff.

29 F. Plasser, P. Ullram and H. Waldrauch, *Politischer Kulturwandel in Ost-Mitteleuropa: Theorie und Empirie demokratischer Konsolidierung* (Leske & Budrich, Opladen, 1997).

30 Sometimes civil movements transform themselves into political parties, as had been the case in Poland, Slovakia, the Czech Republic or the Baltic States.

31 W. Merkel, *Systemtransformation. Eine Einführung in die Theorie und Empirie der Transformationsforschung* (Leske & Budrich, Opladen, 1999), p. 135.

32 Z. Mansfeldová, 'Zivilgesellschaft in der Tschechischen und Slowakischen Republik', *Aus Politik und Zeitgeschichte* 6–7, 1998, p. 15.

33 M. Szabó, 'Die Zivilgesellschaft in Ungarn vor und nach der Wende', *Aus Politik und Zeitgeschichte* 6–7, 1998, p. 21.

34 A. Ágh, 'The "Comparative Revolution" and the Transition to Democracy in Central and Southern Europe', *Journal of Theoretical Politics* 2, 1993, pp. 231–52.

35 A. Smolar, 'From Opposition to Atomization', *Journal of Democracy* 1, 1996, p. 28.

36 A. Ágh, 'The "Comparative Revolution"'.

37 A. Smolar, 'From Opposition to Atomisation', p. 29.

38 *Ibid.*

39 A. Vari, 'Civil Society and Public Participation: Recent Trends in Central and Eastern Europe', available online: http://www.sfu.ca/cdrc/research/civil soc/vari.htm, 1998, p. 36.

40 *Ibid.*

41 Freedom House, 'Nations in Transit: Civil Society, Democracy and Markets in East Central Europe and the newly Independent States', available online: http:// www.freedomhouse.org/nit 98/, 1998.

42 K. Ertsey and F. Miszlivetz, 'Hungary: Civil Society in the Post-Socialist World', report prepared for the North–South Institute, Ottawa, 1997, p. 10.

43 Freedom House, 'Nations in Transit'.

44 For the concept of 'Defective Democracy', see W. Merkel, *Defective Democracies* working paper no. 132 (Instituto Juan March, Madrid, 1999).

45 M. Bútora and Z. Bútorová, 'Slovakia's Democracy Awakening', *Journal of Democracy* 1, 1998, pp. 80–95.

46 *Ibid.*, p. 89.

47 Of course this has also to with the fact, that the governments of these two countries respected the constraints of the rule of law and the new democratic constitution much more than had the semi-authoritarian Mečiar Governments.

48 R. Putnam, *Making Democracy Work*.

49 A. Smolar, 'From Opposition to Atomization', p. 33.

50 J. Rupnik,, 'The postcommunist divide', *Journal of Democracy* 1, 1999, p. 60.

51 R. Putnam, *Making Democracy Work*, pp. 65ff.

52 Except from the Gypsy-population, which is discriminated against socially and eco-
    nomically in the Czech Republic as in the other Central European countries (this
    applies also for the West European countries).

53 Here, there is clearly an important empirical suggestion for studies which not only
    include the known items of political culture but more intensively research the con-
    nection between civic engagement and social capital, as Robert Putnam has done
    in relation to Italy and the USA.

54 In this respect, the ROP-leader Jan Olszewski criticised the 1995 election success of
    Kwaśniewski by saying that large parts of the population had now ceased to belong
    to the Polish nation, see M. Mildenberger, 'Zwischen Konsens und Polarität. Zur
    Entwicklung der demokratischen politischen Kultur in Polen', in *Aus Politik und
    Zeitgeschichte* 6–7, 1998, pp. 39–45.

55 A. Wolff-Poweska, 'Politische Kultur in den postkommunistischen Gesellschaften',
    in W. Weidenfeld (ed.), *Demokratie und Marktwirtschaft in Osteuropa* (Verlag
    Bertelsmann-Stiftung, Gutersloh, 1995), p. 49.

56 A. Vari, 'Civil Society and Public Participation'.

57 *Ibid.*, p. 48.

58 Freedom House, 'Nations in Transit'.

59 *Ibid.*

60 A. Vari, 'Civil Society and Public Participation', p. 77.

61 Freedom House, 'Nation in Transit'.

Mainly sunny with scattered clouds: political culture in East-Central Europe

Introduction

In this contribution we look at the *subjective* side of democratic consolidation, the political culture of the population in post-communist societies. Democratic consolidation in our understanding means the process of stabilising the minimal formal criteria of a democratic regime in a polity, namely pluralism, competition in free and fair elections and its prerequisites, and government according to basic civil rights and the rule of law.[1] The anchoring of these principles at the level of mass attitudes is important since a lasting divergence between the institutional structure and the rules of the game on the one hand and basic patterns of orientations on the other is likely to cause friction which could undermine the functioning of the new system. This holds especially true for the new democracies in Central and Eastern Europe where the consolidation process proceeds simultaneously with a process of economic transformation and where the institutional structure is less firmly established than in traditional democracies.[2]

Furthermore, the existence of democratic orientations on the mass level is likely to work as a barrier against authoritarian tendencies on the part of (some) political actors. Conversely, widespread antidemocratic sentiments might prove a fertile ground for radical political movements or populist leaders.

Following Almond's seminal concepts of policy culture, process culture and system culture[3] as well as Easton's distinction between specific and diffuse support,[4] this chapter starts with the public evaluation of the performance of the new political systems, followed by evidence on satisfaction with democracy. Next, we concentrate on indicators of specific support (trust in collective actors). The final part deals with the core of democratic orientations, e.g. the assessment of party competition and the preference for democratic rule *vis-à-vis* authoritarian alternatives. In this way, evidence will throw light on progress towards democratic consolidation in East-Central Europe.

The data basis is provided by representative mass surveys conducted by the

Table 2 *Regime transformation: expectations and reality (1991–99)*

	BG	RO	RUS	UA	PL								H							
	99	99	99	99	91	92	93	94	95	97	98	99	91	92	93	94	95	97	98	99
My personal expectations of regime change have been . . . (in %)[a]																				
Exceeded or largely fulfilled	24	22	8	4	28	13	16	14	27	37	35	26	18	9	10	13	10	13	22	23
Rather disappointed:																				
I expected more	43	47	39	40	41	41	38	46	47	41	44	43	56	55	42	55	54	53	58	51
Seriously disappointed: none of my expectations have come true	22	22	27	36	19	30	29	24	16	12	13	18	13	19	31	17	23	20	14	15
Confirmed: I was right in never expecting any good to come of it	9	8	26	17	10	12	15	15	8	8	5	11	11	14	14	11	12	11	5	11
No response	2	1	1	3	2	4	4	1	2	2	2	2	1	2	3	3	1	3	1	–

	SK								CZ							
	91	92	93	94	95	97	98	99	91	92	93	94	95	97	98	99
My personal expectations of regime change have been . . . (in %)[a]																
Exceeded or largely fulfilled	17	18	7	30	14	13	14	18	29	26	23	27	40	29	21	17
Rather disappointed: I expected more	56	55	46	52	57	55	51	46	52	49	54	49	45	50	55	53
Seriously disappointed: none of my expectations have come true	19	16	29	11	17	19	26	21	10	14	14	13	9	15	16	19
Confirmed: I was right in never expecting any good to come of it	8	10	17	6	12	12	9	13	8	9	9	10	6	4	8	10
No response	1	1	1	1	–	1	–	2	1	1	–	–	–	1	–	1

Note:

[a] Discrepancy between percentage given and 100% = no response.

Source: FESSEL-GfK, *Politischer Kulturwandel in Ost-Mitteleuropa* (1991–99).

Table 3 *Failure of politics – Central and Eastern Europe*

| | Politics are failing in important matters: | | | |
| | *Sometimes/seldom/never (%)[a]* | | *Often/all the time (%)* | |
	1995	*1999*	*1995*	*1999*
Austria [b]	54	na	45	na
Hungary	37	41	62	57
Bulgaria	na	40	na	58
Slovak Republic	46	30	53	69
Romania	na	27	na	73
Poland	42	24	57	75
Czech Republic	65	21	35	79
Ukraine	na	11	na	89
Russia	na	10	na	89

Notes:
[a] Discrepancy between percentage given and 100% = no response
[b] 1996 not 1995
   na = not asked
Source: FESSEL–GfK, *Politischer Kulturwandel in Ost-Mitteleuropa* (1995 and 1999);
FESSEL–GfK, *Politische Indikatoren* (1996) [for Austria]

market research group GfK of Vienna at regular intervals between 1990/91 and 1999 in Hungary (H), Poland (PL), the Czech Republic (CZ) and Slovakia (SK) (PKOM project).[5] Additional information is drawn from surveys in Russia (RUS), the Ukraine (UA), Bulgaria (BG) and Romania (RO) as well as from studies on the political culture in now-established post-authoritarian democracies, e.g. Austria (A), Western Germany and Italy.

General performance

The beginnings of the great transformation in 1989 were accompanied by much hope and expectation that the establishment of a new order would result in both more wealth and social justice as well as in a rather idealised political system (see Table 2).[6] Many people expected a quick improvement of the economic and social situation. Even more, the very concept of democracy prevalent in Central and Eastern Europe included not only institutional, procedural and liberal–individualistic dimensions, but assumptions about economic and social progress.[7] But as early as 1991, system change had failed to fulfil the hopes of roughly two-thirds of citizens in East-Central Europe (ECE). Disappointment was highest in 1992 and 1993 when economic and social hardships reached their peak and the working of the new political systems did not correspond to the widespread popular idealisation of democracy (see Table 3).

In the following years, one finds a gradual improvement in Poland and the Czech Republic with Hungary following somewhat later. The development in Slovakia was more erratic due mostly to domestic political events. When the Czech Republic faced growing economic problems and internal political strife in the late 1990s, the evaluation of how much of the original expectations had come true worsened accordingly. There is, however, a remarkable difference between the East-Central European countries on the one side and the Ukraine and Russia[8] on the other; in the latter two countries, there are very few people whose expectations have either come true or even been exceeded by real developments. A majority of the population feels very disappointed or had never expected anything good to come out of the transformation in the first place, and the developments then taking place confirmed their dim prognoses.

Politics' positive associations diminished in most Central European countries between 1991 and 1995 or remained on a very low level, as in Poland.[9] This process of disillusionment can also be illustrated by the increasing number of people who notice political mistakes and failures: in 1995 about one-third of Czechs and half of Poles and Slovaks thought that politics was failing on important matters often or all the time. Four years later this view was shared by 69 per cent in Slovakia, 75 per cent in Poland and 79 per cent in the Czech Republic. Only Hungarians, who showed a rather negative attitude already in 1995 presented a more positive view in 1999. There are also considerable doubts whether democracy is able to deal with the problems the countries are facing. The number of such sceptics varies between 26 per cent in Romania and 31 per cent in Poland on the one hand and is around 44 per cent in Slovakia and Bulgaria on the other. Again, the successor states of the former Soviet Union stand out for their overall pessimistic outlook (Table 4).

There are both objective and subjective reasons for the rather sceptical assessment in the areas of policy and process culture. For most East-Central Europeans, economic transition – at least in its early stages- has meant considerable economic loss and more worries, especially about jobs which were more or less guaranteed under the old regime. While various degrees of economic recovery took effect at different times and in specific ways in each country, individual households generally did not begin to feel this until the late 1990s, and even then only to a limited degree. Furthermore, most people thought that only small groups of the population (most notably enterpreneurs and members of the old nomenclatura) were among the 'beneficiaries' of economic reform, while large and important social groups (especially workers, women and retired persons) were designated as 'losers' of this process. Generally speaking, social and economic developments were considered uneven and slanted.[10] The new political institutions took considerable time before they were able to function properly, a process aggravated by the fact that the majority of the political and administrative personnel either had to be recruited from rather inexperienced representatives of the former opposi-

Table 4 *Capability for problem solving – Central and Eastern Europe*

	Democracy is capable of dealing with the problems the country faces (%)[a]		Democracy is not capable of dealing with the problems the country faces (%)	
	1997	1999	1997	1999
Austria	na	72	na	23
Romania	na	74	na	26
Poland	64	61	31	36
Czech Republic	51	55	49	42
Slovak Republic	58	55	41	44
Hungary	52	54	43	42
Bulgaria	na	54	na	44
Ukraine	na	42	na	52
Russia	na	19	na	54

Notes:
[a] Discrepancy between percentage given and 100% = no response
na = not asked
Source: FESSEL–GfK, *Politischer Kulturwandel in Ost-Mitteleuropa* (1995 and 1999);
FESSEL–GfK, *Politische Indikatoren* (1999) [for Austria]

tion or remained in post unchanged. With the particular exception of Poland, the new elite lacked a sufficient anchoring in society,[11] and the structures of political integration were weak, thus creating an intermediary vacuum. Confronted with the high level of positive expectations with the onset of system change, it was clear that disillusionment had to follow. This was especially the case in the successor states of the former Soviet Union, where both the economic and the political transformation took place in only an incomplete form, economic crisis remains an ongoing experience and the public institutions (among others) are characterised by a combination of high claims for political control and low efficiency in implementation.[12]

Disillusionment or disenchantment, however, is a two-sided process: on the one hand, it can be interpreted as an indicator of growing discontent; on the other, it can be a sign of growing realism. People may become more realistic not only about the time necessary for the delivery of material benefits and the functioning of the new economic and political system, but about the very concept of democracy. Comparing the data on the meaning of democracy by Simon[13] for the early 1990s with the relevant data from the PKOM-project in 1995, one finds indeed a shift from idealistic to realistic conceptions. The latter is characteristic of established democracies where more emphasis is put on 'formal' (e.g. institutional and rule of law) aspects at the expense of social and economic opportunities and expectations.

Satisfaction with democracy

Although the indicator 'satisfaction with democracy' is strongly influenced by evaluations of government performance, economic development for example,[14] it can serve as a first hint of progress towards regime consolidation:[15] 'There is no objective criterion by which to determine how widespread satisfaction must be before we can talk of a stable democracy. However, it is implausible to assume that a democracy is in jeopardy if a majority of citizens are content with the political system'.[16]

PKOM's data series on satisfaction with democracy[17] points to trend patterns and developments which are highly specific to each country, and does not present a united picture (see Table 5). Crises of economic adaptation, the social costs of transformation, structural and functional deficiencies, political polarisation and conflict among rival elites all account for fluctuating levels of satisfaction in the individual countries. Temporary increases of dissatisfaction in some countries contrast with a general move toward consolidation in others. Discontinuity, rather than linearity, is the key characteristic of the dynamics of system satisfaction in the reform countries of ECE.

In Hungary, satisfaction with democracy declined between 1991 and 1993. Towards the end of the 1990s satisfaction increased somewhat, but remained at relatively low levels until the economic situation improved significantly; in 1998 and 1999 six out of ten Hungarians were very or fairly satisfied with democracy and the whole political system. The development in Poland was similar, with a big increase of satisfaction after 1995 but a considerable decline in 1999. In the Czech Republic the levels of satisfaction were higher and rather stable until 1997 when the economic downturn and instability within the governing coalition caused a definite worsening in public attitudes. The situation in the Slovak Republic appears to have been rather volatile and unstable. Satisfaction with democracy rose in 1992, the year national independence was attained. The following year was, however, marked by growing disillusionment. In 1994 the share of individuals satisfied with Slovak democracy again increased, only to plummet in 1995 to its lowest level since 1990. This volatility remained characteristic also for the following years although the shifts were somewhat less pronounced. These ups and downs correspond fairly well to the troubled politics of the new state, political developments having evidently a bigger impact on satisfaction than the economic situation.

Nevertheless, in 1999 all Central European countries reveal a majority of more or less satisfied citizens, thus showing a striking difference not only to the (economic) crisis years but even more to the situation in the Ukraine and Russia, where only 30 per cent and 24 per cent respectively express some kind of political satisfaction.

In any case, these data on trends and levels of satisfaction with democracy in East-Central Europe should not be over-played. Apart from some methodical problems, which still plague this indicator, a comparison with a manifestly

Table 5 *Satisfaction with democracy – Central and Eastern Europe*

		PL	H	CZ	SK	BG	RO	UA	RUS
In general, are you satisfied with democracy and the whole political system? (%)[a]									
Very satisfied	1990			14	9				
	1991	5	2	4	2				
	1992	1	3	4	1				
	1993/1[b]	2	1	6	2				
	1993/2[c]			4	2				
	1994	2	1	3	3				
	1995	4	1	3	2				
	1997	5	0	5	4				
	1998	7	2	2	2				
	1999	3	1	1	1	3	2	1	2
Fairly satisfied	1990			60	55				
	1991	62	56	72	56				
	1992	54	55	69	68				
	1993/1[b]	35	33	73	61				
	1993/2[c]			60	29				
	1994	43	47	59	70				
	1995	59	42	72	43				
	1997	74	45	68	51				
	1998	73	62	52	40				
	1999	58	58	54	52	50	42	29	22
Not satisfied	1990			19	28				
	1991	32	39	24	41				
	1992	39	40	26	29				
	1993/1[b]	57	64	20	36				
	1993/2[c]			35	67				
	1994	53	48	37	27				
	1995	37	57	25	25				
	1997	19	52	27	47				
	1998	19	36	46	57				
	1999	38	41	44	46	46	56	70	75

Notes:
[a] Discrepancy between percentage given and 100% = no response
 Missing figures: no data for this year
[b] First poll
[c] Second poll
Source: FESSEL–GfK, *Politischer Kulturwandel in Ost-Mitteleuropa* (1990–99)

consolidated democracy such as Austria calls for a prudent interpretation of the data. The level of political satisfaction in the Czech Republic in 1995, as well as in Slovakia in 1994 and in Poland in 1997 and 1998, was approximately the same as in contemporary Austria. Furthermore, the amount of dissatisfaction in East-Central Europe at the end of the first decade after the new regimes were established is not higher than in post-authoritarian Southern European countries during their first phase of consolidation.

Trust in institutions

While the indicator 'satisfaction with democracy' suffers, in the terminology of Easton's seminal model, from a blurred distinction between diffuse and specific support, trust in institutions is first and foremost an indicator of specific support.[18] It differs widely even in consolidated Western democracies where different levels of trust reflect especially whether an institution's public profile is primarily corporate or predominantly centred around a leader or representative;[19] and whether it is seen as a competitive (hence contentious and partial) or a 'neutral' and 'all-encompassing' body.[20]

Trust in institutions, however, is also of importance for any analysis of diffuse system support:

- The overall level of institutional trust would seem to indicate the extent of diffuse political support. However a high level of trust in some institutions may also either compensate for low or declining confidence in others or cushion and blunt the effect of their temporarily deficient credibility.
- If the level of confidence in predominantly hierarchical and authoritarian institutions (e.g. armed forces) differs greatly from that in institutions of political control and/or pluralist politics, liberal-democratic consensus is likely to be vulnerable.
- Different levels of confidence in non-competitive executive institutions, on the one hand, and government and/or parliament, on the other, indicate similarly divergent patterns of functional and/or attitudinal democratic consolidation .
- No full assessment of levels of trust is possible unless we understand the dynamics and development of trust in each particular institution, as well as confidence in each institution relative to the others.

For these reasons, our analysis of trust in institutions in East Central Europe does not limit itself to political institutions in the narrower sense, i.e. to institutions which compete in elections and have 'directly and indirectly' acquired democratic legitimacy in the process. We also include executive institutions, as well as other associations which, taken together, constitute societal and political pluralism.

Starting with political institutions, our findings indicate that confidence in presidents depends to a considerable degree on their institutional role. If it is a strong and powerful executive position, as in Russia or, to a certain extent,

Table 6 *Trust in institutions (1998)*

	Sums (%) of grades 5,6,7 on a scale of 1 = not trust to 7 = high trust in %				
	CZ	SK	H	PL	A[a]
President	60	29	53	40	47
Prime minister	50	25	33	36	na
Government	26	21	25	23	26
Parliament	15	25	25	25	27
Political parties	15	15	11	9	17
Trades unions	28	28	15	26	28
Churches	29	42	37	51	35
TV, radio	47	30	45	45	16[b]
Newspapers, other print media	48	34	42	42	
Government authorities and civil service	27	28	32	28	44
Law courts	25	35	39	30	55
Police	29	30	35	32	60
Army	31	58	40	53	41

Notes:
[a] 1997 not 1998
[b] In Austria, TV, radio, print media and newspaper were counted as a single category
Source: FESSEL–GfK/Paul Lazarsfeld Gesellschaft: (NDB) *Neue Demokratien-Barometer* (1998) [for CZ, SK, H, PL]; FESSEL–GfK, *Politische Indikatoren und Legitimität* (1997) [for A]

in Poland until 1995, we find a lack of trust. If, conversely, the president is primarily a moral and balancing agent, and if his executive position is weak and he remains above the daily political bickering, as is the case in Hungary and the Czech Republic, trust is very high and matches West European standards.[21] Governments and parliament generally enjoy much less public confidence, and political parties less still. The case was somewhat different in the Czech Republic where explicit trust in the government and political parties exceeded that of its East-Central European neighbours for a long period. In 1997 and 1998, however, the intensification of political conflicts led to a notable loss of confidence in political institutions, especially government, parliament and political parties.

Trust in institutions of a societally pluralist kind shows considerable nation-specific variation: Poles express a high level of confidence in the Catholic Church, based in large measure on its traditional role as, among other things, a seat and vehicle of national identity and given its deep structural roots in the population. More than 90 per cent of Poles claim to be devout Catholics, and nearly two out of three attend mass regularly. In the other countries, the share of confessionally committed respondents is much smaller. Here, the Czech Republic marks the other extreme: it shows the lowest level of trust in religious institutions. Environmentalist groups, examples of political figures with no party affiliation or salient ideological profile, enjoy high levels of trust which generally exceed those of competitive political organisations. The same holds true for the media, which are considered relatively untrustworthy only in Russia.

Trust in administrative institutions, as well as, in some cases, in courts of law and police forces – precisely those institutions which citizens most frequently encounter – is remarkably low. East-Central Europeans are generally much more wary of the state's public representatives than are Austrians or West Germans. Obviously, East-Central Europeans' past experiences with officials and the judiciary play an important role in this, as do functional deficiencies, doubts concerning the present claim to impartiality, and the widespread conviction that bureaucracies have been left more or less unaffected by transition. As in Western Europe, trust in the executive and judiciary generally exceeds trust in competitive political institutions; but, as a rule, East-Central Europe lacks the 'basic trust' in the web of state institutions which could, if it existed, absorb legitimacy crises of particular political institutions or compensate for their still rather fragile foundations.[22] The low levels of trust on the part of East-Central Europeans appear less dramatic, however, when compared to those which prevail in Russia. There, only the armed forces' public standing seems in any way balanced, while the bureaucracy, police and judiciary are subject to much more severe criticism than their East Central European counterparts. Among East-Central Europeans there seems to be no consensus on whether or not to trust the armed forces: Poles and Slovaks show considerable confidence in their national armies while distrust is predominant in the Czech Republic. Hungary falls between the two.

The patterns in the development and dynamics of institutional trust in East-Central Europe show great divergence. Public confidence in Hungary's political institutions began to wane as early as 1989 and continued in this vein for at least three more years.[23] Following the parliamentary elections of 1994, executive institutions improved their standing somewhat, only to lose it again in 1997. Churches and the army continued to lose credibility. After 1998 practically all institutions in Hungary experienced a strengthening of their public image. This was especially the case for political institutions – probably a consequence of a change in government and parliamentary majority. In Poland, the armed forces and the police were discredited as 'henchmen of the old guard' in the wake of the change of regime, while the Church and new democratic institutions enjoyed a surge of popularity. Soon, however, the latter had all but used up their bonus of confidence: political and pluralist institutions were judged increasingly by their often poor performance during the first years of transformation and consequently suffered a 'punitive' withdrawal of trust. In turn, army and police forces re-emerged in the public consciousness as supposedly neutral agents of order and security. Even trades unions affiliated with the former Communist Party were considered more trustworthy than was Solidarity in 1992 – a trend which, however, proved short-lived. In recent years, the media, the Catholic Church and independent unions improved their confidence ratings, as did the civil service.

Shifting grounds and volatility are salient characteristics of trust in Slovak institutions. With national independence attained, some symbolically charged institutions of the new nation-state (armed forces, government) improved their reputation significantly, while the civil service, police and judiciary remained largely unaffected, and trust in political and/or pluralist institutions declined. Church(es) and the media still have not recovered completely from the loss of confidence suffered once the initial enthusiasm for transition had begun to fade. However, government's confidence bonus also diminished within a few months. Finally, political parties do not seem to have reaped the benefits of independence euphoria at all.

In contrast to this scenario, Czech confidence in institutions has remained stable over a long period of time. The only exceptions to this rule were the Churches and the army. In 1997, however, against the backdrop of slowing economic growth, austerity measures and fierce conflict within the Government, there was an erosion of trust in institutions for the first time.

In all four countries, trades unions with no party affiliation are winning employees' loyalty at the expense of unions associated with Communist successor parties. Finally – and despite all the differences – the Polish, Hungarian, Slovak and Czech Republics are all characterized by a low level of confidence in political parties, most of which rank below other institutions of political pluralism. There is an important difference between this problem of democratic consolidation and that in Austria and Italy,[24] as well as a loose analogy with post-Franco Spain:[25] the role of political parties as agents of democratisation is relatively limited, while that of civil society is correspondingly strong.

Democratic orientations

Decisive for democratic consolidation on the attitudinal level is whether or not democratic rules are accepted as 'the only game in town' by a majority of the population. According to Linz and Stepan,

> attitudinally, a democratic regime is consolidated when a strong majority of public opinion, even in the midst of major economic problems and deep dissatisfaction with incumbents, holds the belief that democratic procedures and institutions are the most appropriate way to govern collective life, and when support for antisystem alternatives is quite small or more or less isolated from prodemocratic forces.[26]

Diffuse support for democracy presupposes the acceptance of a multi-party system, since democracy without pluralist competition and parties would constitute the hybrid 'authoritarian or delegative democracy',[27] prevalent in some Latin American and Asian states. Country-specific variations

Table 7   *Preference for a single-party system in post-authoritarian democracies*

	Only one party (%)[a]										
	A	DW[b]	I	CZ	H	PL	SK	RO	BG	RUS	UA
Do you think it is better for a country to have only one party, where there is a maximum of unity, or several parties, so that diverse views may be represented?											
Early 1950s		21									
Late 1950s	16	8									
1970s	11	8									
1980s–90s	15[c]		6[d]								
1991				6	18	19	14				
1992				8	22	31	14				
1993				8			16				
1994				6	22	23	20				
1995				6	24	24	13				
1997				5	24	29	16				
1998				8	18	22	11				
1999				13	22	23	24	23	23	35	42

Notes:
[a] Missing figures = no data for this year
[b] DW = Western Germany
[c] 1990s
[d] 1980s
Source: FESSEL–GfK, *Politischer Kulturwandel in Ost-Mitteleuropa* (1991–99); Gerlich, Plasser and Ulram (1992)

notwithstanding, a majority of the population in ECE countries favours a multi-party system. According to data from 1999, 86 per cent of respondents in the Czech Republic support pluralist party competition, as compared to three out of four respondents in the other Central European countries as well as in Romania and Bulgaria. Russians and Ukrainians embrace the pluralism of parties with markedly less enthusiasm. In all countries there is a strong correlation between preference for a single or a multi-party system on the one hand and education and age on the other. Among persons with only elementary education and in the highest age group, the preference for a single-party system is clearly higher than average. Lack of interest in politics, affiliation with or closeness to Communist Party groupings and pronounced disappointment with the social and economic consequences of the transition in turn increase a weariness towards pluralist party competition. Periods of exacerbated domestic conflict, power struggles between competing elites or signs of economic downturn similarly trigger scattered resurgences of latent anti-pluralist attitudes.[28] A case in point was the increase in support for a single-party system in Slovakia in 1999, most of which respondents adhere to those parties that lost the 1998 parliamentary elections (see Table 7). However, due

Table 8 *Democratic consciousness in post-authoritarian countries (1999)*

	RUS	UA	BG	RO	PL	SK	CZ	H	E[b]	I[b]	DW[c]	A
Which of the following opinions on democracy and dictatorship do you agree with? (%)[a]												
Democracy is preferable to dictatorship under any circumstances	32	44	54	66	61	64	64	71	70	70	90	90
For people like me, it makes no difference whether we live in a democracy or a dictatorship	20	21	29	14	27	21	22	16	9	10	3	3
In some cases, dictatorship may be preferable to democracy	29	34	16	20	10	15	13	12	10	13	6	5
No response	19	1	1	0	2	0	1	1	11	7	1	1

Notes:

[a] Discrepancy between percentage given and 100% = rounding difference

[b] Spain (E) and Italy (I): data for 1985

[c] DW = Western Germany: data for 1989

Source: FESSEL–GfK, *Politischer Kulturwandel in Ost-Mitteleuropa* (1991–99)

to its inherent passivity, resignation and lethargy, this sort of potentially anti-democratic force does not pose an immediate threat to consolidating democracies, however receptive to populist appeals it may seem. Juxtaposed with the sparse data on the consolidation periods of other post-authoritarian democracies, the findings on post-Communist democracies appear less dramatic. Thus, in the early 1950s, 21 per cent of West German respondents favoured a single-party system, but within a decade this rate fell to just 8 per cent.[29] A similar development took place in the consolidation period of Austrian postwar democracy.[30]

More stability is found regarding the core indicator on diffuse support for democracy, the choice between democracy on the one hand and authoritarian solutions on the other (Table 8). With very few exceptions, between two-thirds and three-quarters of the respondents during the last decade in Central Europe preferred democracy to any dictatorial regime under any circumstances. Poland experienced a dramatic decline in system support in 1992, directly related to the economic and domestic upheavals taking place at the time. However, two years later support for democracy had again reached and surpassed its former level. A similar, albeit less pronounced, development can be seen in the Czech and Slovak Republics, also mainly due to an increased amount of political conflict and economic difficulties (Tables 9(a) and 9(b)).

Table 9(a)   *Democratic consciousness in Central and Eastern Europe*

	RUS	PL	H	CZ	SK
Which of the following opinions on democracy and dictatorship do you agree with? (%)[a,b]					
Democracy is preferable to dictatorship under any circumstances					
1990				72	63
1991		60	69	77	67
1992		48	69	71	68
1993	36			72	60
1994	50	64	73	75	68
1995		65	67	74	66
1997		65	65	68	68
1998	39	68	75	72	76
1999	32	61	71	64	64
2000	39				
In some cases dictatorship may be preferable to democracy					
1990				8	
1991		14	9	7	10
1992		16	8	10	11
1993	20			9	11
1994	27	17	8	11	11
1995		15	11	9	12
1997		18	17	11	18
1998	28	16	10	10	16
1999	29	10	12	13	15
2000	21				

Notes:
[a] Discrepancy between percentage given and 100% = rounding difference
[b] Missing figures = question not asked in this year
Source: FESSEL–GfK, *Politischer Kulturwandel in Ost-Mitteleuropa* (1990–2000)

Declines in support for democracy normally do not lead to a correspond-ing increase of authoritarian attitudes, but rather to an increase in reactions of indifference or despondency on the part of interviewees when asked to specify the form of government they most favour. Such indifference is partic-ularly widespread among those who claim to have been sceptical of system change from the outset, and whose gloomy predictions of its consequences for their lives have apparently been borne out. The 'hard' core of anti-democrats who give preference to dictatorship over democracy amounts to 10 per cent in Poland, 12 per cent in Hungary, 13 per cent in the Czech Republic and 15 per cent in Slovakia. There has been very little fluctuation in this segment over the time period surveyed. Pronounced anti-democratic attitudes prevail, mainly

Table 9(b) *Democratic consciousness in Central and Eastern Europe*

	RUS	PL	H	CZ	SK
Which of the following opinions on democracy and dictatorship do you agree with? (%)[a,b]					
For people like me, it makes no difference whether we live in a democracy or a dictatorship					
1990				12	18
1991		23	18	15	22
1992		30	21	18	19
1993	19			17	28
1994	23	16	16	14	19
1995		17	17	16	22
1997		13	14	19	12
1998	21	14	15	17	7
1999	20	27	16	22	21
2000	16				
No response					
1990				9	8
1991		3	4	1	1
1992		6	2		2
1993	25			1	1
1994		3	3		2
1995		2	5	1	
1997		4	4	2	2
1998	12	1			
1999	19	2	1	1	1
2000	21				

Notes:
[a] Discrepancy between percentage given and 100% = rounding difference
[b] missing figures = question not asked in this year
Source: FESSEL–GfK, *Politischer Kulturwandel in Ost-Mitteleuropa* (1990–2000)

among (former) members of the Communist Party, but also among the unemployed and/or those who are pessimistic about their economic situation and prospects.

Again, the situation is quite different in the Ukraine and Russia where genuine anti-democratic sentiments are much stronger, as are fluctuations in the numbers of both supporters and adversaries of democratic systems.

An even deeper insight into the degree of democratic consolidation can be gained by using such typologies of core democratic attitudes as those developed by Morlino and Montero and Linz and Stepan[31] for the post-authoritarian democracies of Southern Europe and Latin America. These authors define confident democrats as individuals who prefer democracy as a form of government to dictatorship and who are convinced that democracy will be capable of solving the crucial difficulties of their country. Worried democrats basically harbour pro-democratic attitudes but have doubts concerning the problem-solving capacity of democratic systems of government. Alienated individuals remain fundamentally indifferent as to which type of government rules their country. Finally, authoritarians would, under certain circumstances, prefer a dictatorial regime to democracy.

In East-Central Europe, confident democrats constitute a relative majority of 48 per cent in Poland, 47 per cent in Hungary and in the Czech Republic and 46 per cent in Slovakia (Table 10). Worried democrats make up the second largest group. Only in Russia and to a lesser degree in the Ukraine were confident democrats (17 and 32 per cent respectively in 1999) outnumbered by authoritarians (39 and 32 per cent). Predictably, there is evidence of a strong connection between latent authoritarian to anti-democratic attitudes and scepticism regarding democratic government's problem-solving capacity. Linz and Stepan's conclusion that 'preference for the authoritarian alternative is always higher among those not believing in the efficacy of democracy'[32] has thus been confirmed for the case of East-Central Europe.

The changes which occurred in basic democratic orientations remained within the bounds of the broadly defined democratic spectrum, or, in rare cases, turned democratic attitudes into alienated ones and vice versa. Correspondingly, the only notable increase in the number of anti-democrats (1997 in Hungary and the Slovak Republic) did not affect the strength of democratic orientations but was due to a reduction in the number of alienated respondents. This is a remarkable finding, which seems to touch on the core of democratic convictions in East-Central Europe, given the exacerbated economic crisis and the many material and social hardships of economic transformation that a majority of the population has had to cope with for several years.

A differentiated analysis of confident democrats points to three factors critical for the spreading and intensifying of basic democratic orientations in East-Central European countries. First, there is *education*: to an exceptional degree, individuals with higher education tend towards pro-democratic orientations. Given the developed system of education and training in East-Central Europe, the cognitive resources of post-Communist societies lend decisive support to democracy. A second important factor is *evaluations of the old regime*; personal affinity or nostalgic feelings towards the old regime tend to weaken support for democracy as a form of government. Finally, the *initial expectations* in regime change are a third important factor in democratisation: individuals who regard their hopes and expectations of political and economic system change as largely fulfilled are much more likely to become solid democrats than are those whose hopes have been disappointed and who have been disillusioned as a result, or whose expectations have been primarily negative from the outset.

Table 10   *Democratic legitimacy and efficacy in post-authoritarian countries*

	Respondents who answered both indicated questions (%)[a]			
	Confident democrats	Worried democrats	Alienated	Authoritarians
Austria	74	18	3	6
Hungary	47	25	16	13
Czech Republic	47	18	22	14
Slovak Republic	46	18	21	15
Poland	48	14	27	10
Romania	59	8	14	20
Bulgaria	43	12	21	34
Ukraine	32	12	21	34
Russia	17	17	27	39
Uruguay[b]	57	29	29	8
Argentina[b]	55	28	28	11
Chile[b]	38	17	28	19
Brazil[b]	32	16	27	25

Notes:

[a] Discrepancy between percentage given and 100% = rounding difference

[b] Data for 1995, all other countries for 1999

Source: FESSEL–GfK, *Politischer Kulturwandel in Ost-Mitteleuropa* (1999); Juan Linz and Alfred Stepan, *Problems of Democratic Transition and Consolidation: Southern Europe, South America and Post-Communist Europe* (Baltimore, MD, 1996, pp. 227–30)

Comparing the levels of diffuse support for democracy in East-Central Europe, Western Europe, Southern Europe and in post-authoritarian democracies of Latin America, our findings do not suggest that the preference for democracy is weak in ECE countries. Hungarian figures, for instance, indicate support levels which are only slightly lower than those of Britain or Italy. Figures for the Czech and the Slovak Republics and Poland are similar to those culled in Spain in 1989. Compared to the fragility of support for democracy as a form of government in the Russian Republic or in Brazil, the process of anchoring democracy attitudinally seems to have progressed remarkably far in the four countries studied.[33]

Conclusion

A decade or so after the collapse of Communist regimes democratic attitudes have taken hold, with country-specific variations, among a sizeable majority within each society in East-Central Europe. Idealistic and 'material' conceptions of democracy are increasingly replaced by realistic and formal conceptions, pluralist party competition is accepted and authoritarian solutions do not strike a responsive chord. By and large, a democratic system culture has evolved and has proven to be stable even under the high political, economic and social stress resulting from the hardships of the transformation process. The situation is quite different in countries like Russia and the Ukraine, where party competition meets with far less approval and one finds much smaller numbers – especially – of 'confident' democrats and a considerable extent of antidemocratic orientation. Furthermore, the numeric relationship between democrats and authoritarians is rather fluid over time, evidently directly influenced by political and economic developments.

On the other hand, there are unmistakable signs of problems in the field of policy and process culture in East-Central Europe too. Criticism of performance is not limited to the socio-economic realm. With regard to process culture one finds a high level of dissatisfaction about the working of the new political system and the performance of political and administrative institutions. Even more, the impression of political failures and doubts about the problem-solving capacity of the new system have increased over time, Hungary being a partial exception from this trend. Subjective awareness of political competence and assessment of the responsiveness of political elites is less developed in all countries than in established traditional and post-authoritarian democracies. As opposed to countries such as Austria or Italy, where disappointment with elites and below-average evaluation of subjective political competence are embedded in relatively stable institutional structures, the attitudinal consolidation on this meso-level of East-Central European political systems is much weaker; the low affective identification with political parties and the lack of integration into institutional networks are indicators of this, as is the low intensity of political cleavages.[34] Latent configurations of conflict are reflected in structures of political competition only to a limited extent; low levels of trust in both competition-oriented political institutions and executive or judicial institutions alike point in the same direction.

In sum, low levels of political efficacy and responsiveness in conjunction with an intermediary vacuum combine to give the impression of a process culture barely consolidated thus far. Both sets of difficulties were predictable at the start of democratisation. Profound economic system change is invariably linked to high (economic and social) transformation costs; in addition, less wealthy societies – and no amount of differences in economic resilience among East-Central European countries will conceal the fact that none of them are wealthy – only limited means of cushioning social hardship are available there. Against the backdrop of decades of an authoritarian (partly totalitarian) past, a pluralist and democratic process culture will have to evolve step by step.[35] At the beginning of consolidation in Southern Europe, too, temporary setbacks and deficits of integration were felt.[36] Given these obstacles, the process of consolidation has been relatively successful, considerable differences between countries notwithstanding. At the levels of policy and process, there has not been a reverberation of such difficulties on the system level of political culture. Without doubt, however, the creation and extension of pluralist institutions and the correction of deficiencies in social integration, besides increases in material output, will be of central importance in any further consolidation.

Notes

1 Consolidation is thus analytically distinguishable from transition where these criteria have yet to be established; see Fritz Plasser, Peter A. Ulram and Harald Waldrauch, *Democratic Consolidation in East Central Europe*, London and New York, 1998. The minimal formal criteria for a democratic regime are:
   • competition for access to central political institutions and, as a prerequisite, pluralism in political and civil society;
   • competing individuals or parties are granted access to central government institutions through competitive, regular, fair, free and universal elections by secret ballot and with the comprehensive participation of (nearly) all adult citizens;
   • the state does not restrict societal pluralism; rather it supports it by governing according to basic political and civil rights and liberties and the rule of law;
   • Decision making in government institutions takes place within the framework of a system of separate and balanced powers established by law.
   There are neither 'tutelary powers' (see J. Samuel Valenzuela (1992), 'Democratic Consolidation in Post-Transitional Settings. Notion, process and Facilitating Conditions', in Scott Mainwaring, Guillermo O'Donell and J. Samuel Valenzuela (eds), *Issues in Democratic Consolidation: The New South American Democracies in Comparative Perspective*, Notre Dame, 1992) which lack democratic legitimacy, nor areas which are not explicitly subject to the sovereignty of democratically legitimised institutions. See Robert Dahl (1971), *Polyarchy: Participation and Opposition*, New Haven and London; Richard Gunther, P. Nikiforos Diamandourus and Hans-Jürgen Puhle (eds) (1995), *The Politics of Democratic Consolidation. Southern Europe in Comparative Perspective*, Baltimore and London; Juan Linz and Alfred Stepan (1996), *Problems of Democratic Transition and Consolidation: Southern Europe, South America and Post-Communist Europe*, Baltimore).
2 The situation in post-Communist democracies is different from that in postwar (Western) Germany, Austria and Italy where especially the intermediary institutions, e.g. political parties, were much stronger and more deeply anchored in traditional social and cultural cleavages. There was also a considerable continuity in political-elite and rank-and-file levels. See, for Austria, Peter A. Ulram (1990), *Hegemonie und Erosion. Politische Kultur und politischer Wandel in Österreich*, Vienna and Cologne). For a general discussion of the importance of political culture, see among others Larry Diamond (1996), 'Is the Third Wave over?', *Journal of Democracy* 3; Juan Linz, Alfred Stepan and Richard Gunther (1995), 'Democratic Transition and Consolidation in Southern Europe, with Reflecions on Latin America and Eastern Europe', in Gunther, Diamandouros and Puhle (eds), *Politics of Democratic Consolidation*; Wolfgang Merkel and Hans-Jürgen Puhle, (1999), *Von der Diktatur zur Demokratie. Transformationen, Erfolgsbedingungen,*

Entwicklungspfade, Opladen and Geoffrey Pridham (1995), 'The International Context of Democratic Consolidation in Southern Europe in Comparative Perspective', in Gunther, Diamandouros and Puhle (eds), *The Politics of Democratic Consolidation.*

3 Gabriel Almond (1987), 'Politische Kultur – Forschung – Rückblick und Ausblick', in Dirk Berg-Schlosser and Jakob Schissler (eds), *Politische Kultur in Deutschland. Bilanz und Perspektiven,* Opladen.

4 David Easton (1975), 'A Re-Assessment of the Concept of Political Support', British Journal of Political Science 4; *A Systems Analysis of Political Life,* 3rd edn Chicago and London.

5 PKOM-project (Politischer Kulturwandel in Ost-Mitteleuropa) by the Austrian research group Plasser and Ulram. See Peter Gerlich, Fritz Plasser and Peter A.Ulram (eds) (1992), *Regimewechsel. Demokratisierung und politische Kultur in Ost-Mitteleuropa* (Vienna and Cologne); Fritz Plasser and Peter A. Ulram (1993), 'Zum Stand der Demokratisierung in Ost-Mitteleuropa', in Fritz Plasser and Peter A. Ulram (eds), *Transformation oder Stagnation. Aktuelle politische Trends in Osteuropa,* Vienna; Fritz Plasser and Peter A. Ulram (1993), 'Of Time and Democratic Stabilization', paper for the WAPOR Seminar 'Public Opinion and Public Opinion Research in Eastern Europe', Tallinn, 11–12 June; (1994), 'Monitoring Democratic Consolidation: Political Trust and System Support in East-Central Europe', paper for the XVIth World Congress of the International Political Science Association, Berlin, 21–5 August; (1994), 'Politische Systemunterstützung und Institutionsvertrauen in den OZE-Staaten', *Österreichische Zeitschrift für Politikwissenschaft* 4; (1996), 'Measuring Political Culture in East Central Europe: Political Trust and System Support', in Fritz Plasser and Andreas Pribersky (eds), *Political Culture in East Central Europe,* London; (1998), 'Democratic Consolidation in East-Central Europe', in Erich Reiter (ed.), *Maßnahmen zur internationalen Friedenssicherung,* Graz, Vienna and Cologne; Fritz Plasser, Peter A. Ulram and Harald Waldrauch, (1997), *Politischer Kulturwandel in Ost-Mitteleuropa: Theorie und Empirie demokratischer Konsolidierung,* Opladen; *Democratic Consolidation in East Central Europe,* London and New York. The representative surveys were conducted face-to-face with random sampling; N = 1.000 interviews each for H, CZ, PL, SK, RO, BG, UA; and *N* = 2.000 interviews each for H, CZ, PL, SK in 1995 and in Russia.

6 Lubomír Brokl and Zdenka Mansfeldová, (1992), 'Von der 'unpolitischen' zur 'professionellen' Politik. Aspekte der politsichen Kultur der CSFR in der Periode des Systemwechsels', in Peter Gerlich, Fritz Plasser and Peter A. Ulram (eds), *Regimewechsel. Demokratisierung und politische Kultur in Ost-Mitteleuropa,* Vienna and Cologne.

7 János Simon (1998), 'Popular Conceptions of Democracy in Postcommunist Europe', in Samuel H. Barnes and János Simon (eds), *The Postcommunist Citizen,* Budapest; Fritz Plasser, Peter A. Ulram and Harald Waldrauch (1997), *Politischer Kulturwandel in Ost-Mitteleuropa: Theorie und Empirie demokratischer Konsolidierung,* Opladen.

8 The Russian data for this question (1998) were collected before the outbreak of the economic crisis. Russian data for 1999 reflect the popular mood in the aftermath (fieldwork September and October 1999).

9 Plasser, Ulram, and Waldrauch, *Democratic Consolidation in East Central Europe.*

10 See *ibid.*, pp. 183ff.

11 Zdenka Mansfeldová and Máté Szabó (2000), 'Zivilgesellschaft im Transformations-prozeß Ost-Mitteleuropas: Ungarn, Polen und die Tschechoslowakei', in Wolfgang Merkel (ed.), *Systemwechsel 5. Zivilgesellschaft und Transformation*, Opladen.

12 Thomas F. Remington (1997), 'Democratization and the new political order in Russia', in Karin Dawisha and Bruce Parrot (eds), *Democratic Changes and Authoritarian Reactions in Russia, Ukraine, Belarus and Moldavia*, Cambridge.

13 Simon, 'Popular Conceptions of Democracy in Postcommunist Europe'.

14 See David Beetham (ed.) (1994), *Defining and Measuring Democracy*, London and Thousand Oaks; (1996), 'The Democratic Audit: Grundprinzipien und Schlüsselindikatoren politischer Demokratie', in David F. J. Campell *et al.* (eds), *Die Qualität der österreichischen Demokratie*, Vienna; Bettina Westle (1989), *Politische Legitimität – Theorien, Konzepte, empirische Befunde*, Baden-Baden.

15 For a further discussion, see Oscar W. Gabriel (1994), Politische Kultur aus der Sicht der empirischen Sozialforschung', in Oskar Niedermayer and Klaus von Beyme (eds) *Politische Kultur in Ost- und Westdeutschland*, Berlin (1994), 'Politische Einstellungen und politische Kultur', in Oscar W. Gabriel and Frank Brettschneider (eds), *Die EU-Staaten im Vergleich: Strukturen, Prozesse, Politikinhalte*, 2nd edn, Opladen; Gabriel, Oscar W. (1996), *Politische Orientierungen und Verhaltensweisen im vereinigten Deutschland*, Opladen; Mishler, William, and Rose, Richard (1996), 'Trajectories of Fear and Hope: Support for Democracy in Post-communist Europe', in *Comparative Political Studies*, no.4.; Niedermayer, Oskar, and Westle, Bettina (1995), 'A Typology of Orientations', in Oskar Niedermayer and Richard Sinnott (eds), *Public Opinion and International Governance*, Oxford.

16 Dieter Fuchs, Giovanna Guidorossi and Palle Svensson (1995), 'Support for the Democratic System', in Hans-Dieter Klingemann and Dieter Fuchs (eds), *Citizens and the State*, Oxford, p. 342.

17 There was no reference to the 'meaning' of democracy in the question. The scaling (very satisfied, fairly satisfied, not satisfied) differs from the one used by the Central and Eastern Eurobarometer (CEEB). Our choice in this matter was based on the necessity for comparative data about the satisfaction with democracy especially in Austria and Western Germany. The results of CEEB show a similar development for East-Central Europe as well as a high difference in the levels of satisfaction between East-Central Europe and countries like Russia and the Ukraine. Unfortunately, recent CEEB-like data are not available due to a postponement of the study.

18 Ola Listhaug and Matti Wiberg (1995), 'Confidence in political and private institutions', in Klingemann and Fuchs (eds), *Citizens and the State*.

19 See Dieter Fuchs (1989), *Die Unterstützung des politischen Systems der Bundesrepublik Deutschland*, Opladen, p. 116; and Herbert Klages (1990), 'Vertrauen und Vertrauensverlust in westlichen Demokratien', in Peter Haungs (ed.), *Politik ohne Vertrauen?* Baden-Baden, p. 56.

20 On the different levels of trust in parliament found in Switzerland and in the post-authoritarian democracies of (West) Germany and Austria, see Fritz Plasser and Peter A. Ulram (1993 c), 'Politischer Kulturvergleich: Deutschland, Österreich und die Schweiz', in Fritz Plasser, and Peter A. Ulram (eds), *Staatsbürger oder*

Untertanen? Politische Kultur Deutschlands, Österreichs und der Schweiz im Vergleich, Frankfurt and Bern, p. 137.

21 Due to a prolonged struggle between the president and the prime minister plus government and parliamentary majority, the Slovak Republic is an exception to this rule. Trust in the president declined dramatically between 1994 and 1995.

22 Thus, in both Germany and Austria, a public increasingly disgruntled with politicians and parties has, for some time now, also shown less and less confidence in political institutions. In the same period, public trust in the civil service, executive and judiciary has been affected only marginally.

23 László Bruszt and János Simon (1991), 'A "választások éve" a közvéleménykutatások tükrében', in Sándor Kurtán, Sándor Peter and László Vass (eds), *Magyarország Politikai Évkönyve 1991*, Budapest; Gabriella Ilonszki and Sándor Kurtán (1992), 'Traurige Revolution – freudlose Demokratie. Aspekte der ungarischen politischen Kultur in der Periode des Systemwechsels', in Gerlich, Plasser and Ulram (eds), *Regimewechsel*.

24 See Peter A. Ulram (1990), *Hegemonie und Erosion. Politische Kultur und politischer Wandel in Österreich*, Vienna and Cologne.

25 See Leonardo Morlino (1995), 'Political Parties and Democratic Consolidation in Southern Europe', in Gunther, Diamandouros and Puhle (eds), *The Politics of Democratic Consolidation*, and Mark Arenhövel (2000), 'Zivilgesellschaft und Demokratie in Südeuropa', in Merkel (ed.), *Systemwechsel 5*.

26 See Juan Linz and Alfred Stepan (1996), *Problems of Democratic Transition and Consolidation: Southern Europe, South America and Post-Communist Europe*, Baltimore, p.16.

27 See Samuel P. Huntington (1996), 'Democracy for the Long Haul', *Journal of Democracy* 2, p. 9.

28 See Fritz Plasser and Peter A. Ulram (1993), 'Zum Stand der Demokratisierung in Ost-Mitteleuropa' in Plasser and Ulram (eds), *Transformation oder Stagnation*, p. 49.

29 See Frederick D. Weil (1993), 'The Development of Democratic Attitudes in Eastern and Western Germany in a Comparative Perspective', in Weil (ed.), *Democratization in Eastern and Western Europe*, Greenwich and London, p. 211.

30 See Fritz Plasser and Peter A. Ulram (1992), 'Zwischen Desillusionierung und Konsolidierung. Demokratie- und Politikverständnis in Ungarn, der CSFR und Polen', in Gerlich, Plasser, and Ulram (eds), *Regimewechsel Demokratisierung und politische Kultur in Ost-Mitteleuropa*, p. 46.

31 Leonardo Morlino and Jose R. Montero (1995), 'Legitimacy and democracy in Southern Europe', in Gunther, Diamandouros and Puhle (eds), *The Politics of Democratic Consolidation*; Linz and Stepan, *Problems of Democratic Transition and Consolidation*.

32 *Ibid.*, p. 226.

33 See Fuchs, Guidorossi, and Svensson, 'Support for the Democratic System', p. 349; José Ramon Montero and Mariano Torcal (1990), 'Voters and Citizens in a New Democracy: Some Trend Data on Political Attitudes in Spain', in *International Journal of Public Opinion Research* 2, p. 126; Morlino and Montero, 'Legitimacy and Democracy in Southern Europe', in Gunther, Diamandouros and Puhle (eds), *The Politics of Democratic Consolidation*, p. 238.

34 Plasser, Ulram and Waldrauch, *Politischer Kulturwandel in Ost-Mitteleuropa;* Plasser, Ulram and Waldrauch, *Democratic Consolidation in East Central Europe.*

35 By comparison, the totalitarian period in Western Germany (1933–45) and in Austria (1938–45) was much shorter; the destruction of traditional subcultures and networks of civil society remained incomplete. The Franco regime in Spain never tried a thorough political penetration of civil society. Furthermore, during the last years before the political transformation, Spanish economic, societal and cultural institutions and attitudes had begun to approach patterns found in democratic West European societies. See Linz, Stepan and Gunther, 'Democratic Transition and Consolidation in Southern Europe, with Reflections on Latin America and Eastern Europe', in Gunther, Diamandouros and Puhle (eds), *The Politics of Democratic Consolidation*, pp. 98 ff.

36 Morlino and Montero, 'Legitimacy and Democracy in Southern Europe'; Leonardo Morlino (1995), 'Political Parties and Democratic Consolidation in Southern Europe', in Gunther, Diamandouros, and Puhle (eds), *The Politics of Democratic Consolidation*.

Parties in the process of consolidation in East-Central Europe

From Burke to Weber parties have been classified according to the dominance of two elements inherent in any party organisation: ideology and patronage. As in Weber's typology of ideal types of legitimate rule only *traditional* and *rational* systems are on the same level of abstraction. The type of *charismatic* leadership is slightly different because it does not exclude rational and traditional elements of the functioning of the system. The same applies to the adaptation of these categories to developing party systems: charismatic parties are even to a greater extent than in Weber's overall classification hardly a pure type in budding democracies. In the rare cases they exist, they do not exclude programmatic and clientelistic features. Kitschelt,[1] who offered this threefold typology, was aware that over time and across party families *the mix of incentives* constituting voter–party linkages varies considerably. Once party systems enter the phase of consolidation the continued support of voters rests on habituation and, in the long run, on socialisation. But post-Communist parties, because of their structural weaknesses, have less socialising capacities than did former mass parties in the waves of democratisation after 1918 and 1945.

Party research by those scholars who previously were not interested in the details of Eastern Europe and who until 1989 never went east of 'Checkpoint Charlie' in Berlin, have usually chosen to classify whole party systems and have neglected individual parties and specific conditions of party formation in various post-Communist countries.[2] The cleavages thus have been simplified and reduced to one (post-Communists vs. democratic umbrella organisations) or two dimensions (economic populists vs. market liberals and secular libertarians vs. religious traditionalists).[3] Some of these hasty typologies became dated by the end of the 1990s. New attempts have sought to list and to classify more carefully individual parties in various countries on a number of dimensions.[4]

What is the consolidation of party systems? This may be measured in terms of such variables as fragmentation, polarisation, volatility or 'critical elections' which lead to a de-alignment or realignment.[5] The criteria of a party system's consolidation can be varied. I propose the following two principal categories:

1 clear cleavage structure reflected in programmatic parties;
2 organisational structures and linkages, sub-divided into;
- a minimum of violence and extremism;
- the acceptance of a division of labour between interest groups and parties;
- the existence of a minimal membership organisation and the limitation of factionalism;
- normal volatility and the absence of 'critical elections';
- a certain efficiency of parties in coalition building.

In this more differentiated way, it is possible to explore the strengths and weaknesses of party development in the first decade of regime change in East-Central Europe. This will be done within the broad context of post-Communist Europe as a whole.

Cleavage structure reflected in programmatic parties?

The development of a clear cleavage structure is mainly achieved in the era of democratisation. The demand that a clear cleavage structure be reflected in distinguishable programmes sounds like a postulate based on West European standards. In post-modern times, programmes play a diminishing role – in spite of some comparative studies.[6] Are post-Communist parties 'loosely knitted anarchies' and the more modern or post-modern parties of the future? Even in East Germany, the weak party structure has not been compensated for by the enormous colonising impact of West German parties. Is the loose framework of *cartel parties* in Eastern Europe pre-modern or post-modern? The answer probably depends on the context of a modernised political regime.

In East-Central Europe (ECE), as in developing countries, parties emerged with sweet-sounding names, which are irrelevant because *every ism 'is a some-body-ism'*. In Russia, names like 'Our House Is Russia' do not strengthen confidence in the durability of an organisation. In East-Central Europe, there are few such groups since the decline of the forum-type parties which started with all-embracing labels. Later, mostly right-wing groups in post-Communist states preferred names such as 'Union of National Salvation' (Bulgaria, 1997), *Ojczyzna* or 'Fatherland' (Poland, 1991). Sometimes even the post-Communists accepted this type of name, for instance the 'National Salvation Front' of Iliescu (Romania, 1990).

In an unstructured and open political market many *political entrepreneurs* believed they saw their chance. Sometimes they were adventurers, such as Tyminski in Poland. Though the electoral market seemed to be unrestrained by past identities and while the rules of entry in some countries initially were relatively lax,[7] hardly any of these demagogues were successful in forming a permanent charismatic party.

Charismatic leadership sprang up occasionally. But it rarely managed to transform itself into a continuous party organisation:

- either the charismatic leader *kept aloof* from parties and strengthened presidential powers, as did Yeltsin,
- or he tried to organise a party of *his followers,* such as Walesa, with little success because his quasi-party hardly managed to pass the threshold into the Sejm,
- or – in the case of the hegemonial power of post-Communists – the leaders used the framework of a party in a rather *bureaucratic* and *un-charismatic* way, such as Iliescu or Milošević, or tried to outmanoeuvre the constitutional primary and secondary institutions via direct appeals to the people.

In no case did the ideal type of charismatic party develop. Even the right-wing parties offered leaders with a limited charismatic appeal, from Csurka in Hungary to the leaders of right-wing extremist parties in Romania. Not even Zhirinovskyi in Russia had a lasting charisma for the voters. Mečiar in Slovakia tried to develop as a charismatic leader and failed because he exaggerated his capacity in conflict with his president and half of the electorate. In May 1999 he failed to be elected as president of Slovakia.

Under these conditions, the *mix of incentives* consisted rather of various degrees of *programmatic elements* and *patronage*. What Kitschelt called 'patrimonial communism', oddly enough, offered both: the programme was more developed than in most bourgeois parties and the clientelistic networks of patronage were an important incentive to support the party. This was true even of the East German PDS, which offered substantial help to people not yet accustomed to living in a society where the state did not provide automatically the minimum support (*Zuteilungsgesellschaft* – distributional society) but where the claims had to be funnelled into the administration (*Antragsgesellschaft*).

After the disintegration of the forum-type of party, the parties gradually differentiated their programmes and the successor organisations developed into normal parties. Sometimes the erosion of the forum led to new functional groups competing in the political arena or they revived the old label for a coalition of groups uniting their forces, such as in Poland.

The former *regime* type (*dictadura* or *dictablanda*) and the mode of *transition* (e.g. the collapse of negotiated revolution) became of secondary importance to the functioning of the system. Only a third subtype of the second typology with continuity of the middle-level elite of the ancient regime has some impact in so far as the parties are more or less irrelevant, as in Serbia. Romania – in spite of so many misgivings and forecasts – did not stick to this type of regime, though party democracy is still far from functioning in a consolidated way.

Institutional factors such as the *choice of the regime* (purely parliamentary or semi-presidential types of regime) and the choice of the *electoral law* (mostly proportional systems in multi-member districts) determined the phase of constitutional engineering. In some regimes, not yet democratised, majority systems were applied. The third option was a combined electoral system (Bulgaria, 1991; Lithuania, 1992; Russia 1993 and 1995; and the segmented or parallel system in Hungary),[8] which was mostly interpreted as the compromise of old and new political forces. It existed also in Albania (1997), Lithuania (1992, 1996), Russia (1993, 1995), Ukraine (1998), Croatia (1992, 1995). Since very few scholars are knowledgeable in the details of electoral laws, this institutional factor has largely been neglected. But certain changes, such as the *increase of thresholds* – as in Poland – has reduced the number of parties from six to five (1993–97) and changed the number of non-represented votes from 6.2 per cent (1991) to 34.3 per cent (1993) and 11.8 per cent (1997). Similar results happened when Latvia, between 1993 and 1995, increased the threshold from 4 to 5 per cent. Only in Hungary did the change, from 4 per cent to 5 per cent, not alter the number of parties (six) and of unrepresented votes (15.8 per cent in 1990, 12.9 per cent in 1994).[9]

But this does not mean that in the pre-consolidation period the threshold clauses prevent fragmentation of party systems *per se*. Estonia, Latvia, Russia, Slovakia and Slovenia developed at least seven parties in spite of their thresholds.

Federal Germany experimented after the war fairly rigidly with a threshold of 5 per cent in order to reduce party-system fragmentation and political extremism. But – on the other hand – not all concentrations of party systems are due to the threshold. The percentage of non-represented votes generally decreased with consolidation. The main reason in post-Communist Europe was the reshuffling of forum-type movements of the former forces in opposition (Bulgaria SDS–ADF: 1991, 1994, 1997; and in Poland AWS: 1996). In other countries where the forum group remained disintegrated, such as in the Czech Republic, the party system was able to absorb two smaller parties, thus diminishing the number of unrepresented votes.

Since the Hungarian electoral law was a case apart in East-Central Europe and coincided with a relatively stable party system, it has been considered the only one which had a shaping impact on the party system structure.[10] More cautious observers,[11] however, have asked whether the stable party system was really due to the electoral law or whether, rather, it was the other way around: the electoral law had structurally consistent effects because of the relative stability of the party system.

Research on comparative electoral systems has developed three main criteria for the evaluation of electoral formulas: *representation* of votes from the population, *concentration* of the party system; and the impact on voter *participation*. Pure proportionalism had only positive impacts on representation. Most other systems fulfilled sufficiently two of the three functions. Only a personalised proportional system, such as the German additional-member system or the mixed-member system in New Zealand, had positive results on all the three levels.[12] But this system has not been introduced in East-Central Europe. Most systems – with the exception of Hungary's parallel or segmented system – represent variations of proportional electoral law in multi-member constituencies which normally have positive impacts only on the concentration of the party system.

On the whole, the systems have been modified too frequently and the time span for comparison is too short to prove the one-sided preference of some authors for certain electoral systems, as in the case of Sartori who, in fact, generalised from Italian conditions and preferred to combine the semi-presidential system with absolute majority votes as in France.

Other authors claim that electoral institutions cannot be considered in an isolated way. The combination of the regime type and the electoral formula is said to count. Semi-presidentialism and proportional electoral law have been declared as the most detrimental option of a mix of institutions.[13] But even this controversy is difficult to solve. On the one hand semi-presidentialism – as in Bulgaria – can be restricted in competences concerning cabinet building (in Austria even this function has withered away because of the latent grand coalition of the two major parties). On the other hand, we still do not know whether the egg or the hen has priority. Are governments unstable because semi-presidentialism does not promote clear party cleavages, or are semi-presidential systems necessary because the party lines and the cleavages between social groups are still blurred and unclear – as some authors argue?[14]

The institutional variables help to channel the party-building process. But they are only one determinant. They:
• influence whether clear-cut parties or loose coalitions predominate;
• influence the development of modern mass parties or post-modern cartel and framework parties with little organisation and few members;
• have an impact on the fragmentation of parties and the volatility among them.
But they hardly explain the number of parties and their confrontation or co-operation within a party system. There are sometimes parties *without* a system. Russia comes close to this type, and this has something to do with the fact that parties in a three-quarter-presidential system under Yeltsin had hardly any impact on the fate of the Government. In East-Central Europe, however, party systems *have* developed. The importance of each party can be determined in terms of its availability for coalition (*Koalitionsfähigkeit*) or in terms of being excluded from feasible governmental coalitions in the country.

Since a theory of party-system formation for *all* the countries is impossible, the result is normally a hybrid theoretical product, e.g. a typology. *Modes of transition* and *types of former Communist regime* have been classified as a *causa remota* (distant cause). One can even go back to *pre*-Communist experiences, though this pre-dictatorship perspective was more rewarding in the democratic waves after 1945 and in the 1970s in Western Europe, since in ECE only Czechoslovakia had had a real democratic experience. Pre-Communist memories may also go back to non-democratic traditions. This was the case most frequently with agrarian parties.

Thus, three types of party have been differentiated:
• old historical parties
• post-Communists and
• new parties.

The question is, however, *how new is new*? The neo-democratic parties which sprang up after the disintegration of the umbrella-groups and the forum-type parties were mostly new, even when they went back to traditions of the anti-Communist opposition. Old agrarian parties were historical but were handicapped by the erosion of agriculture. Moreover, the transformation of collective agriculture had undermined the smallholders – both in fact and frequently also in the minds of those who remained in agriculture. Not even the powerful German 'Bauernverband' managed to convince the former East German collective farmers to turn in great masses back to smallholding farms. Ethnic groups frequently had forerunners, but in terms of organisation and personnel they were predominantly new. Some of the historical parties managed to enter even governmental coalitions, but they played a minor role in them, as in the Czech Republic, Slovakia and Hungary.

Two historical forces were handicapped in their revival: the *Christian Democrats* and the *Social Democrats*. Unlike the democratic wave of 1945, in which these two groups became the major forces in Western Europe, the same did not happen in Central and Eastern Europe. Already, in the case of Spain, predictions that a Christian-Democrat group might be the leading force after the Franco regime were proved wrong. The centre–Right umbrella organisation UCD was also possible because the episcopate, after the experience of too close relations between the Christian movement and the state, did not push for the formation of a Christian party. This was even more the case in the much more secularised post-Communist systems. Christian-Democrat parties are normally feasible only in countries with large Catholic populations. In Hungary and in Slovakia they were initially present and relevant for government in 1994, but they later declined. In Poland, Catholic Electoral Action (WAK) of 1991 was transformed into the *Ojczyzna*, which moved further to the Right and was hardly comparable to Western Christian Democrats.

The Czech Republic seemed at the end of the 1990s to be the most Western country because there the Christian Democrats remained relevant and the Social Democrats became the strongest party in 1998. The process has its parallel in East Germany. The PDS was hardly stronger than the Communist Party KSCM (13.2 per cent in 1990). But since in both cases the post-Communists did not manage to transform themselves into a socialist party of the Western type – as happened in Poland and Hungary[15] – the Social-Democrat Party in question enjoyed more political space.

In fairly consolidated countries such as Hungary[16] the professionalism of the HSP was used to explain its success. But the comeback of the social-democratised post-Communists did not meet expectations everywhere. In Lithuania this can hardly be explained only by the fact that the come-back came too early (1992). In the Hungarian–Romanian comparison it has been argued[17] that the Hungarian party – because of early liberalisation – preserved closer personal and ideological continuity with its Communist predecessor than did its Romanian counterpart. Maybe this is true of the cadres. But even

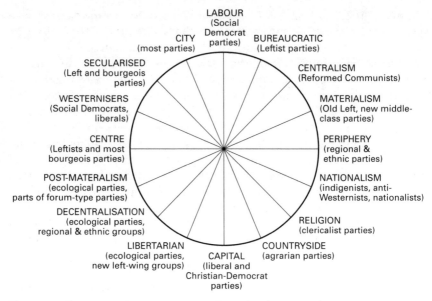

Figure 1 *Cleavages and party systems in Central and Eastern Europe*

the replacement of former top elites in Romania did not necessarily lead to a more Social-Democrat policy perception.

So, basically two camps are visible in the process of consolidation: the reforming socialists and the democratic camp.

Only occasionally has the latter developed a liberal camp from the outset, such as the Hungarian SZDSZ and FIDESZ. More often they developed along liberal conservative lines, or even in a conservative nationalist direction.

Can we integrate these groups into the *ideological families* which have developed in Western Europe since the French Revolution? If we take party ideology seriously, we surely can use most of the labels of the traditional cleavages. Not all of them fit into the Rokkan matrix. In my scheme of eight possible cleavage lines, sixteen party groups are feasible (Figure 1). Fortunately, in no country did all of them come to the fore. In the West, Finland and Italy came closest, for a while, to representing most of them even in parliament. Only a few of these cleavages are linked to the special situation of Central and Eastern Europe, such as Westernisers and traditionalists, though even these categories had equivalents in the nineteenth century, in Spain for instance. In countries of an orthodox tradition, this cleavage tends to be more acute than in Catholic or Protestant countries.

Stein Rokkan had emphasised mainly two dimensions in his scheme of social cleavages, translated into parties: the class conflict and the centre–periphery cleavage. Social cleavages in post-Communist systems also developed quite differently from Western experiences. The conflict between *labour* and *capital* was emphasised for forty years by Communist ideology, but it remained incomplete because of the absence of a capitalist party. The *centre–periphery* conflict, on the other hand, came to the fore, since it was suppressed from the public agenda by the old regime. Capitalists made some hapless attempts to found business lists in Bulgaria. In some countries, such as Poland, the GDR and Czechoslovakia, these lists were hidden under the disguise of 'parties of beer friends'. All of them remained weak, because they failed to link capitalist interests with the interests of other bourgeois groups, as did liberal, conservative and Christian Democrat parties in the West. Social-Democrat formations were under-represented as well, unless they were reconstructed post-Communists. In Lithuania (1992), Poland (1993), Hungary (1994) and Estonia (1995), the reforming Communists succeeded in representing workers who felt underprivileged in the transitional societies (see Figure 1).

The *centre–periphery conflict* was sometimes exaggerated in its impact, especially in the GDR. It was used to explain the pro-Christian-Democrat vote of the workers in Thuringia and Saxony as a protest against the centre of Berlin, though the SED (Party of Socialist Unity) elite came predominantly from those areas. Ethnic and regional conflicts sometimes have been strengthened by the cleavage of *secularised society* vs. *clericalism*, especially in Poland.

The scheme of eight cleavage lines remains crude and does not reflect the individual weights of the respective cleavage poles. Studies in party platforms have emphasised different cleavages, such as the Left–Right dimension, the dimension of political rights and the cleavage between conservatives and welfare-state socialists.[18] But even this empirical simplification of the cleavage structures shows similar results for the party system as developed by this author. The typology of cleavages should be linked with the typology of revolutionary changes after 1989.

The *party families* are normally derived from Rokkan's concept of social cleavages. *Ideologies* are reflections of major conflicts in the countries. In Western Europe we normally have few deceptive self-stylisations of party names. In Eastern Europe, there are blatantly misleading names such as 'liberal democratic' for Zhirinovskyi's group in Russia. In the countries of Central and Eastern Europe, the names are often fanciful, different from Western parties' appeal to 'union' or *rassemblement*. Nevertheless, most of the groups in the long run can be located ideologically, even if their programmes are hardly differentiated from other parties' programmes or are misleading in the light of the policy goals which these parties pursue in practice. Sometimes the labels have shifted as in the case of the Polish WAK (nationalistic Christian Democrats).

Other criteria include the 'integration in transnational federations' and the 'policies' which these parties pursue.[19] These criteria can hardly be applied in Eastern Europe in a period of transition because their acceptance in international party federations was slow. The third criterion, policy performance, is still hard to assess, because of lack of governmental experience or because the parties were many and unstable – such as the seven parties under Prime Minister Hanna Suchocka in Poland (1992–93) – so that policy performance is hard to ascribe to individual parties. Thus, the easiest way is the most super-ficial one: to trust the declarations of parties and their programmes as Klingemann did.[20] There are two ways of allotting groups to party families:

1 *By constructing simplified kinds of programmes*, such as civic liberal, neo-populist, technocratic-right and technocratic-left.[21] In this case we run into even greater difficulties. Is the Romanian 'National Salvation Front' really 'technocratic-Right' though preferring to define itself as 'left'? This approach has the drawback that very different groups, from Social Democrats to Christian Democrats, are lumped together as 'civic liberal'.

2 By using the *traditional labels of the European cleavages* (see Figure 1). Also in this case there are difficulties in classification. Was the Polish WAK Christian Democrat or was it from the outset right-wing nationalist? Nevertheless, the more consolidation progresses, the more the programmes really begin to reflect the policy positions.

The conventional classification of party families also has the advantage of relativising variations in non-ideological 'technocratic' attitudes. Many parties which in the West have a civic liberal touch are highly technocratic and étatiste in Eastern Europe because of the Communist heritage in outlook. Party research faces the difficulty that the ideological labels developed in the West hardly fit in Eastern Europe.[22] Alternative typologies, however, tend to oversimplify the cleavage structure in post-Communist countries in a still more misleading way.

None of these typologies explains, however, how likely it is that party systems in Eastern Europe will acquire a clear programmatic structure. Kitschelt[23] clas-sified the variable of the 'pre-Communist heritage' and patterns of Communist rule as well as the democratic constitutional framework in order to get some hold on the *programmatic structuring* of the post-Communist party systems. Political science which tries to be explanatory rather than descriptive – and typologies cannot cover the fact that they are in a pre-stage of theorising – will try to find some correlations between the timing of industrialisation (based on the size of the agricultural sector at the time of Communist take-over), political constitu-tion (based on existence of parliamentary or 'more presidentialist constitutional designs' and the existence of proportional or pluralist representation), demo-cratic transition (erosion or collapse) and system duration (duration of pre-Communist (semi-)democracy). Though the indicators are vague, the index of chances for programme-based party formation shows a ranking which we could have guessed: on top are the Czech Republic and Hungary, at the bottom Russia and Serbia. But what do we learn from this? Is Hungary really below the Czech Republic if we carefully compare the programmes and especially their impact on policy making – just because Hungary had less pre-Communist democratic expe-rience and its early industrialisation was considerably below the Czech level? If we measure this indicator, do Communist efforts of delayed modernisation not count? Hungary certainly, already under Communism, came closer to the Czech part of Czechoslovakia, which – like the GDR – did not benefit from Communist industrialisation (unlike Slovakia) but rather found its former level lowered.

Comparisons after the fall of Communism between Austria and the Czech Republic, which co-existed in a single state until 1918, demonstrate this. Austria, especially in Alpine areas, until 1918 was rather underdeveloped. Bohemia and Moravia, however, produced two-thirds of the manufactured goods of the Habsburg Empire before 1918. By 1989 Austria's industry was three times stronger than the Czech manufacturing sector. This is not to say, as some authors do, that there are no regular patterns and that Central and Eastern Europe in terms of 'traditional cleavage research' is still a 'no-man's-land'.[24] But most correlations to date either predict truisms or are nonsense. Thus, it is necessary to continue to work with descriptive typologies in turning now to consider the other category of a party system's consolidation.

Organisational structure and linkages in the era of consolidation

The limited strength of extremist parties

Compared to the countries of the Commonwealth of Independent States (CIS), the East-Central European systems successfully established their parties in the process of democratic constitution making. But this achievement was not yet a guarantee of a completely consolidated party system. There were several further prerequisites, such as the limited influence of extremist groups, the acceptance of a division of labour between interest groups and parties, limited factionalism, the normalisation of volatility and a certain efficiency in the process of coalition building.

Research on party families, so far as it takes seriously the criterion of policy making, is mostly concentrated on parties working loyally within the regime. One criterion, according to Linz and Stepan,[25] emphasises that 'democracy' has to be 'the only game in town'. Neither the military nor even the churches or business veto groups could disturb the game. The military remained – according to the Communist tradition – remarkably passive in the consolidating democracies. The church interfered only occasionally in countries such as Poland or Slovakia. The orthodox tradition hardly gave the church a very independent role against the state. This has not changed. The population in a consolidating regime must be psychologically strong enough to tolerate frustrations without resorting to violence. But this does not mean that there are no organisations that would not like to play another game in town, but their scope for propaganda and their alternatives in terms of non-compromised regimes have diminished. Even in Western societies this is not very different. When Zeman and the Social Democrats came to power in Prague in 1998, he said that 'since the elections another standing order is valid'.[26] Whatever precisely he meant, it was not another constitution or another system that he had in mind, but just some minor rules of the game.

Extremism is particularly dangerous in transitional regimes where an ideological vacuum has been left by the former Communist regimes. The 'avant-garde of Communism' in the party had abused the working class, so that large groups of the latter turned to the Right. Normally, reformist Communists are considered less dangerous than the radical Right, and in many countries (Lithuania 1992, Poland 1993, Hungary 1994, Estonia 1995) they have proved that they were not determined to lead the system back into a 'different Republic'. In the countries considered here, right-wing extremists are most threatening in Romania, but they do not obtain above 10 per cent of the vote. The Czech Republicans had some impact until 1996. Csurka's MIEP (5 per cent in 1998) remained a marginal phenomenon in Hungary. Even in Poland the right-wing extremists have declined (ROP 5.6 per cent in 1997). In the Slovak Republic, the National Party (SNS) has generally obtained around 8 per cent of the vote. As in many Western countries, the dangers of right-wing extremism are present, but come not so much from organised movements in the political arena but rather in the form of *ad hoc* violence and latent authoritarian attitudes.[27]

Division of labour between parties and interest groups

Most parties in the West sprang from social movements and the borderlines between groups and parties remained blurred. The British Labour Party has shown these atavistic traits with elements of a collective membership. The *left* with its movement orientation and the *right* with its corporatist holistic view of the society had therefore some potential to undermine the privileged position of the parties. Somewhat similarly, post-Communist systems have shown remnants of the 'national front idea' because functional groups in some countries were running for parliament to support the post-Communists.

Trades unions played a role in Poland as fragments of the Solidarity movement. *Business lists* (Bulgaria) and 'beer drinkers', as the disguised form of business interests, present initially in Czechoslovakia, Poland and in the GDR, were mostly listed under 'liberal groups'. FIDESZ in Hungary quickly abandoned its functional character of a youth group. *Pensioners* entered the political scene as in the West, but remain marginalised (Czech Republic 1998: 3 per cent). *Agrarian parties* played a role in Hungary, Bulgaria and Romania, but modernisation and industrialisation under Communist rule did not offer them a great future in a consolidating democracy.

The division of labour between parties and interest groups is progressing. Where parties still have close links to groups, as in Hungary, they have sometimes – even the Christian Democrats – developed a network of *conveyer organisations*, interest groups which supported the Party.[28] On the whole, in ECE the lack of an authentic division of labour produced a less intimate relationship of organised interest groups and parties. This remains true even in East Germany, even though interest groups as well as parties have entered the country from the old Federal Republic without showing the same co-operation patterns as in the West.

Limited factionalism

Rational choice coalition theories discovered that there is coalition building not only among parties but within parties.[29] In Western democracies, factionalism was strongest in parties with a hegemonic position, such as the Israeli Mapai, the Indian Congress Party and the Italian Democrazia Cristiana. Traditional elements of *clientelism* reinforced factionalism. Post-Communists were said to be the most clientelistic because they preserved the 'old-boy-networks'. Oddly enough, these groups, which had just abandoned the verdict of the old Leninist principles against factionalism (*krugovchina*), had no major problem with it now, fighting as they did rather defensively for a slow path of transition to a market economy. Either they remained rather authoritarian, as did the Czech post-Communists, or they transformed into Social Democrats, as in Hungary and Poland.

Factionalism as a *pre-stage* to splitting was found only in the Romanian National Salvation Front, from which a Social Democrat-minded group under Petre Roman broke off before the 1992 elections. Oddly enough, after a transitional stage, Roman initially kept the old name SFN, whereas Iliescu adopted the misleading name 'Party of Social Democracy in Romania' (PDSR).[30]

Factionalism in East-Central Europe has frequently been the consequence of *overlapping cleavages*: there were different opinions on economic strategies (Poland, Czech Republic), national conflicts (Slovakia), right-wing leanings of some parts of a party (Csurka in Hungary, WAK in Poland), or personal cliques which were strongest in semi-presidential systems where the president interfered permanently in the political process (e.g. Poland under Walesa). Factionalism in these countries was only a by-product of volatility, especially as a precursor of 'critical elections' which led to a realignment of groups.

Reduction of volatility

Only immobile systems know no volatility. But very high fluctuations of voters, on the other hand, are a sign of the non-consolidation of party systems. 'Critical elections' (see Table 11) happened during regime change in Western Europe (France, twice in 1951, Portugal in 1987) as well as in Central and Eastern Europe (Slovakia in 1998, Bulgaria in 1997), on the occasion of the third free elections (in Hungary, already with the second post-founding election in 1998). Perhaps this indicates that the *time-span of consolidation* is more important than the *number of elections* held after the 'founding elections'. The case of Romania, with the decline of its post-Communists in 1992 and 1996, and the rise of the Democratic Convention and Roman's Social Democrats without huge volatility the second time, was unusual. On the whole, comparisons with the transitions of post-1945 and the 1970s showed that Central and Eastern Europe is above the level of volatility in these earlier democratisation processes. This is hardly

Table 11 *Volatility after the founding elections of new democracies (Second–Fourth Waves)*

2nd wave			
Austria (1949, 1953, 1956)	11.7	3.6	5.6
France (1946, two times 1951)	3.7	6.0	21.3
Germany (1953, 1957, 1961)	20.1	8.2	10.4
Italy (1948, 1953, 1958)	25.3	10.5	4.0
3rd wave			
Greece (1977, 1981, 1985)	19.1	24.1	5.0
Portugal[a] (1979, 1983, 1987)	11.0	2.7	25.7
Spain (1979, 1982, 1986)	10.8	42.5	11.9
4th wave			
Bulgaria (1991, 1994, 1997)	11.9	4.9	30.3
Czech Republic (1992, 1996, 1998)	15.9	27.4	10.6
Hungary (1994, 1998)	22.7	37.0	–
Poland (1993, 1997)	33.8	37.3	–
Romania (1992, 1996)	43.0	13.7	–
Slovakia (1992, 1994, 1998)	20.6	25.5	42.1

Note:

[a] Portugal's 1980 election omitted because there was little change

surprising, because the former countries had had more democratic experience before their dictatorships as a point of orientation than most East European countries, with the exception of the Czech Republic. The thresholds for entering parliament have reduced the fragmentation of party systems, but have increased the rates of volatility because voters had therefore to integrate into a reduced number of parties.

My figures differ from Cotta's.[31] Because of unclear fusions and the connections of lists the data for Poland and some other countries are occasionally 'enlightened guesswork'.

Fragmentation and efficiency in coalition building

High volatility and factionalism may be confusing, and budding democracies can survive many hardships. But voters are more sensitive when the coalition-building function of new democracies does not work. In Poland, the continual reshuffling of governments during Walesa's presidency also had an impact on electoral behaviour. When Hanna Suchocka led a coalition of seven parties which fought each other still in the elections of 1991, there was little chance for the voter to assess the individual performance of the various parties.

Programmes of parties should differentiate among themselves. In the first period they resembled each other very much. Only in a few cases (e.g. in Hungary) did these programmes set priorities for concrete policies. When the forum-type parties disintegrated, a paradox was visible: the more fragmented the parties in parliament, the less clear was the representation of the great social interests in the legislative assembly. Clear social support groups have to be organised. As long as major groups – such as *capital* and *labour* – have not yet found a political home, the consolidation of the political market is impossible.

The degree of *fragmentation* in the party systems obviously has an impact on the capacity for coalition building in the system. This was evident in the early period, with many taxi parties in the first stage and low barriers for parliamentary entry in some countries (Poland until 1993, Romania until 1992). In the latter case, Iliescu lowered the thresholds deliberately in order to keep the democratic camp fragmented. Nevertheless, fragmentation was hardly the main problem in Central and Eastern Europe, with the exception of Slovenia and Latvia. This recalls the experiences in the transitions of the 1970s. Only Spain was slightly above the European average according to Rae's fragmentation index.[32]

Two more indicators are important in evaluating the coalition-building function of party systems:

- the development of a clear alternative of *government* and *opposition*; and
- the numerical possibility of creating *minimal winning coalitions* out of *the centre parties* as they turn for partners to the Right or to the Left.

East-Central Europe and South-East Europe show that few regimes have developed really competitive party systems. But we should not be too demanding: Western Europe has had many minority governments, e.g. in Scandinavia and the Netherlands. They exist even in Westminster-type systems such as Canada – in spite of alternating governments without coalitions. Oversized grand coalitions were common in Austria and the Benelux countries, and then briefly in Germany (1966–69). Other countries suffered from the hegemonic position of one party, such as the Gaullists until 1981 or the Democrazia Cristiana in Italy until 1994. So it should come as no surprise that the government- and coalition-building patterns in transitional democracies have varied considerably (Table 12).

Comparisons with Western systems (Table 2) show that the performance of consolidating systems in post-Communist states has not been so bad after all. There are no completely weakened parties in a charismatic semi-presidential system, as is shown under Walesa in Poland and under Iliescu in Romania. After the Second World War there were 'reconciliation governments' in some regions, but reconciliation concerned the new system's parties. The former 'fascist' groups remained irrelevant and irreconcilable. The difference in Central and Eastern Europe has been that the post-Communists remained relevant, and in some cases also reconcilable, when they seriously transformed into Social Democrats, as in Hungary or Poland. The cleavage old–new regime made more alternations possible than in Western Europe after 1945 and in the 1970s.

Table 12 *Governmental and coalition-building patterns in transitional democracies*

| | Weak parties in semi-presidential systems with charismatic leadership | Grand coalitions and oversized reconciliation coalitions | Alternating competitive systems | Hegemonic party systems | |
				New democratic forces	*Old post-communist forces*
Western Europe					
France (5th Republic)		France (until 1947)	Germany		
		Austria (until 1966)	Greece		
		Spain (1970s)	Portugal		
			Spain (1990s)		
Eastern Europe					
Russia and other CIS countries		Poland (1989–92)	Bulgaria (1994, 1997)	Czech Republic (until 1998)	Romania (until 1996)
			Hungary (1994, 1998)	Lithuania (until 1992)	Yugoslavia
			Poland (1993, 1997)	Hungary (until 1994)	Belorussia

Hegemonic systems of the new democratic forces eroded quickly. Only in the Czech Republic did this process take until 1998. The old post-Communist forces remained hegemonic in many CIS states and Yugoslav successor states (with the clear exception of Slovenia). But in the countries *really* eligible for democratic consolidation their power disintegrated, even in Romania (in 1996).

Minority governments or *oversized coalitions* are usually common in transitional processes. In some respects the countries between Poland and Romania did better than most Western countries, e.g. in terms of alternating governments. Cabinet stability was above average only in Hungary and was extremely low in Poland and Bulgaria. But there are trends towards normalisation in most systems (Table 12). In fragmented party systems small groups sometimes acquire an exaggerated blackmailing power. The pensioners did not enter the Czech Parliament – in spite of many forecasts. The ethnic groups, however, have an important function in providing majorities, such as in Slovakia, Bulgaria and maybe, with increasing consolidation, also in Romania.

In the early period of democratisation, the first three variables discussed above were dominant. With consolidation, coalition-building was decisive for the development of party systems.

Conclusion

Most East-Central European systems – slowly this applies even to Poland – belong to the type of *moderate pluralism*. Party identification is naturally low, lower even than indicated by the figures for Southern Europe.[33] First surveys show that accounted for little more than one-quarter of the voters, even in the most developed political systems such as Czech Republic or Hungary.[34] Surveys in new democracies from Poland to Slovakia demonstrate that the electors were mostly able to locate themselves on a scale of Left and Right: most of them clustered around the centre. Only the Czechs showed more inclination to place themselves on the Right.[35] This self-placement may be distorted because the term 'Left' in some countries was discredited.

Party identification even declined after the first frustrations with democratisation, as the figures for in East Germany show. *Membership density* is diminishing more drastically – because the initial level was lower than in Western Europe. Only Hungary and the Czech Republic came close to Western averages (4–6 per cent).[36] Most parties oscillate between 15,000 and 40,000 members.[37] Confidence in parties is also extremely low compared to most other institutions, as in Western Europe.[38]

Nevertheless, it is noteworthy that parties play a prominent role in post-Communist democracies. Forecasts that *corporatism of social organisations* might dominate over an irrelevant 'facade' of party democracy did not materialise. *Round Tables* did not develop into a permanent form of corporatism.

Cartel parties (Katz/Mair) or parties of professional elites (von Beyme), 'loosely knitted anarchy' (Lösche) or 'framework parties' (Raschke) have been denounced in the West. But the more post-modern forms of parties were developed in Central and Eastern Europe. This seems to be a fair compromise between the anarchical–libertarian forms of organisation, which the torch-bearers of 'civil society' preferred to the organisational bias of the old regime, and the classical modern mass parties. An idealised civil society as a 'third road', far from capitalist modes of organisation, has hardly developed. Fortunately, however, an imperfect form of party democracy in Central and Eastern Europe reflects already a minimal *civil society*.

I agree with Philippe Schmitter[39] that 'the basic weakness of parties in these neo-democracies is that virtually all the difficulties that they have been experiencing are also being experienced by contemporary parties in archaeo-democracies'. The parties in East-Central Europe may well turn out to be more modern or to be the post-modern parties of the future. The parties are still to date 'guardians of access to political power', just as West European parties have streamlined the networks of decision making on various levels. A 'Party Leviathan' has been rediscovered, as in legislative studies of the United States. This, so far, is not possible in most East European parliaments. It is highly doubtful that the parties of East-Central Europe are as central in co-ordinating the networks of organised interests, regional units, bureaucratic experts as in the West. The habit of lobbying state agencies on the part of interests during the time of the erosion of Communism is still widespread, certainly in the successor states of the Soviet Union.

A different type – sometimes of a mafia type – of interest representation is still prevalent also in East-Central Europe. So the centrality of parties is less clear than in the West. But it is still worthwhile studying the parties in post-Communist countries, although we sometimes overstate the party role. We do this less for particular theoretical reasons, but rather because the networks of interest aggregation and lobbying remain relatively secret. It is easier to collect data on elections or the party composition of governments than to trace influences in everyday governmental or parliamentary decision making. Even in the West this is difficult, unless the influences are as well documented as they are in the United States or in Germany.[40]

Only with a decision-making study will we be able to decide to what extent the parties shaped the process of consolidation. There is no doubt that they were central during the first stage of democratisation, i.e. the phase of constitutional engineering. The institutions were normally a compromise between their competing constitutional ideas. Sometimes their divergence of views slowed down the process of final constitution making, as in Poland and Hungary. In times of consolidation the parties also play a vital role. The functioning of party democracy, especially coalition making, is one of the main criteria for consolidation. Unlike the delegated or illiberal systems within countries from the former Soviet Union, the consolidation of the party systems in East-Central Europe is proving quite successful although, in several key respects, conclusions have to be tentative.

Notes

1 Herbert Kitschelt (1995), 'Formation of Party Cleavages in Post-Communist Democracies', *Party Politics* 1: 4, pp. 447–72, esp. 449.
2 Attila Ágh (1995), 'Partial Consolidation of the East-Central European Parties. The Case of the Hungarian Socialist Party', *Party Politics* 1: 4, 491–514, esp. 491.
3 Kitschelt, 'Formation of Party Cleavages', pp. 466f.
4 Dieter Segert *et al.* (eds) (1997), *Parteiensysteme in postkommunistischen Gesellschaften Osteuropas.* Opladen, Westdeutscher Verlag, pp. 401f.
5 Wolfgang Merkel (1998), *Systemtransformation.* Hagen, FernUniversität, pp. 187ff.; Leonardo Morlino (1995), 'Political Parties and Democratic Consolidation in Southern Europe', in Richard Gunter *et al.* (eds), *The Politics of Democratic Consolidation.* Baltimore, Johns Hopkins University Press, pp. 315–88; esp. 319.
6 Hans-Dieter Klingemann *et al.* (eds) (1994), *Parties, Policies and Democracy.* Boulder, Westview.
7 Jan Bielasiak (1997), 'Substance and Process in the Development of Party Systems in East Central Europe', *Communist and Post-Communist Studies* 30: 1, pp. 23–44, esp. 25; Scott Mainwaring, (1998), 'Party Systems in the Third Wave', *Journal of Democracy* 9: 3, pp. 67–81, esp. 75ff.
8 Dieter Nohlen and Mirjana Kasapovic (1996), *Wahlsysteme und Systemwechsel in Osteuropa.* Opladen, Leske and Budrich, p. 174.
9 Figures from Timm Beichelt (1998) 'Die Wirkung von Wahlsystemen in Mittel- und Osteuropa', *Zeitschrift für Parlamentsfragen* 4, pp. 605–23, esp. 615.
10 Wolfgang Merkel (1997), 'Parteien und Parteiensysteme im Transformationsprozeß', in Wolfgang Merkel and Eberhard Schneider (eds), *Systemwechsel 3. Parteien im Transformationsprozeß.* Opladen, Leske and Budrich, pp. 337–71; esp. 343.
11 Florian Grotz, ' "Dauerhafte Strukturprägung" oder "taktische Wahlarithmetik"? Die Auswirkungen des ungarischen Wahlsystems in den 90er Jahren', *Zeitschrift für Parlamentsfragen* 4 (1998), pp. 624–47; esp. 646.
12 Nohlen and Kasapovic, *Wahlsysteme*, p. 187.
13 Lijphart, Arend (1992) 'Constitutional Choices for New Democracies', *Journal of Democracy* 3, pp. 72–84; Juan J. Linz and Alfred Stepan (1996) 'Toward Consolidated Democracies' *Journal of Democracy* 7: 2, pp. 14–33.
14 Herbert Döring, 'Parlamentarismus, Präsidentialismus und Staatstätigkeit', *WeltTrends* 16 (1997), pp. 143–70.
15 Agh 'Partial Consolidation'.
16 *Ibid.*, p. 503.
17 Grigore Pop-Eleches (1999), 'Separated at birth or by birth? The Communist successor parties in Romania and Hungary', *East European Politics and Societies* 13: 1, pp. 117–47; esp. 147.
18 Hans-Dieter Klingemann (1994), 'Die Entstehung wettbewerbsorientierter Parteiensysteme', in Wolfgang Zapf and Meinolf Dierkes (eds), *Institutionenvergleich und Institutionendynamik.* Berlin, Sigma, pp. 13–38.

19 M. M. Gallagher *et al.* (1995), *Representative Government in Modern Europe*. New York: McGraw-Hill, 2nd edn, p. 15.

20 Klingemann, 'Die Entstehung'.

21 Andrew C. Janos (1994) 'Continuity and Change in Eastern Europe: Strategies of Post-Communists Politics', *East European Politics and Societies* 8: 1, pp. 1–31, esp. 26.

22 Attila Ágh (1998), 'The Role of Political Parties: Political Culture and Electoral Behaviour', in Attila Ágh, *The Politics of Central Europe*. London, Sage, pp. 101–38; esp. 122.

23 Kitschelt 'Formation of Party Cleavages', p. 454

24 Margaditsch Hatschikjan (1994), 'Offenheit und Omnipotenz. Stärken und Verlockungen der neuen Parteiensysteme in Osteuropa', in M. Hatschikjan and Peter R. Weilemann (eds), *Parteienlandschaften in Osteuropa*. Paderborn, Schöning, pp. 171–82; esp. 179.

25 Linz and Stepan, 'Toward Consolidated Democracies' p. 15.

26 Berthold Kohler (1998), 'Noch keine Ferien für die böhmische Koalition. Die Sozialdemokraten lassen nach dem Wahlerfolg in Prag ihre Muskeln spielen. *Frankfurter Allgemeine Zeitung*; 15 July 1998, p. 5

27 Klaus von Beyme (1996), *Transition to Democracy in Eastern Europe*. Basingstoke, Macmillan.

28 Zsolt Enyedi (1996), 'Organising a subcultural Party in Eastern Europe. The case of the Hungarian Christian Democrats', *Party Politics* 2:3, 390.

29 James N. Druckmann (1996), 'Party Factionalism and Cabinet Durability', *Party Politics* 2: 3; pp. 397–407.

30 Attila Ágh (1998), *Emerging Democracies in East Central Europe and the Balkans.* Cheltenham, Elgar, p. 283.

31 Maurizio Cotta (1995), 'Structuring the New Party Systems after Dictatorship: Coalitions, Alliances, Fusions and Splits during the Transition and Post-Transition Stages', in Geoffrey Pridham and Paul Lewis (eds), *Stabilising Fragile Democracies*. London, Routledge, pp. 69–99, esp. 71.

32 Merkel, *System transformations*, p. 188

33 Morlino, 'Political Parties and Democratic Consolidation in Southern Europe', 331

34 Matthew Wyman *et al.* (1995) 'Place of "Party" in Post-Communist Europe', *Party Politics* 1: 4, pp. 535–48, esp. 545.

35 Radoslaw Markowski (1997) 'Political Parties and Ideological Spaces in East Central Europe', *Communist and Post-Communist Studies*, 30: 3, pp. 221–54, esp. 225.

36 Petre Kopecký (1995), 'Developing Party Organizations in East Central Europe. What Type of Party is Likely to Emerge?', *Party Politics* 1, pp. 515–534, esp. 524.

37 Dieter Segert (1997), 'Parteien und Parteiensysteme in der Konsolidierung der Demokratien Osteuropas', in Wolfgang Merkel and Eberhard Schneider (eds), *Systemwechsel 3*, pp. 57–97; esp. 65.

38 Richard Rose (1995) 'Mobilizing Demobilized Voters in Post-Communist Societies', Party Politics 1: 4; pp. 549–64

39 Philippe Schmitter (1999), 'Critical Reflections on the "Functions" of Political Parties and Performance in Neo-Democracies', in Wolfgang Merkel and Andreas Busch (eds), *Demokratie in Ost und West. Für Klaus von Beyme*. Frankfurt, Suhrkamp, pp. 475–95, esp. 491.

40 Klaus von Beyme (1998), *The Legislator. German Parliament as a Centre of Political Decision-Making*. Aldershot, Ashgate, pp. 48ff.

Early democratic consolidation in Hungary and the Europeanisation of the Hungarian polity

Hungary was a focus of international attention in the first ten years of its democratisation process and a substantial amount of literature has discussed its progress. After these ten years, one may begin to summarise the results of its democratisation process; but it is even more important now to outline the new problems facing Hungary in the second decade of democratisation. Thus, this chapter has two main messages. The first is about the past, the first decade, for some years ago Hungary completed the stage of democratic transition. The second message is about the present, given that Hungary has entered the new stage of early consolidation that characterises its second decade.

Hungary is no longer a 'transition country' with a mixed economy and a transformation recession, because it has now embarked on the stage of economic and political consolidation. Already by 1998 the third free and fair elections had taken place, and since 1996 there has been a sustained economic growth of about five per cent. Thus, the basic economic and political criteria of democratic consolidation have been met domestically, and with NATO membership the international situation of Hungary has begun to be secured. However, Hungary – like the other ECE countries – has not repeated the South European (SE) way of democratisation that took place in a bipolar world and with an active promotion of democracy, i.e. with substantial economic and political assistance from the West. Therefore, the Hungarian transition was more difficult and took longer than had been the case in Southern Europe. Thus, the East-Central European democratisations have to be separated from the former Third Wave as a Fourth Wave. They have entered the new stage of early consolidation that makes them markedly different from the previous SE democratisations, which took much less time to consolidate. This chapter argues that democratic transition has left behind a series of unresolved issues to be addressed in the new stage of democratic consolidation. Also, the external factors have been less beneficial than in SE, so that the domestic and international circumstances together necessitate highlighting this special period. The terms and concepts of Fourth Wave democratisation and its early consolidation suggest the need for a new approach to the systemic change theory in ECE based on the experiences of the first decade in order to express its markedly region-specific features.[1]

These two messages can be also taken as hypotheses to be discussed in this chapter, which focuses on the particular character of the early consolidation in Hungary in the ECE context. Hungarian democratisation has usually been described as an elite-driven process, although it was much more a 'mass-driven' process than is often recognised, involving a relatively strong, organised civil society, conceived here as a plurality of competing and conflicting intermediary associations representing interests in a multi-actor society. There is not the space here to fully develop this argument but it is enough to mention that at all of the turning-points of the democratisation process there has been active public mobilisation, which has tended to promote democracy. It began with the 'movement parties' in the late 1980s, and continued with peaceful mass demonstrations in 1991–93, organised by the movement called Democratic Charter, to prevent an authoritarian renewal orchestrated by the incumbent national-conservative Government, and it witnessed the robust development of civil associations in the second half of the 1990s. I fully endorse the 'interactive approach' emphasising the two-way flow of causality or circular interaction between politics and economy, and between institutions and actors. Nevertheless, this chapter concentrates on the overall results of the democratisation process rather than its public actors and competing elites.[2]

First, I introduce the achievements of democratic transition in the field of institution building in which I distinguish between macro-, meso- and micro-politics. Macro-politics concerns the level of the most important institutions, such as the government, the president and parliament, with the entire system of checks and balances, including the Constitutional Court. Meso-politics is represented by the largest socio-political actors as well as by functional and territorial organisations like business interest organisations, trades unions and chambers, and regional or county self-governments. Micro-politics works at the level and in the sphere of civil society or voluntary organisations. After institution building, I discuss the shortcomings of the Hungarian democratic transition: a great number of tasks remain to be addressed during early consolidation, and these have created new contradictions as well as the emergence of a performance crisis. Finally, I give an overview of the recent stage of the Europeanisation of the Hungarian polity and I argue that EU requirements have demanded the completion of consensual democracy. As a conclusion I outline the common features of the ECE democratisations and point out the specifically Hungarian features.

The achievements of democratic transition in the Hungarian polity

Hungary had in 1989 an early constitution-making process that led through all-party negotiations to a basically constitutional type of democracy. The

Hungarian Constitution of 1989, and its amended version in 1990, provide an extensive system of checks and balances, on the one side, and allow for a participatory democracy with an organised civil society as autonomous self-governments in meso- and micro-politics on the other. The Constitution was a blueprint for institution building that came to an end in the late 1990s, closing the period of democratic transition. This process of basic democratisation in the Hungarian polity may be briefly outlined by analysing the main fields of transformation in

- macro-politics in general;
- the party system;
- the stabilisation of executive power; and
- the consolidation of the Parliament.

After reviewing the achievements, it is necessary to identify the remaining tasks left by democratic transition for early consolidation and their connections with further Europeanisation.

Democratic institution building and the balance of powers

Government–president relationship: In April 1990 the then two largest parties, the conservative Hungarian Democratic Forum (HDF) and the liberal Alliance of Free Democrats (ADF), concluded a pact about constitutional changes, including the introduction of the prime ministerial system and thirty-six qualifying acts to be passed as two thirds' majority laws. As a result, in the macro-political power triangle Hungary has a prime-ministerial government, a largely ceremonial president and a very active but not too strong parliament. The relationship between the 'strong' government and the 'weak' president was finalised by the Constitutional Court in a series of decisions in the first parliamentary cycle (1990–94) that led at the same time to the Constitutional Court becoming an influential political actor. Both Árpád Göncz (1990–2000) and Ferenc Mádl (2000–) are politicians who have enjoyed strong popular consent. They have represented indeed the 'strength of a weak president' through their political behaviour and moral standing, so that since the early 1990s there has been no tension around the president of the republic. Even the election of the second president, Ferenc Mádl, took place with wide support from the parliamentary parties.

The role of the prime minister has been more controversial, and therefore the exact balance in this triangular relationship in the early 1990s was burdened by short-term considerations on the part of the first head of government. The first Government wanted to establish 'simple majority rule', but public opinion stood firmly behind the very popular president against the increasingly unpopular prime minister. Finally, the relationship between prime minister and president of the republic was clarified and stabilised, hence there is no dual executive power in Hungary. The Hungarian polity is a rather clear case of parliamentary democracy where the centre of power is the prime minister. The president of the republic remains the guardian of democratic institutions with some authority in controlling the powers of both government and parliament.[3]

Government–parliament relationship: Constitutionally Hungary has a strong, German type of prime-ministerial government. The prime minister can only be dismissed through a constructive vote of non-confidence. It is not the government but exclusively the prime minister who is answerable to parliament, since he/she can replace ministers without the approval of parliament. The constitutional model of prime-ministerial government has weakened the classical control function of parliament, but new control institutions were created instead by parliament, such as the Ombudsman. The strong executive, however, exercises its power mostly in and through parliament, above all through its simple parliamentary majority. Hence, the idea of complete separation and counter-positioning of the executive and the legislative power is meaningless in the Hungarian polity. Their relative separation is both necessary and functional, but one has to have in mind that the government works organically with parliament. For instance, the most important decisions of the government have always been formulated as legislative acts. Nevertheless, the system of the 'constitutional acts' or two-thirds' majority laws (thirty-six acts) prevents the government from dominating parliament completely through its simple majority and making constitutional changes on its own because it needs the support of the opposition for the amendments to these 'fundamental laws'. The parliament was the central site of political life during democratic transition, so the political parties concentrated on their activity in parliament, although the final word or the decisive role in policy making still belonged to the government. As Robert Jenkins observes:

> The policy process in Hungary remains highly centralized, with basic decisions made by the government (the prime minister and ministries), which is the primary initiator of legislation. Due to the strength of the prime minister's position, the independence of the ministries from the parliamentary control, and party centralization, Parliament exercises only limited influence in the development of policy.[4]

Government–Constitutional Court relationship: The consensual character of Hungarian democracy – and, in addition, the relative weakness of the parliament and the overwhelming strength of the government – has made the Constitutional Court a main political actor in balancing the government. Jon Elster summarises this new construction's advancement beyond the classical triangle of powers in the following way: 'Although the rule of a constructive vote of no confidence ensures that government has some independence from parliament, the strongest constraint on the legislature is provided by the Constitutional Court.' Hungary, in fact, has one of the most powerful constitutional courts in the world, with extensive powers in the *ex ante* and *ex post* scrutiny of legislation and with a monopoly over the interpretation of the Constitution. Elster noticed already in the early 1990s that '[t]he Hungarian Court has been by far the most active one. In the last few years it has emerged as a major political force, and has in fact been characterized as the most powerful constitutional court in the world.'[5]

The period of democratic transition was marked by confrontation between successive governments and the Constitutional Court; but the latter has been successful in preventing arbitrary actions by them. In general, the Constitutional Court opposed the Antall Government of 1990–93, mainly on issues of public law in order to create a proper balance between the major power centres, and the Horn Government of 1994–98 on issues of socioeconomic legislation due to its drastic management of the economic crisis. Introduced on 12 March 1995, and called 'The Bokros package' after the finance minister, it influenced the course of Hungarian politics profoundly for some years and radically reduced social and health services in the public sector, but the decisions of the Constitutional Court reinstated some of them by defining the basic public services according to the Constitution. Finally, after ten years and under a new leadership, the Constitutional Court has turned from these substantial issues to more formal and procedural issues, hence, it has to a great extent become de-politicised.

Consolidation of the party system in Hungary

The multi-party system emerged in Hungary very early on, in September 1987, with the organisation of the Hungarian Democratic Forum (HDF). Thus, at the first free elections, in the spring of 1990, there was already a competitive multi-party system. Compared to the other ECE countries, Hungary's party system has been stable from the very beginning, since the same six parties were elected to the First (1990–94) and the Second (1994–98) Parliament. Apart from the HDF, these parliamentary parties were the Hungarian Socialist Party (HSP), the Alliance of Young Democrats (Fidesz), the Independent Smallholders Party (ISP), the Alliance of Free Democrats (ADF) and the Christian Democratic Party (CDPP). The ISP and CDPP were historical parties that re-established their continuity from the early post-war period, while the other parties were organised in the late 1980s. Actually, Fidesz was earlier an acronym for the Alliance of Young Democrats but the name of the AYD was abandoned in the mid-1990s and the name of Hungarian Civic Party was added to Fidesz, i.e. Fidesz–HCP (for simplicity's sake I use only the name Fidesz in the following discussion).

These parties scored almost the same results at the first two free and fair elections, except for the change in the leading position between HDF and HSP in 1994. Thus, seemingly, there was considerably more volatility among voters at the second elections, although it was not so much voters changing their

Table 13   *Results of the three elections: seats in the Hungarian Parliament (1990–98)*

	1990				1994				1998			
	ID	TL	NL	All	ID	TL	NL	All	ID	TL	NL	All
AFD	35	34	23	92	16	28	25	69	2	5	17	24
Fidesz	1	8	12	21	–	7	13	20	90	48	10	148
HDF	114	40	10	164	5	18	15	38	17	–	–	17
HSP	1	14	18	33	149	53	7	209	54	50	30	134
ISP	11	16	17	44	1	14	11	26	12	22	14	48
CDPP	3	8	10	21	3	5	14	22	–	–	–	–
PHJL	–	–	–	–	–	–	–	–	–	3	11	14
Independent	11	–	–	11	2	–	–	2	1	–	–	1
All	176	120	90	386	176	125	85	386	176	128	82	386

Notes:
ID: individual districts; TL: territorial lists; NL: national list
[a] After the elections, in the First and Second Parliaments, some independent MPs joined parties

views as the leading party altering its character: the HDF became a centre-Right party from having been a large umbrella organisation, and its former Leftist voters went back to the HSP. Again, there was only one change at the third free elections, in 1998. The CDPP dropped out of parliament and was replaced by the Party of Hungarian Justice and Life (PHJL) (see Table 13). But this extreme Rightist party was not completely new in Parliament in 1998, since it had been a 'parliamentary party' in the First Parliament, first as a fraction within the HDF then it had split from HDF in 1993 to form an independent party.

At the recent stage in the emergence of the Hungarian party system in its early consolidation, the HSP and Fidesz have emerged on the political scene as dominant parties. The HSP appeared already in 1994, by its landslide victory at the elections, as a large centre-Left party, and Fidesz in 1998, by unifying the smaller Rightist parties, as a large centre-Right party. Thus, from the late 1990s the Hungarian party system has become bipolar, with about 80 per cent of public support behind the two largest parties. This structure, with two big parties and some smaller ones, is similar to West European party systems, and the Hungarian parties have also developed their contacts with the major European party internationals. It can be interpreted as the 'external' Europeanisation of the Hungarian parliamentary parties and party system, still without their 'internal' Europeanisation, that is without the full internal adjustment of party structures and practices to West European standards. There is no doubt that 'transnational linkages' have played a decisive role in party developments in ECE in general and in Hungary in particular.[6]

The stabilisation of central government

The competences of Hungarian government changed much between 1990 and 1998 due to the emergence of the private market economy. The Antall and the Horn Governments in the cycles of the First and Second Parliaments still acted as collective governing bodies, unlike a truly German type of prime-ministerial government, as had been envisaged. This meant a constitutional transfer without a proper institution and/or policy transfer. The all-embracing Prime Minister's Office (PMO), according to the German model, was established only in 1998, by the Orbán Government. The new and re-organised PMO has improved the performance of central government, although it has induced controversies about the over-extension of executive power as a whole at the expense of other centres of power as well as intergovernmental relations between central and local government. Altogether, the new PMO, the 'flagship' of central Government, has transformed the workings of executive power beyond recognition. It has acted within the incumbent Government like a super-ministry, managing the control and co-ordination of the major policy-making processes of the individual ministries.

The ministerial structure of successive Hungarian governments has not altered too much and by the Third Government it may be considered as stabilised. The number and profile of the individual ministries has remained more or less the same over the three government cycles. Both the Antall and Horn Governments had thirteen ministries, and the present Government – by separating the Ministry of Education and the Ministry of Culture – has fourteen ministries. As a contrast to this structural consolidation, coalition politics have been very turbulent in Hungary, albeit both the Antall and Horn Governments served the full four-year term. The first coalition government consisted of three centre–Right parties – the HDF, ISP and CDPP – and two constituent parties suffered party splits due to tension in the coalition. This national conservative coalition was seriously defeated in the 1994 elections. The second, socialist–liberal, coalition fared better, since the HSP and AFD formulated a written coalition agreement with detailed policy commitments. Yet, from time to time the level of tension was high between the governing parties and contributed to their electoral defeat, although this defeat was mainly caused the result of drastic economic crisis management. The incumbent new national-conservative coalition has also revealed tensions between the two major partners, Fidesz and ISP, and the minor partner, HDF, has been downgraded, but these coalition parties have also been kept together during the Third Parliament because of their common interest in staying in power.

Democratic transition as parliamentarisation

In democratic transition, the Hungarian Parliament was the model and mother institution, indeed. Research has shown that the Hungarian political system as a whole became 'parliamentarised', meaning that all the other macro-political institutions grew out from parliament and followed the model of the parliament, i.e. copied its procedures and behavioural patterns to their own practices. The same applies to all other meso- and micro-political institutions. Thus, the process of democratic transition began within parliament and then developed as the parliamentarisation for the Hungarian polity. One could notice even an over-parliamentarisation, that is an overwhelming role for the Hungarian Parliament, with the parties as the quasi-monopolistic actors of political life – termed as over-particisation. Wolfgang Merkel has confirmed in his book *Systemtransformation* that these tendencies have surfaced in the ECE countries in general and have presented obstacles to consolidation.[7]

This overwhelming role of both parliament and parties was very marked in the first half of the 1990s, although by the end of democratic transition this unbalanced situation in macro-politics decreased; yet more than ten years on, it has not disappeared completely. Hungary has certainly been a clear case of the 'rise of parliaments' versus the so-called 'decline of parliaments' in the West. It is still an open question, however, whether with the full consolidation of the Hungarian polity parliament will keep its central or privileged position in political life. Democratic transition after the first free elections brought about the parliamentarisation of Hungarian politics because parliamentary rules and patterns of politics became generally accepted and applied by all the other political institutions. Similarly, early consolidation in Hungary has also begun in the Parliament, since this new stage of parliamentarisation has induced the consolidation of parties and, vice versa, the relatively consolidated party system has produced an early consolidation of the Hungarian Parliament. This is reflected in the achievements of institution building. Democratic institution building in the Hungarian Parliament can be characterised by the following major processes:

- Standing Orders: the Second Parliament passed new and coherent Standing Orders (the official name in the Hungarian Parliament for House Rules) on 30 September 1994. This 'constitution of parliament' ensures the democratic and efficient working of the Hungarian Parliament. It is democratic because it safeguards the rights of the opposition and it is efficient because it regulates clearly the division of labour between the plenary and committee sessions and their tasks.
- Legislative production: the Hungarian Parliament has by and large completed the legal systemic change, that is it has passed the most important acts for the new social, economic and political order. It has standardised its legislative production by passing about 100 laws every year with about another 100 parliamentary decisions of various kinds. Although obviously there is still a need for further amendments, all thirty-six acts earmarked as two-thirds' majority laws or 'constitutional laws' have already been passed (see Table 14).
- Committee system: the First Hungarian Parliament inherited a rather well elaborated system of parliamentary committees. This system has been

Table 14 *Legislation in the Hungarian Parliament (1990–99)*

	1990	1991	1992	1993	1994	1995	1996	1997	1998	1999
New Acts	29	55	50	61	43	67	75	82	49	84
Amendments	48	38	42	60	56	59	55	77	45	42
Decisions	55	73	92	103	75	128	120	126	95	109
All	132	166	184	224	174	254	250	285	189	235

gradually extended and committees have become more involved in legislative work. The MPs have an extra financial incentive to get involved in committee work, since they get extra pay for participating, and the 'backbenchers' have also a political ambition for career promotion through committees. The Third Parliament has twenty-two standing committees with 483 members; that is, some MPs sit on two or three committees. Parliamentary committees have been developed more or less according to the structure of the ministries, the majority of them having a 'departmental' character.

- Party fractions: with the consolidation of parties, the parliamentary fractions ('fraction' is the usual name on the Continent for parliamentary party groups) have also become consolidated, and 'fraction hopping' or 'political tourism' has come to an end. In the First Parliament fifty-six out of 386 MPs (about 15 per cent) left their party groups. HDF, the largest party of the ruling coalition, split and PHJL emerged as a new party within the Parliament. In the Second Parliament forty-nine MPs (about 12 per cent) changed their seats, mostly due to the crisis in the CDPP fraction, which now ceased to exist. There was erosion also in the HDF fraction, and the MPs from both fractions moved to Fidesz. These changes led to the emergence of Fidesz as the largest centre-Right party and thus to the consolidation of the bipolar party system. In the first two years of the Third Parliament the only change has been that five Fidesz MPs and one AFD MP have become Independent, since both the party identities and the political commitments of the MPs have stabilised.
- Incumbency retention rate: after the 'transitory parliament' (1985–90), in the First Parliament (1990–94) only 5 per cent of former MPs were re-elected. In subsequent elections, however, their percentage has grown to a great extent. In 1994, 35 per cent of MPs were re-elected to the Second Parliament (1994–98) and in 1998 45, per cent to the Third Parliament (1998–2000). Altogether, in the Third Parliament, half of the MPs elected have previous parliamentary experience, with some MPs re-elected from the First Parliament to the Third Parliament. This percentage is well below the Western average of 70–80 per cent, though such a high percentage is, however, necessary both for the professionalisation of the MPs and for the application of the seniority principle in the organisation of parliamentary life.

It is possible to indicate some general features of democratic institution building in the Hungarian case. Above all, the increase in the institutional capacity
of the Hungarian Parliament has been easier than that in its cultural capacity,
or the professionalization of the MPs due to the low incumbency retention
rate. This paradox of institutional and 'cultural' development continued
through the democratic transition as a whole, and its solution is a task for
democratic consolidation. *The Political Yearbook of Hungary* has published
all the data on Parliament every year, and parliamentary research has shown
that, as an early sign of maturation, most MPs have accepted the Left and the
Right as their major options of political orientations. Unlike in the First
Parliament, in the Second and the Third Parliaments more than two-thirds of
the MPs consider the Left–Right division as the major dividing line in political life in general and in parliament in particular. The learning process of the
MPs is still very slow, since half of them are uncertain of re-election and,
therefore, prepare themselves for the other options of life, primarily for business careers. Due to this attitude, the level of attendance of parliamentary sessions among the MPs has been rather low. It was only 72.4 per cent in voting
procedures and much lower in the discussions in 1999. This lack of discipline
on the part of the MPs irritates the public and alienates ordinary people from
'high' politics.

Institution building in meso- and micro-politics

The institution building in the 1990s was very asymmetrical, since the emergence of the meso- and micro-political institutions was very much delayed compared to that of the macro-political institutions. Although Hungary already
had an active civil society with 'movement parties', the development of meso-
and micro-politics still lagged behind that in macro-politics. The constitutional
framework was in place for these spheres but was not yet complemented by the
actual formation and activity of the institutions concerned. However, sustained
economic development in Hungary since the mid-1990s has changed the social
construction of democracy beyond recognition. It has created new conditions
for the development of meso- and micro-politics as well, since these institutions
needed economic stability and growth for their own establishment. Altogether,
as Terry Cox and Bob Mason conclude in their *Social and Economic
Transformation in East Central Europe*, by the late 1990s 'key elements of a new
institutional framework have been established' in meso-politics as well, such as
professional and economic chambers, top business and trades union organisations and their common Interest Reconciliation Councils.[8]

The contrast between institution building in macro-politics on the one side
and in meso- and micro-politics on the other has not yet completely disappeared. It can be described as high and balanced institution density in macro-
politics versus low and weak organisation density in meso- and micro-politics,
through which the asymmetrical character of institution building has come to

the surface very markedly. Nevertheless, in democratic transition there was a significant development of the institutional structure in meso- and micro-politics as well. Organised interests developed a tripartite structure of the (national) Interest Reconciliation Council that played an important conflict-management role during the long socio-economic crisis, although even the socialist–liberal Government failed to institutionalise this sphere completely and coherently. Similarly, the system of local and territorial self-government was established in the early 1990s but has remained unfinished since, e.g. the status of the traditional counties versus the newly planned regions has been left open. In short, although an extended structure of meso-politics has been built up, this sphere has not been completely regulated and the inter-relations between the central government and the territorial self-governments have largely remained undecided. The Constitution has stipulated unambiguously that territorial and local governments constitute an independent branch of power. Still the resources have not been granted, so they may pursue independent activities. This has produced their indirect dependence on central government. This unfinished and asymmetrical character of the system of democratic institutions has been one of the major reasons for the low performance of the political system as a whole, since there has been a permanent clash about competences between central government and the territorial and functional self-governments.

The same controversial development or internal asymmetry in micro-politics can be illustrated on one side by the robust development of civil society organisations since 1989. In 1997 there were already 51,032 non-profit organisations in Hungary. In fact, by 2000 there were more than 60,000 non-profit organisations, although about half are, so to say, 'sleeping', not fully active. On the other side, however, these civil associations have been mostly concentrated in the capital and some well-developed regions; and civil society has been 'sleeping', indeed, in the remainder of the country. In addition, this new sector of the civil associations has been very asymmetrical in development, both regionally and *socially*. It is primarily the new middle class that has organised these civil associations, and the other strata of society have for the most part remained without self-organisation and self-protection.

The conventional wisdom in the democratisation literature declares that transition is mainly a period of institution building and that the consolidation period in its turn brings about the development of political culture. While this is more or less true, institution building continues in the consolidation period at the level of meso- and micro-politics. Actually, in civil society these two dimensions – the institutional and the cultural – are now merging, more closely in micro-politics but also in meso-politics. It means that political culture is becoming institutionalised in the form of implemented and materialised values. Thus, the current definitions of consolidation, e.g. by Plasser, Ulram and Waldrauch in *Democratic Consolidation in East-Central Europe*, presuppose the completion of institution building in meso- and micro-politics as well, parallel with the institutionalisation of democratic values, since '[i]nstitutions may be defined as societally stabilised patterns of behaviour and interaction'. This approach reconciles the institution versus culture dualism at meso- and micro-levels following Robert Putnam's work on the vital role of civic communities in democratic consolidation. In the same vein, Jacques Thomassen and Jan van Deth state that 'this civic culture is embodied in and reinforced by the membership of all kinds of civil and political organiza-tions'.[9]

Actually, the completion of institution building at meso- and micro-levels through the institutionalisation of democratic values is a tremendously big task, and is necessarily left mostly for the consolidation period of democrat-isation. But this delay in a 'cultural revolution' and the emergence of civil society is bigger in the ECE case in general than it was in SE. This task has also been more closely connected with the problems of 'performance' of the political system. Mainstream research on democratic consolidation in ECE has moved towards analysing the 'improving' and 'deepening' of democratisa-tion by consolidation, i.e. through enhancing its performance. This urgent need clearly indicates the shortcomings of democratic transition and the new tasks of Hungarian development in consolidation.

The performance crisis and the attempted presidentialisation of democracy

The emergence of democratic institutions has produced a series of new contradictions, in particular the contrast between the democratic character and the low performance of the new institutions. This contrast continued through the period of transition as a whole in all ECE countries, with Hungarians being the most critical due to their higher expectations. Support for democracy was around 70 per cent in Hungary in the 1990s, but approval for the functioning of democracy tended to be around only 20 per cent. In other words, procedural legitimacy of the new democratic system was present but the performance legitimacy was still largely missing. General or 'diffuse' support for democracy has not developed in Hungary because a large part of population has had a negative view about the functioning of democracy. As a result of this performance crisis, there has been in Hungary a large percentage of 'dissatisfied democrats'.[10]

The lack of performance legitimacy or, simply said, the low performance of the new institutions has culminated in the period of early consolidation becoming a one of 'performance crisis'. It has become the major bottleneck for further democratisation and also for Europeanisation. The serious short-comings and structural problems in the workings of the Hungarian polity make a profound modernisation unavoidable. The resolution of the recent performance crisis to make way for a drastic increase in system performance necessitates a switch from 'democratisation' as creating a merely formal or procedural democracy to political 'modernisation', that is, to a significant improvement in all the three criteria of policy making (effectiveness, efficiency and efficacy).

The low performance of the political system has been visible to the Hungarian public, first of all in the very slow procedure at the courts, taking usually two–three years. At the level of parliamentary decision making there has been a great number of new acts – about fifty – to be amended year by year. Actually, the legal re-regulation of social, economic and political life as a whole has been a very painful task and it has demanded a high number of new regulations to be passed concerning various levels of the political system. The deregulation process, i.e. the elimination of outdated regulations from the former system, has been a big task in itself, and its delay and the controversial forms it has assumed have sometimes produced legal gaps and near chaos in some fields. People have also witnessed competition for power within the checks and balances system, for example between the Ombudsman's Office and the Constitutional Court. Due to the high crime rate people generally have been dissatisfied with the Office of the Chief Public Prosecutor. For an improvement, some have considered increasing its independence from government, while others have wanted to restore ministerial control over it. Last but not least, Europeanisation has also been a major reason for the performance crisis, although, as discussed later, it has been or will be even more important for its solution. Legal harmonisation and structural adaptation in all fields to the high complexity of EU regulations have put a tremendous burden on the political system, well beyond its capacity to cope with the European policy universe.

Domestically, one of the main reasons for the low performance of the new democratic institutions has been the asymmetrical character of the Hungarian polity, that is the insufficient development of meso- and micro-politics. No doubt, consolidation as a new stage presupposes the revival of organised civil society with the inclusion of all relevant social groups and their interest representations in political life as a means of helping to overcome the performance crisis. Meso-politics has suffered a lot from the dominance and exclusiveness of party politics. At the level of meso-politics consolidation means that the autonomy of socio-political actors will be completed and respected. Paradoxically, this new development embracing many actors and 'veto points', can aggravate in some fields the already severe situation of low performance in the political system. Namely, some steps were taken by the second government towards lessening the asymmetrical character of the Hungarian polity (e.g. by extending the system of territorial self-governments). These efforts, at least temporarily, proved to be counter-productive by increasing the duration and difficulties of decision making, but in the longer run they will be effective and citizen-friendly.

Parallel with the asymmetrical character of the Hungarian polity has been a second major reason for its low performance – what may be called the *fragmented* character of the polity. As discussed earlier, Hungary has established a consensual type of democracy according to the 1989–90 Constitution. It is, however, an unfinished democratic constitution, since it contains many contradictions and legal gaps. It is true that the harmonisation of the main power centres – or the elaboration of a coherent structure of macro-politics with precise relationships among the major institutions and actors – has created much tension in all ECE countries. This has been especially felt in Hungary, given the markedly consensual character of democracy with its extended system of checks and balances. In my view, Hungary has created not only an asymmetrical but a fragmented democracy. The separation of powers was overburdened with many overlapping competences, and some institutions were not completely developed. This fragmented state of democracy appears mainly in macro-politics, while the asymmetrical character of democracy, in turn, concerns first of all meso-politics, that is, the underprivileged position of social and territorial actors. Democratic transition created, by and large, a balance of powers at the formal–legal level among macro-institutions like government, parliament and president. But it did not solve the problem of the fragmented and asymmetrical democracy, so this problem has been left for early democratic consolidation.

Hungary has developed an extensive system of checks and balances. Beyond the Constitutional Court, there have been other important institutions, like the Ombudsman, the National Bank, the State Audit Office and the chief public prosecutor's Office, and the National Judicial Council has also been separated from the Ministry of Justice in order to supervise the courts. All these institutions have become independent of government and have been attached to and are controlled by parliament. So instead of the traditional control of the executive by the legislative power, parliament controls the government mostly indirectly, through these new institutions, including of course the Constitutional Court. This huge system of institutions has worked well in that it has produced a large number of decisions (see Table 15). This system of checks and balances has been reasonably successful in controlling the executive but, due to its fragmented structure, it has been unable to eradicate the contradictions, legal gaps and areas of overlap that have hindered the good performance of the democratic polity as a whole.

There have been two possible solutions to the performance crisis: turning to a more majoritarian democracy or completing a final breakthrough towards consensual democracy. The Antall Government tried the first, the Horn Government the second. Now the Orbán Government has made a renewed attempt at establishing a quasi-majoritarian democracy. Therefore, in the present parliamentary cycle there has been a heated political debate between the Government and the Opposition about the type of democracy. Two governing parties (Fidesz and ISP) have openly stated their wish to turn to a majoritarian type of democracy, and in turn the opposition parties (HSP and AFD) have argued for the completion of a consensual democracy.[11]

Table 15 *Decision-making output (1990–99)*

	1990	1991	1992	1993	1994	1995	1996	1997	1998	1999
Gov	32	188	177	185	190	179	242	288	245	228
CC	84	180	167	145	149	169	239	191	150	229
Om	0	0	0	0	0	0	3353	2477	2556	2308
SAO	28	52	72	38	31	54	158	59	44	37

Notes:
Gov = governmental decrees; *CC* = Constitutional Court decisions; *Om* = issues treated by the three Ombudsman Offices (citizenship rights, personal data protection and minority rights) which began their activities in 1995, so the figure for 1996 includes also 1995's decisions; *SAO* = reports of the State Audit Office
Source: Political Yearbook of Hungary (2000, p. 503)

However, this debate has not remained at a merely theoretical level. In 1998 a new attempt began, indeed, to create a majoritarian type of democracy by the new centre-Right Government. The new coalition has aimed at concentrating all executive powers in central government in order to cut short the decision-making process and to enhance the policy-making capacity of the political system as a whole. The Government has used all possible means to the – partial or complete – exclusion of other actors, first of all the opposition parties, from the policy-making process. Moreover, in Central Europe there is still a living conservative tradition of a strong state, so different from the current idea of the 'effective state', advocated nowadays by the leading global institutions like the World Bank. Therefore, when conservative governments try to turn to majoritarian democracy they copy not so much its present models from the West, such as the often-mentioned Westminster democracy, but instead turn to Hungarian authoritarian traditions from the past, from the late nineteenth century or the interwar years. These traditions show a combination of formally democratic procedures with, in practice, deep penetration of the system from the government to the working of public administration and, to a great extent, to some vital sectors of the private economy as well, in the spirit of power concentration and strict state hierarchy.

The efforts to return to majoritarian democracy or to establish a presidential-type of democracy in a parliamentary disguise can be noticed most in three fields:

1 In the prime-ministerial system the Prime Minister's Office (PMO) plays a central role, as it does also in Germany and Spain. The present government has completed this constitutional 'import' by establishing a big central organisation similar to the Chancellor's Office in Germany. It is a very powerful organisation but its working does not lead *automatically* to majoritarian democracy. However, in its over-extended form, the Prime Minister's Office, controlling closely all ministries and extending its powers well

beyond the traditional competences of its German model, has become the symbol of the recent effort at majoritarian democracy in Hungary. The PMO has also acquired the function of interest reconciliation. In both functions it has tried to influence and control civil society, putting pressure on the media and on the top civil organisations. The individual ministries have lost power and influence by this power-concentration process.[12]

2 In 1998 a form of simple majority rule began in the Third Parliament whereby the Government has tried to circumvent the qualified or two-thirds' majority laws by 'reinterpreting' them. The most effective way of reducing the role of the Opposition, the media and the public at large in parliamentary affairs has been the introduction of the three-week working cycle in the Third Parliament. The first week is for plenary sessions, the second for committee meetings and the third for constituency work (albeit only 45 per cent of the Hungarian MPs have their own single-member or individual constituency). This cycle runs counter to the Standing Orders, and the Constitutional Court ordered Parliament to stop this practice or else to rearrange it by amending the Standing Orders before the end of 1999, but nothing has happened. MPs have continued the practice of the three-week cycle, disregarding the ruling of the Constitutional Court and claiming that they have not violated but only 'reinterpreted' the Standing Orders. As a result, the Hungarian Parliament has been devalued: as a political actor it has played a much less important role in the recent parliamentary cycle than it did in the First and the Second Parliaments.[13]

3 The incumbent government has pursued a policy of confrontation not only with other political actors but with social and territorial actors and organisations. Meso-politics has not been further developed: on the contrary, its capacity and competences have been reduced, and this has enhanced its asymmetrical character. The imperfect yet fairly effective system of the tripartite Interest Reconciliation Council (established in 1989) has been abolished and an Economic Council has been organised instead. This is only a consultative body without actual powers, convened twice a year. Parallel with this, the National Labour Council has also been established in the competitive sector, with restricted negotiating powers. By these transformations, the whole system of interest reconciliation and concertation has become meaningless. Not only the trades union confederations, but even the business interest organisations and territorial self-governments have been marginalised as partners.

All these efforts to establish a quasi-majoritarian democracy can be summarised as the tendency towards presidentialisation in Hungarian democracy by the incumbent prime minister. The prime minister has very rarely attended parliamentary sessions so far. He has also avoided parliamentary control through parliamentary questions by shifting the duty to answer them to the other ministers who are, indeed, his 'secretaries'. Like an American president, the incumbent prime minister has introduced a series of yearly

'Messages to the Nation' in early February, at the beginning of the political season. But these messages have taken place outside of parliament, with the prime minister addressing only his own followers in a ceremonial building and televised through the public TV channel. This prime minister with a presidential approach has not been ready to negotiate or communicate regularly with the leaders of the Opposition or with prominent social and business actors. He has sent only his own delegates to other organisations in order to express the fact that he is above other actors and it is not his duty to negotiate with them.[14]

Consequently, the full conflict between majoritarian and consensual approaches faces come into being in Hungary only after the successful completion of democratic transition. Therefore, early consolidation faces a higher level of political and social conflict than did the transition phase, except for the short initial period of systemic change in 1989–90. In some ways, history repeats itself, because the same conflict or the model of 'tyrannical majority' was attempted in the early 1990s, during the period of the first national-conservative Government. The problem of majoritarian democracy has recently re-appeared markedly in Hungary as a contradiction between long-term and short-term tendencies, i.e. between the most developed consensual democracy and the strong effort of the incumbent government in favour of power concentration. Thus, Hungary can be considered a classic case of the high level of conflict produced by early consolidation. However, under the new circumstances of Europeanisation, and given the structural determinants of former developments in consensual democracy, these majoritarian efforts are likely to fail. It is not by chance that the efforts of the third government to establish a quasi-majoritarian democracy in Hungary have already met with strong international and internal resistance.

The Europeanisation of the Hungarian polity

The Europeanisation of the Hungarian polity can also be divided between the periods of democratic transition and democratic consolidation that have developed more or less in parallel with the association and (pre-)accession stages of Hungary's involvement with European integration. The structural accommodation process in Hungary in the period of democratic transition and EU association experience was to some extent successful. The European Commission in 'Agenda 2000' issued its 'certificate' in July 1997 as the Commission's opinion on Hungary's application for membership of the European Union. However, the accession process has brought a new challenge to the Hungarian Polity, and meeting this challenge has proven to be more difficult than the former one. I distinguish in the Europeanisation of the Hungarian polity between the general and *particular* accommodation periods. The major tasks of structural adjustment in the first period covered mostly the general democratisation of the Hungarian polity, and in the second the much more detailed adjustment to the whole body of *acquis communautaire* has come to the fore.[15]

Hungary, like all of the associated countries, has established an institutional system for its contacts with the EU, the Association Council, the Association Committee and the Joint Parliamentary Committee. These intermediary institutions have served as channels for hard and soft policy transfer. That is, they have mediated both mandatory requirements and expectations in policy making. These joint institutions have been instrumental in the Europeanisation of the Hungarian polity but their elitist character has meant that their influence has been too remote and indirect even for most politicians, leaving aside the population at large. In addition, Hungary has created its own domestic institutional organs to manage Europeanisation. The Integration Secretariat has been established in the Ministry of Foreign Affairs, regulating both political and economic affairs, and supervising the activities of the ministries that have organised their own departments of European affairs.

These are only the top organisations, however; and while they are very important for Hungarian political and business life, they are too remote from them, and even more so from the life of the average citizen. In this new decade Hungary has to accomplish a breakthrough from a predominantly elite-led Europeanisation to a much more civil society-oriented European integration. The establishment of the intermediary organisations has also begun, although mostly as consultative fora and not involving participation in decision making, e.g. the trades union confederations have a European Integration Council and within its framework the government provides them with information four times a year. But, what is more important, both the organised interests and the territorial self-governments have directly contacted their EU counterparts (UNICE–ETUC in ECOSOC and the Committee of Regions) and they have regularly received information and support. The Hungarian regions have opened their common office in Brussels to gain direct access to information. Yet, the government is not yet ready to involve these actors in the domestic preparations, and even less ready to invite them to participate in the EU accession negotiations. The necessary 'parliamentarisation' of EU negotiations has also been missing so far in Hungary. Obviously, parliament has to serve as a forum for interest aggregation at the national level and it has to establish its own Grand Committee to take an active part in the EU negotiations, as it was in the case of the latest entrants (Austria, Finland and Sweden). The EU sub-committees have to be given much more scope for decision making in order to cope with the complexity of the EU 'policy universe' and to be prepared for 'comitology'. Thus, parliamentarisation together with an organised civil society could have been a major step towards the elimination of the performance crisis.

I have suggested above that the EU is both a reason for and a solution of the performance crisis. Indeed, the EU has clearly formulated the demand for the end of the performance crisis in the ECE countries. 'Agenda 2000' has clearly stated that the interest of the EU is 'to assess how democracy actually works in practice'. Instead of merely accepting the *acquis* as legal harmonisation, the EU has emphasised more and more its demand on the candidate countries to implement them in order to eliminate the 'implementation gap'. Hence, even officially, the performance crisis has become the biggest obstacle to the Europeanization of the Hungarian polity. The demand for increased administrative capacity to apply the *acquis* has figured in all country reports as a major requirement since the publication of the 'Agenda' for Hungary in 1997. However, significant improvement in the performance of the Hungarian political system, above all in the implementation of the EU requirements, presupposes the completion of consensual democracy or, simply put, the acceptance of the autonomous role of social and economic actors. In this respect, there has been a clash between the EU requirements and the efforts of the incumbent Hungarian Government to establish a quasi-majoritarian democracy. It is not by chance that the country report of the European Commission in October 1999 criticised the Hungarian Government for its majoritarian efforts. This criticism concerning power concentration by the incumbent government at the expense of the meso-politics and its actors was even more severe in the ECOSOC report on Hungary issued on 1 March 2000.[16]

The EU has always had a concept of consensual democracy and has in particular developed a demand for minority protection and representation in the decision-making bodies. Otherwise, there has been a long debate about the nature of the EU polity, including the character of its democracy and/or its democratic deficit. But, without entering into this discussion, I think that by and large the multi-actor character and the multi-level governance of EU policy making definitely proves its consensual character. At least, these above-mentioned consensual features have been part of the EU institutional system and Hungarian governments have to reckon with this.[17]

The increase in the consensual character of the EU institutions means that the particular requirements as entry conditions have been constantly redefined by the latest EU summit. Somewhat paradoxically, the EU has set higher standards for applicants than for its own members. The Amsterdam Treaty rigorously limits flexibility, since new members cannot have any 'opting out'; that is, they have to accept all decisions, including e.g. the Schengen *acquis*. This paradox, however, has played a positive role because it has pushed the ECE states, including Hungary, towards consensual democracy. Actually, the correction of the present 'asymmetrical' democracy means the establishment of those particular institutions in meso-politics in Hungary that are vitally needed for EU integration in order to fit into the system of EU institutions. Thus, the top organisations of organised interests are vital for social dialogue. In addition, some kind of regional assembly in Hungary is necessary to represent the territorial interests both in the Committee of Regions and at home. The present decade is about the early consolidation of the Fourth Wave democracies in ECE connected with accession to the EU, and its difficulties are as big as they were in the period of democratic transition.

Conclusion: the specifics of Hungarian democratisation

Hungarians have always appreciated the Polish breakthrough towards democratisation in the late 1980s. They have thought, however, that Hungary began everything earlier and more deeply in its own gradualist and evolutionary way. After the 1956 revolution this evolutionary approach and attitude in accepting compromise became the dominant pattern of Hungarian political culture, so that conflict-seeking politicians have never been popular in the democratisation period either. The population at large still remembers the significance of the early start in the second half of the 1980s, and there is still nostalgia for the Németh Government (1988–90), considered by many Hungarians as the government that prepared and initiated systemic change. Despite this revolutionary transformation, Hungarians have kept a strong continuity in this respect, notwithstanding both economic and political changes.[18]

Democratic transition, with its need for drastic economic crisis management and profound changes in the enterprise structure, was very painful in Hungary, but support there for extreme political forces has always been lower than in other ECE countries, or even in Western Europe. Hungarians have been very patient: there have been few mass demonstrations against poverty and high unemployment because Hungarians, allegedly famous for their pessimism, have actually been optimistic about economic recovery. They have, however, been very active politically in the defence of democracy, in recent years often demonstrating against right-wing extremism. At the civil-society level Hungary may be one of the most active participatory democracies in ECE.

At the institutional level Hungary has been a clear case of parliamentary democracy. Although this direction has also been strengthened in the other ECE countries, Hungary may be considered as that ECE country in particular where the parliamentarisation of democratic transition and consolidation has developed most. Similarly, as a result of its negotiated transition, Hungary has built up a system of consensual democracy, more developed in both qualitative and quantitative terms than elsewhere in ECE. In Hungary there has always been a strong emphasis on both the checks and balances system and on participatory democracy, including the involvement of organised civil society in decision making in relation to its constitutional design.

As we have seen, the problems of asymmetrical and fragmented democracy with a performance crisis have also derived from this consensual constitutional design, being easier to draft than to implement. The future will revolve around this topic, how Hungary manages to realise its potential for a genuine consensual democracy. For sure, there has to date been no significant political support for majoritarian tendencies. Transition fatigue after so many changes has also been felt in Hungary, but there has been no decline in the support for EU membership as there has been after 1997 in other ECE countries. Hungarians think that the worst is over, and this belief helps them to cope with the difficulties of the second decade of democratisation, too. Although they usually deny it, Hungarians are still proud to belong to the vanguard of the Fourth Wave transformations.[19]

Notes

1 In this chapter I summarise only briefly the democratic institution building in Hungary based on my former publications (e.g. Attila Ágh (1998) *Emerging Democracies in East Central Europe and the Balkans*, Cheltenham: Edward Elgar, pp. 73–112). I focus here on the new contradictions of early consolidation, indeed, 'ten years after'. The volumes of the Political Yearbook of Hungary (published annually by the Hungarian Centre for Democracy Studies since 1988), edited by Sándor Kurtán, Péter Sándor and László Vass, have collected all the data on Hungarian political life. All of my data are taken from these volumes.
2 Concerning the interactive approach, see the introductory chapter by Geoffrey Pridham (2000), 'Democratization of Balkan countries', in Geoffrey Pridham and Tom Gallagher (eds), *Experimenting with Democracy: Regime Change in the Balkans*, London and New York: Routledge, pp. 5–6. I introduce here some new concepts step-by-step to characterise the new situation more than a decade later. First, I briefly describe early consolidation; then comes the asymmetrical and fragmented character of the Hungarian polity are discussed together with the concept of performance crisis; and, finally, the debate between majoritarian and consensual concepts of democracy is considered. Not wishing to dwell upon the problems of procedural versus substantive democracy, I merely indicate here that these terms are parallel with those of transition and consolidation. Consolidation may also be connected with the 'quality of democracy'; as a stage in the process, it ends when a consolidated democracy emerges. I note also that most recent authors formulate the criteria of consolidation as overlapping with those of consensual democracy.
3 As a result of the Hungarian negotiated transition, the 'Polish solution' of a strong president was rejected in Hungary. The presidents have been elected by the Parliament for five years. Some parties have wanted a direct, popular election of the president, but this point has not created a deep cleavage between the political parties. The Hungarian intelligentsia played a very important mobilising role in preparing for democratic transition, and the same may be noticed now concerning the 'needs' assessment' for democratic consolidation.
4 Robert Jenkins (1999) 'The role of the Hungarian nonprofit sector in postcommunist social policy', in Linda Cook, Mitchell Orenstein and Marylin Rueschemeyer (eds), *Left Parties and Social Policy in Postcommunist Europe*, Boulder, CO: Westview Press, p. 176
5 Jon Elster (1992) 'On majoritarianism and rights', *East European Constitutional Review* 1: 3, pp. 22, 24.

6 Geoffrey Pridham has pointed out in several writings the significance of the trans-national party contacts for the development of the ECE party systems; see his recent paper, 'EU eastern enlargement, informal integration and transnational link-ages: towards party-political convergence in Europe?', paper presented at the Budapest UACES Conference, 6–8 April 2000.

7 Wolfgang Merkel (1999) *Systemtransformation*, Opladen: Leske & Budrich, pp. 161, 496. In the 1990s I co-edited a series of books in English analysing the phe-nomena of over-parliamentarisation and over-particisation in Hungary, see e.g. Attila Ágh and Sándor Kurtán (eds), *Democratization and Europeanization in Hungary: The First Parliament, 1990–1994*, Budapest: Hungarian Centre for Democracy Studies.

8 Terry Cox and Bob Mason (1999), *Social and Economic Transformation in East Central Europe*, Cheltenham: Edward Elgar, p. 124.

9 Fritz Plasser, Peter Ulram and Harald Waldrauch (1998) *Democratic Consolidation in East-Central Europe*, Basingstoke: Macmillan, p. 13, and Jacques Thomassen and Jan van Deth (1998), 'Political involvement and democratic attitudes', in Samuel Barnes and János Simon (eds) *The Postcommunist Citizen*, Budapest: Erasmus Foundation, p. 142. See also Dieter Fuchs and Edeltraud Roller (1998), 'Cultural conditions of the transition to liberal democracy in Central and Eastern Europe', in *ibid.*, p. 40.

10 See the public opinion data in Plasser *et al.*, *Democratic Transition*, pp. 87, 97.

11 See e.g. an interview with László Kovács, the Opposition leader, under the title, 'We do not share the concept and practice of democracy of the incumbent coali-tion government', published by the Budapest daily *Magyar Hirlap*, 15 January 2000.

12 There was a government reshuffling in the summer of 2000 which has even increased the power concentration in PMO and extended its competences.

13 During the Third Parliament even the definition of 'party fraction' has become vague and elusive. The electoral law puts a threshold of 5 per cent for the parties to enter parliament but the Standing Orders demand fifteen MPs for establishing a party fraction. These two criteria have come into conflict in the Third Parliament, since the PHJL reached the 5 per cent threshold but had only fourteen MPs (later twelve MPs), and the HDF did not reach the threshold but had seventeen MPs from the individual single-member constituencies. After a long constitutional debates both have been accepted, so the government has created two fractions in its support.

14 I have recently discussed the majoritarian–consensual democracy debate at length in my paper, 'Early consolidation and the crisis of the fragmented democracy: the majoritarian–consensual democracy debate in Hungary', in *West European Politics* vol. 24, No. 3 (July 2001). I briefly summarise it here. Jon Elster warned as long ago as 1992, in his above-quoted paper, about the danger of 'new despotism' through majoritarian tendencies.

15 I have described the Hungarian accession capacity and EU institutions in detail in my paper, 'Europeanization of policy-making in East Central Europe: the Hungarian approach to EU accession', *Journal of European Public Policy*, 6: 5 (1999). See also Alan Mayhew (1998), *Recreating Europe: The European Union's Policy towards Central and Eastern Europe*, Cambridge: Cambridge University Press.

16 'Agenda 2000. For a stronger and wider Union', Bulletin of the European Union, Supplement 5/97 (Luxembourg: European Commission 1997), (referred to as 'Agenda 2000'), p. 40; and 'Agenda 2000. Commission opinion on Hungary's application for membership of the European Union', *Bulletin of the European Union* Supplement 6/97 (Luxembourg: European Commission, 1997), p. 72.

17 Many analysts consider the EU polity as a consensual–consociational democracy; see e.g. J. H. H. Weiler (1997), 'Legitimacy and democracy of Union governance', in Geoffrey Edwards and Alfred Pijpers (eds), *The Politics of the European Treaty Reform*, London and Washington: Pinte, pp. 280–3.

18 The Government of Miklós Németh (1988–90), which initiated the profound economic and political reforms, has been very popular with Hungarians. As the recent public opinion surveys conducted by Ferenc Gazsó have shown, the popularity of the three ensuing governments has been the following: Horn (38 per cent), Orbán (17 per cent), Antall (16 per cent), none of them (17 per cent) and don't knows (12 per cent); see his research summary on party support edited by the József Attila Foundation (Budapest, February 2000, p. 19). During the period of Németh Government there were very active contacts with Spain to benefit from its democratization experiences, noted also by Samuel Huntington *The Third Wave* (1991), Norman and London: University of Oklahoma Press, pp. 101, 127, as the most characteristic demonstration effect.

19 At the time of writing this paper, the results of the latest public opinion surveys by the largest institutes show the lack of popular support for the majoritarian effort. The level of support for the HSP and Fidesz are the following percentages, respectively: 44, 32 (Szonda Ipsos) and 45, 36 (Tárki). The trend changed in favour of the HSP in July 1999. The first national conservative Government had also lost its popular support in 1994 because of its authoritarian–majoritarian tendencies. As far as EU support is concerned, according to a public opinion poll in late 1999, the fullest support is 63 per cent in Hungary, but only 46 per cent in Poland and 35 per cent in the Czech Republic (*Magyar Nemzet*, 25 November 1999).

The development of democratic institutions in post-Communist Poland

Democratisation and the electoral process

Elections were vital to the post-Communist democratisation process in Central Europe as well as to some elements of incipient consolidation. They were not the only motor of party system development, but they were the main such impetus, with new parties emerging at every election. Elections were less effective as vehicles of political participation and policy responsiveness; none the less discontent did not result in the mobilisation of anti-democratic forces. Protest groups made demands of democratic governments and disaffection led to electoral defeat for incumbent governments. Yet most stable democracies have serious flaws; and the insufficiencies of Central European democracy did not seem notably more profound than those of many other European democracies.

A system of free and fair competitive elections is the most important institutional mechanism of a functioning liberal democracy. It is the linchpin of all contemporary definitions of democracy. For some observers the very fact of holding competitive elections in Eastern Europe in 1990 confirmed that these political systems could now be regarded as 'democratic'.[1] This suggested that the events and processes which occurred before the election took place constituted the 'transition', while the subsequent events and processes were deemed part of a process of 'consolidation', itself closely associated with the routinisation of the electoral process.[2]

Such approaches quickly generated a response, pointing out that free elections do not alone make a democracy; free elections are a necessary but insufficient condition of democracy. Stress on elections risked falling prey to the 'electoralist fallacy'.[3] However, this view in turn needs to be qualified. There are three dimensions to the 'fallacy'. The first refers to a situation where elections provide a facade to hide the real locus of political power. This type of 'electoralist non-transition' occurs, for example, where the military 'retains such extensive prerogatives that the democratically elected government is not even *de jure* sovereign'.[4] This does not apply in Central Europe (though it may well apply to Russia, with its networks of economic oligarchies).

The second and third dimensions relate to the conceptualisation of democracy itself, namely whether it is conceived as a set of procedures or an essential 'substance'. Even procedural democrats should not equate a single, free, competitive national election with the achievement of 'democracy'. It is not the end of 'transition' but the beginning. It is the start of a *process* because the essential core of representative democracy is not just one moment of choice but a repeated process of competitive elections. The concept of liberal democracy has implications of process, since a 'free election' is predicated upon the notion of a subsequent free election, ensuring that power continues to reside with the people, providing them with a means for judging the quality and responsiveness of their representation and a method of orderly succession in government. It is this assumption of continuation that builds representation and accountability into the system: the electoral mechanism becomes a continual process for ensuring that representatives represent those whom they were elected to serve and are accountable to them (with accountability tested at the next election). Thus the routinisation of the electoral process is a condition of democracy itself, not of its 'consolidation'.

Participatory (substantive) democrats do not necessarily challenge the institutional format of representative government, but emphasise the insufficiency of elections for ensuring accountability and representation. They seek maximum inclusion, multiple mechanisms of participation and the democratisation of social institutions such as political parties and pressure groups or the workplace itself.[5] This participation deficit certainly applies to all post-Communist states, where the inherited political and socio-psychological obstacles to social self-organisation were legion. It has ideological elements too: whether in stressing the putative character of *homo sovieticus*, dependent and incapable of much initiative;[6] or in decrying the *trahison des clercs* and the perpetuation of old inequalities.[7] It is best regarded as a deficit, since its rigorous application would presumably leave all democracies labelled 'unconsolidated'.

The role of elections in a contemporary democratising polity is indeed different from that of a long-established democracy. Firstly, the conditions of democratic elections must often be established simultaneously and in parallel with their implementation. With the gradual democratisation of Western Europe, by the time the concept of 'free, democratic elections' gained currency, a whole series of these prior conditions was already in place for their realisation, if only imperfectly.

'Free elections' do not occur in a vacuum. An ideal–typical free election is a microcosm of democratic process and practice, both confirming and sustaining 'democracy'. It requires a capacity for public administrative efficiency and integrity to establish a register of eligible voters, to demarcate constituency boundaries, to confirm candidacies, to set up polling stations, to print ballots, to count votes and apply electoral formulae. It requires the capacity for free expression and public debate to ensure that the electoral mechanism embodies competition, i.e. that choices are meaningful. It requires freedom of association and assembly to develop some set of organisational linkages with society in order that candidates may be trawled/extracted and offered as 'representative'; historically, political parties provided such linkages and evolved and developed with major extensions of the franchise.[8] Lipset and Rokkan's model, for example, identified class, religious, centre–periphery and rural–urban conflicts as cleavages nurtured and consolidated not just by political parties but by meso-structures of civil society, such as trades unions, churches, local communities and the like.[9]

A free election also requires sufficient sense of political community and consensus to ensure acquiescence in, if not positive acceptance of, the results. It requires the embeddedness of the rule of law to make sure that rules are upheld, that disputes are resolved non-violently, that the winners take their seats. It also requires that the government generated by the electoral process should constitute the effective decision makers for society. Authoritative control of a territory, the rule of law and the acknowledgement of civil liberties are all fundamental features of the democratic state. Uncertainties about the state's boundaries and the community of citizens (the problem of 'stateness'[10]) may provide huge obstacles to democratic transition, and their resolution is surely a condition of consolidation.

Historically, in both the United States and Western Europe, it was liberalism's stress on the rule of law, limited government and individual rights that provided these prior conditions. The ensuing challenge of democracy, with its stress on popular sovereignty, to liberalism, emphasising the autonomy of the individual citizen and the need for limited government, created liberal democracy, replete with both philosophical and practical tensions.

Although the growth of 'democracy' was closely associated with the extension of the franchise, where liberalism was weak the 'democratic institutional context' making representation 'fair' and 'meaningful' was not necessarily in place: there were many 'electoral non-transitions'. The franchise was quite wide for the Russian Duma in 1906, but the Duma itself had virtually no power. Prussia had universal adult male suffrage from 1867, but again, parliament had little authority. Neither could be regarded as a democracy. The prerequisites were not in place and elites were not committed to democratic processes. This is why concepts such as 'electoral democracies' or 'delegative democracies' are of little use: these are not democracies; rather they are what used to be called 'quasi-democracies' or 'facade democracies'.

The question of *when* a country becomes 'a democracy' thus admits of no easy answers. Democracy is not a fixed, permanent end-state. Indeed, all democratic countries may still be regarded as 'democratising', for since the nineteenth century a major aspect of their political agendas has centred on the question of how to make the political systems *more* democratic: by extending the suffrage, by strengthening representative assemblies, by changing electoral laws to remove perceived flaws, by acknowledging new rights, by enhancing access to information . . . Democracy has been invented and reinvented ever since the first claim to democracy by the United States. As democratic discourse penetrated ever more deeply into the political fabric, vastly varied demands were and are justified by appeals to democracy. When democracies further democratise, they do in an evolutionary fashion, through existing institutional processes.

This distinction is not clear-cut either: Poland, Hungary and the Czech Republic democratised in this fashion after the profound changes of 1989–90. They marked the inauguration of democracy with free elections and contin- ⚡ ued to democratise through lawful mechanisms and processes. In Poland what might be termed an eight-year period of democratic transition can be neatly divided into two distinct parliamentary periods: one, from 1989 to 1993, of great institutional flux, conflict and uncertainty – but also of great achievement in setting Poland on a sound course of political democratisation and economic transformation; and a second of greater stability and, ironically, a relative conservatism. The final passage of a new Constitution and the removal of the socialist-led Government in 1997 after further elections broadly confirmed Poland's acceptance of the democratic 'rules of the game' and gave a good indication in concrete terms of the effective consolidation of democracy.

As the Introduction to this book makes clear, democratic consolidation initially involves the removal of uncertainties about features of the newly installed regime, like the nature of the constitution and general parameters of elite behaviour. Poland's acceptance of its new Constitution in 1997 and the emergence of a new pattern of elite behaviour reflected in the acceptance of democratic norms by the socialist government installed in 1993 (originally the object of widespread suspicion because of its roots in the former Communist regime) represented the removal of such early uncertainties. This opened the way for the institutionalisation of the new democracy, and reflected the progressive internalisation of the appropriate rules and procedures of democratic political life. As Poland developed as a parliamentary democracy structured along standard Western lines, in terms of party competition and government established on that basis, it was the institutionalisation of a party system and that of the parliamentary process within which it operated (aspects that receive most of our attention in this chapter) that provided the primary area of democratic consolidation. Both processes depended on the effective development of the electoral process, and this too was a major factor in the consolidation of Polish democracy.

One does not need to adhere to a strictly procedural conception of democracy to judge that the holding of competitive elections was the single most important factor driving the dynamic of democratisation and facilitating the consolidation of a new democratic order. Elections constitute a major step in the emergence of a party system and offer a sequence of developmental contexts for parliamentary institutionalisation. Poland's fourth competitive election since 1989 thus once more saw major government change and gave a strong indication that subsequent changes would take place within a democratic framework.

Poland's relatively numerous elections between 1989 and 1993 may well have been occasioned by the unfortunate structure of the first two democratic parliaments, the weakness of the basis they offered for effective party government and the general atmosphere of political turbulence. But these were not the result of some broadly conceived national characteristic or arbitrary concatenation of specifically Polish historical events. Questions of political sequence and the staging of particular phases of democratisation were important. To start with, Poland's status as a trend-setter of democratisation in the Communist world did not make its own path any easier. By holding the elections of June 1989 it made a major contribution to changing the whole structure of regional politics and, indeed, the entire global order, but it still had to face its own particular tribulations of regime change.

In doing so it turned its own half-way house of the initial 'contract' Parliament (the semi-democratic body that emerged from the bargain struck by the Communist leadership with Solidarity in 1989) into an immediate anachronism while giving an enormous boost to the pluralisation of its own society and that of East-Central Europe more generally. The relationship between regime pluralisation and socio-political change thus became a particularly uneven one in Poland, and its electoral sequence produced more problems for democratisation than was the case in some other countries. The pluralisation of Polish civil society was already well advanced when the first fully competitive election was held in October 1991, so the different aspects of democratisation were to this extent out of phase.[11] But the frequency of the early elections in Poland had certain advantages in accelerating the pace of an admittedly tortuous path of institutional development. The very discontinuity of Polish development and the shortening of parliamentary terms acted as a kind of self-regulating mechanism that protected the system against some of the consequences of its own operation.[12] In this fashion, the very turbulence of political change in Poland made its own contribution to the country's democratisation.

Party development in Poland

Overview 1989–99

The Polish 1989 agenda for change was not one of 'free' elections. Nor was the semi-competitive 1989 election designed as, though it proved to be, a plebiscitory occasion for passing judgement on the regime. Still 1989 may be classed along with the first free elections elsewhere in 1990 as a 'founding election', effectively a referendum on the Communist system. In this sense these elections marked the formal start of the process of democratisation, notable in Poland, Hungary and Czechoslovakia (and Slovenia) for their ringing popular endorsement of system change. Since only Hungary had anything resembling coherent political parties, the others generated elites that were in large part 'accidental', if united by their anti-Communism and desire for democracy. The formation of political parties then took on a central importance in the process of democracy building in its early stages.

Parliamentary elections were central to the development of the emerging party system in Poland, but presidential elections also played a role. The main dividing line between the old regime and the new was the 1989 election: while not fully competitive, it ended the effective monopoly of the Communist Party.

Successive elections then shook up various elements of the party system in different ways. 1989 broke the old PZPR (Communist Party) and brought Solidarity to the fore, but the 1990 presidential election destroyed Solidarity as a unified 'umbrella' movement. The 1991 parliamentary election demonstrated a continuing fragmentation of the Polish political scene: 111 myriad 'parties', groups and local committees contested the election, with some sixteen or so (under twenty-nine labels) gaining parliamentary representation and no party gaining more than 12 per cent of the vote. This chaotic parliamentary pluralism found its echo in weak, divided government and vertiginous changes in the political parties.

Introducing electoral thresholds to reduce the 'extreme' proportionality of the electoral system had the desired effect in 1993, when six parties entered Parliament; but about one-third of voters were effectively disenfranchised. The right wing constituted only a tiny presence in the *Sejm*, while the successor parties, the Social Democrat Party and Peasant Party, with little more of the vote, gained almost two-thirds of the seats.

The Social Democrat Aleksander Kwaśniewski's narrow presidential victory in 1995 strengthened the Left, but it also reflected and intensified a renewed polarisation of the Polish political scene. It did not serve and perhaps retarded the cause of party development. Only the Alliance of the Democratic Left (*Sojusz Lewicy Demokratycznej*, SLD) proved capable of mounting an effective campaign on behalf of its candidate. The remarkable revival of the non-party incumbent Lech Wałęsa in the first round provided no scope for the inter-party alliances characteristic of two-round majoritarian electoral systems. It demonstrated the importance of personality and the role of key individual actors in the unevenly institutionalised political system. Wałęsa's representation of the Right had no organised political basis, and it was for this reason that his personal defeat had a major impact on the developing party system.

Indeed, the presidential election shocked the fragmented ex-Solidarity parties into a new realism. The Solidarity trade union united numerous small parties and pressure groups under a new umbrella, AWS (Solidarity Election Action), and won a substantial victory in 1997. The number of parties in the *Sejm* fell to five (plus the German Minority). Two large blocs now dominated, AWS and the SLD, with the pivotal Freedom Union (*Unia Wolności*, UW) sandwiched between them, along with the now emaciated Peasant Party (*Polskie Stronnictwo Ludowe*, PSL) and on the fringe a small clerical nationalist party, the Movement for Rebuilding Poland (*Ruch Odbudowy Polski*, ROP).

In October 1998 local elections confirmed the growing importance of the established political parties, especially at provincial level (in the communes local committees took most seats). AWS and SLD continued to dominate: together they took 64.5 per cent of the vote. The Freedom Union saw its vote drop in comparison with 1997, as it appeared to take most of the blame for the failures of the Buzek Government. Outside parliament the Solidarity-inspired social-democratic Labour Union (UP) struggled to remain relevant. Its alliance with the PSL and the Pensioners' Party (KPEiR) in the local government elections was not very successful; and the UP distintegrated further,[13] losing hope of retaining a national presence. Only the PSL benefited from the alliance, though it was soon to find itself challenged by the mobilising capacity of the extra-parliamentary peasant Self-Defence (*SamoObrona*).

Evolution of the parties

Ten years after the Round Table election of June 1989 the political parties had undergone profound evolution. Up to 1993 the incipient Polish party system was characterised by a few credible parties along with a multiplicity of small ones possessing few resources and weak organisational links. Only the Social Democrat and the Peasant Parties could claim genuine bonds to their constituencies, but the former in particular continued to bear the stigma of its origins. Other parties, with the partial exception of the Democratic Union and the KPN, remained little known to the public. Party programmes were largely indistinguishable, and politicians were not seen as representing people's interests but rather as arrogant, corrupt and self-serving.[14] Leading figures changed their political allegiance frequently as the parties split, merged and changed partners.

In 1993 the number of parliamentary parties was sharply reduced (to six), but at the cost of generating an unrepresentative legislature that excluded the post-Solidarity Right. However the election also confirmed the full electoral legitimacy of the Democratic Left Alliance (SLD). Indeed, on the eve of the election one survey found that nearly half the respondents were indifferent to the idea of an SLD victory, while another 23 per cent were pleased.[15] The Social Democrat Party itself made the transition from a position of parliamentary isolation to governance with a degree of grace, while the high degree of policy continuity pursued by the SLD–PSL coalition (1993–97) confounded those opponents who had predicted a nightmare scenario of Communist restoration.

The dual shock of the 1993 election and the presidential victory of the SLD's Aleksander Kwaśniewski in 1995 spurred the small post-Solidarity parties to unity, culminating in AWS's electoral success in 1997. By this time the four significant parties – AWS, SLD, PSL and UW[16] – were increasingly experienced and professional, waging sophisticated election campaigns bearing little comparison with the palpable amateurism of 1991. All were 'programmatic parties'[17] standing on electoral platforms based on reasonably clear ideological principles and many specific policy proposals, albeit with considerable overlap among them. By now the early confusion of voters had given way both to increased public recognition of the main political actors and a stronger sense of party responsiveness. As late as September 1995 polls were still indicating public alienation: 58 per cent did not feel that any party represented their attitudes and interests.[18] The formation of AWS made a big difference. Six months before the 1997 election a CBOS survey found that 87 per cent of respondents could identify a party representing the 'interests of people like you'.[19]

At the same time the parties in power made full use of the extensive patronage opportunities available. These extended beyond the scope of the political to include scores of boards of directors and government agencies. Jadwiga Staniszkis referred to a 'cartel party system' by 1999, controlling access to the political market, co-operating under the guise of conflict.[20] This judgement is unpersuasive, but it indicates the difficulties of fitting the new parties into easy typologies.

Ideological divisions

Much has been written about the applicability of the 'Left–Right' divide to the party systems of the emerging democracies. Polish parties clearly identified themselves as 'Left' (the SLD and the moribund UP), 'Right' (AWS and the defunct ROP), and 'centre' (the PSL and the UW). This division held quite well in terms of value orientation, with AWS and ROP representing traditional Catholic values, SLD and UP being firmly secular, and PSL and UW embracing both traditionalist and secular elements. The policies of AWS and SLD in 1997 were clearly consonant with these values: they were divided over attitudes to the role of the Catholic Church, abortion, divorce, sex education, contraception, 'pornography' and a host of other social issues. For AWS this was particularly important. Along with its programme of 'historic reckoning', religion was its key identifying marker, binding together its heterogeneous elements. The link between patriotic sentiment and Catholic values formed a focal point of the 1997 programme, with the nation conceived of as a 'family of families' and the State to be firmly grounded in natural law.[21]

SLD in contrast linked itself firmly to traditions of 'European social democracy'. It 'supported a secular state with equal treatment for all, regardless of world view'. It elevated 'the rights and dignity of women, including the right to choose motherhood' (*prawo do wiadomego macierzyństwa*) to a high position in its election manifesto.[22] The Freedom Union, on the other hand, contented itself with support for the Concordat and a brief reference to the principle of 'amicable demarcation of the spheres of Church and state and their mutual co-operation for the common good'.[23] UW excluded moral–social issues from the coalition agreement and (mostly) left them to the individual consciences of its deputies. In practice only a handful of UW deputies voted with SLD or abstained after 1997 in order to support the coalition (which survived to June 2000), although notable exceptions included the refusal to vote to override the presidential veto of new anti-pornography legislation.

PSL for its part declared the principles of Catholic social doctrine a 'natural' part of its programme and ideology; 'we neither battle with the Church nor fall on our knees before it; but neither will we permit its marginalisation in public life'.[24] Its electoral broadcasts placed more stress on the Catholic Church and in Parliament its deputies mainly voted with AWS. In sum, the combined weight of AWS, UW, PSL and the few ROP deputies skewed the parliamentary party system to the Right on a secular–clerical axis after 1997.

The position was somewhat different in regard to the persistence of the historical division between the Communist establishment and the opposition. In one sense the divide was clear: on the one side the successor parties, SLD and PSL, versus the Solidarity parties, AWS and UW, on the other. AWS kept the division alive with its strongly anti-Communist rhetoric (it referred to the Social Democrats as 'Communists'). It kindled and rekindled the lustration issue. Yet to impute direct historical continuity would be to underrate the considerable changes in all four parties, as well as to exaggerate the extent to which the old divisions remained salient for society as a whole.

The heirs of Solidarity themselves remained keenly divided. Representatives of the old Solidarity 'ethos' became less visible in UW after Balcerowicz (himself only marginally associated with the Solidarity Opposition before 1989) became leader. AWS was not only anti-Communist but anti-liberal, with an antipathy to Balcerowicz's economic strategy running deep within the Solidarity trade union and most of AWS's other constituents. Moreover, UW was noted for its self-conscious cosmopolitanism and its less radical religiosity. With the partial exception of its self-styled 'conservatives', AWS attitudes to the successor PSL were in fact far more positive than those to UW, rooted deep in Solidarity.

On socio-economic issues the Polish ideological spectrum was skewed leftwards, within the framework of a general commitment to 'continuing reform' and a Western-oriented foreign policy based on NATO membership and EU accession. At the same time there were undoubted tensions between elites determined to press ahead with privatisation and maintain strict control over public finances and constituencies which demanded continuing protection from the dislocations arising from the move to the market economy. Poland's 'shock therapy', launched by Finance Minister Leszek Balcerowicz in 1990, had left an enduring impression; and both AWS and the Social Democrats contained strong champions of economic interventionism, not just from their respective trade union wings. Still, this broad consensus found expression in the high degree of policy continuity after 1989, regardless of the complexion of government.

Despite common perceptions of the fragility of Poland's new democracy in the early 1990s – in view of the fragmentation of the Parliament elected in 1991 and the instability of the governments it first installed, both of which occurred against a background of rapid economic transformation, soaring unemployment and declining GDP – the early problems of transition were rapidly overcome and the Polish prospects for democratic consolidation soon brightened. This rapid turnaround took place for a number of reasons. Polish 'shock therapy' was introduced at an early stage of post-Communist transition, and certainly with greater intensity and before any such measures in other East-Central European countries, but for this reason its early negative effects passed earlier and clear signs of economic recovery already made themselves felt from mid-1992. Poland regained its pre-1989 level of GDP well before any other East-Central European country, although this was as much due to the depressed state of its economy through the 1980s as to any miracle worked by economic 'shock therapy'.

The fragmentation of Poland's first freely elected Parliament and the problems of government formation and coalition maintenance that emerged on that basis were, too, more the consequence of an inappropriate electoral mechanism (proportional representation with no threshold) than some endemic defect of Polish political culture. This was rectified in 1993, and the pattern of party representation in Poland since then has not been very different from that in other countries of East-Central Europe. In this sense, the economic and political aspects of post-Communist transformation were not so closely linked as many observers suggested at the time, and reform of the pattern of electoral procedures did much to counteract the political instability that many saw as threatening the transition to democracy in Poland, let alone its consolidation. Once a more appropriate electoral mechanism was introduced, though, the advantages of early 'shock therapy' became more widely apparent, and the pattern of radical economic change and greater parliamentary stability proved to be highly positive for democratic development in Poland.

Those who anticipated the rapid emergence of a strong liberal party clearly reflecting the interests of the new capitalist entrepreneurs were mistaken. The small (if pivotal) UW was the nearest Poland came to this, with its *laisser-faire* leader stressing fiscal responsibility, privatisation and a reduced role for the state (Balcerowicz was once again deputy prime minister and minister of finance between October 1997 and June 2000). Even as its Social Democrat element weakened, UW retained a measure of ambiguity in its economic liberalism, with a vocal chorus reminding its leader of the need for compassion and social sensitivity. At the same time SLD also retained the allegiance of its own entrepreneurs.

In terms of ideology, therefore, all four parties had distinctive but overlapping ideologies within a common commitment to (some form of) democratic capitalism. There was relatively little programmatic structuring around economic issues and the two dominant electoral blocs embraced considerable heterogeneity in each. However the depth of the secular–religious divide between the two main blocs left a psychological gulf between AWS and the SLD (if not vice versa). The *perception* of the historical divide was also significant. It appeared to convince UW that its electorate would not tolerate an opening to the Left (although an opinion poll in May 2000 suggested that a SLD–UW coalition was the most popular combination, with 28 per cent support.[25]) This in turn left SLD leader Leszek Miller with little immediate hope of a strategy postulating the availability of UW as a potential coalition partner. In both Hungary and Slovakia the successor parties had proved able to work in coalition with parties originating in the anti-Communist opposition.

It seems a mistake however to see the party system as 'complete' by the end of the first decade, though this view was held by some observers.[26] 'Partial consolidation' would be more accurate, as sources of potential fluidity and change remained. In particular, much would depend on changes in party organisation, the nature of the new electoral system, and the nature of electoral mobilisation.

Comparative perspectives on party system formation

In most countries of the region three democratic elections further to the early 'founding' or 'constrained' ballots have now been held. In East-Central Europe something of a common two-party or two-bloc system seems to have emerged in the parliaments of four of the five countries.[27] One should not exaggerate the level of 'systemness' that can now be detected, and the broad pattern that seems to have formed represents at best an early development whose future is by no means assured. But in the relatively short period of ten years the emergence of such a pattern is quite striking, and from this vantage-point a process of relatively successful post-Communist development and even democratic consolidation in East-Central Europe can be identified.

Despite such problems of party growth and the general challenge of institutional development, the pattern of party representation in contemporary East-Central European parliaments has become both clearer and more positive in its implications for stable democratic government. Both the fragmentation of the Polish Parliament in 1991 and the virtual absence of right-wing representation in that elected in 1993 were largely overcome, though new uncertainties emerged with the collapse of the governing coalition in June 2000. In Hungary the strong dominance of the Left after 1994 has also been moderated. In Slovakia an opposition coalition won through in 1998 and brought to an end the long-lasting dominance of Vladimir Mečiar, although any further judgement on the nature and structure of Slovak politics must depend on the performance of the apparently rocky governing coalition. Slovenia, on the other hand, sits more firmly in the group of increasingly consolidated parliamentary democracies but remains dominated by a single party as the core of changing coalitions.

In Hungary and the Czech Republic, as in Poland, a strikingly similar structure of parliamentary party representation emerged, with two major parties each attracting around 30 per cent of the vote and together gaining a decisive majority of seats in the legislature. In each country there is also a third party whose level of electoral support places it in a somewhat stronger position than other minority parties. This points to the emergence not so much of two-party/bloc system, on the Westminster model, but more of a two-and-a-half party system in keeping with the proportional systems of other Western countries.

In the case of Poland's Freedom Union this position took it into a thirty-month governing coalition with the Solidarity Electoral Alliance. In Hungary the shrinking Democratic Forum proved a more amenable coalition partner for Fidesz than the Smallholders, but all three had to join forces to form an effective governing coalition. For a long time the continuing pariah status of the Communist Party in the Czech Republic barred it from deriving much political advantage from its reasonably strong parliamentary presence, but signs emerged that this situation might change as the Czech minority Social Democrat Government reconsidered its position in the summer of 2000. Significant differences in terms of governmental alignment thus accompany the broad similarities now apparent in the pattern of parliamentary party representation.

The establishment of parliamentary practices

As institutions, both political parties and parliaments have been regarded as critical components in the establishment of a democratic order. Parties provide indispensable forms of linkage between government, legislators and a democratic public, while parliaments form the arena in which the major societal interests meet and interact to form a viable democratic synthesis. This is no less true of contemporary processes of democratisation in East-Central Europe than in previous cases of regime change.[28] Different theorists may argue the priority of either institution, and specialists in each area of political organisation promote the special role of *their* particular agency in democratisation. But in practice it is the parallel development of both and the establishment of a reasonably harmonious working relationship between them that promotes democratisation and facilitates consolidation.

The conditions of the Polish democratic breakthrough exerted their own influence on the course of later political change. While it was the Solidarity movement that led the way to political transformation and regime change throughout the region as much as in Poland itself, it did not provide favourable conditions for the structural development of a democratic order in terms of the institutionalisation of party politics or commitment to the growth of parliamentary activity. In contrast to Hungary in this respect, party development did not progress with much despatch, and the activists of the Solidarity movement initially showed a distinct lack of enthusiasm for party politics.[29] Neither were they always eager to enter parliament and engage in the mundane aspects of organisation politics and legislative activity. The *Sejm* elected in 1989 showed a clear division between old and new forces, and Solidarity representatives were reluctant to lose their political purity and ethical superiority by entering parliament.[30] Both major institutions of liberal democracy were thus often regarded in a negative light, and the organisational development of a liberal democratic order was made that much more arduous in Poland.

The 'contract' *Sejm* elected on the basis of the agreement reached at the Round Table negotiations in 1989 thus had a distinctly problematic inheritance from the Communist period. Neither were conditions for harmonious parliamentary political activity or effective institutional development produced by the first fully free election of October 1991. Elected without a threshold to satisfy the interests of the contending groups in the previous Parliament, it too was sharply divided and characterised by acute political fragmentation. The pattern of representation was inherently unstable and party affiliations in the short-lived Parliament were very fragile. More than a quarter of all deputies, 123 representatives in all, switched party membership during the short life of the fragmented parliamentary body.[31]

Underlying the instability of Poland's first Parliaments and the low level of party development was a fundamental uncertainty surrounding its constitutional order. For some years Poland's new democracy had to operate according to the prescriptions of an amended Communist Constitution, which provided a somewhat more viable governing framework with the passage of the Little Constitution in December 1992. It was, nevertheless, far from satisfactory (not least in defining the balance between parliamentary and presidential powers) and still represented essentially the compromise devised in April 1989 which now had to operate under radically different conditions.[32] The passage of a new Constitution in May 1997, not long before the socialist-led Government lost power to a right-wing coalition in September, thus marked a further decisive step towards consolidation.

But overall, and despite the turbulent conditions and messy institutional arrangements of the early transition period, considerable progress was eventually made in terms both of parliamentary and party system development. The structural development of a revived *Sejm*, the influx of a younger generation of deputies, intensified activity and a range of constitutional innovations all reflected a growing parliamentary capacity to perform new democratic functions and a heightened level of political effectiveness.[33] The severe public dissatisfaction with the performance of new democratic institutions and the wave of disillusionment with post-Communist realities that succeeded the elevated political and economic aspirations accompanying the end of Communist rule eventually bottomed out, and the popular mood also gradually improved. The lowest net approval ratings for the *Sejm* were seen in July 1991 as well as between January and May 1993 – and thus towards the end of the two highly troubled Parliaments of the early transition period.[34] Although the sober realities of democratic political life meant that there was no return to the highly positive views expressed in 1989 and 1990, neither did the particularly negative opinions expressed between 1991 and 1993 re-emerge until mid-1999, when problems surrounding the governing coalition led to even higher levels of popular dissatisfaction.[35]

Associated with the general fluidity of political structures, and the problems of institutional development that have affected both parties and parliament in Poland, there has also been extensive ambiguity surrounding Solidarity as the country's primary agent of democratisation, its leading though multi-faceted political force and dominant national symbol. Solidarity representatives were doubtful from the outset both about transforming the social movement into a formal party and the nature of their involvement in the 'dirty' world of parliamentary politics. The unique context of the hyper-representative and highly fragmented Parliament in 1991 provided new opportunities for coping with such anxieties. While offering the newly emerged competitive parties an uncertain and very loosely structured framework for political activity, it gave Solidarity a good opportunity to present itself in rather a different guise, for which it was eminently well suited – that of an interest group representing a critical segment of Polish society. In this way its representatives could step aside from the struggle to gain legislative authority and resign from the competition for executive power. Its strategy in this context was relatively clear: it hoped to supervise government and influence the authorities' decisions without actually participating in the central processes of political rule.

Under the conditions that prevailed in early post-Communist Poland, it has been claimed, Solidarity was able to combine the role of interest group and political representative quite satisfactorily, although 'the situation was not always effective from an organisational point of view'.[36] Such a conclusion is something as an understatement, as it was precisely to this position and to the Solidarity trade union vote in 1993 that the fall of the Suchocka Government could be attributed, following which a left-wing Government ably managed by Communist-successor parties was in power for a full four years. A fundamental rethink among right-wing forces in Poland occurred after the election of Social Democrat leader Aleksander Kwaśniewski to the presidency in

November 1995. Solidarity's development away from the restricted role of interest group and its redefinition as a political force began before that, though, and it re-emerged as the author of a major constitutional initiative in the summer of 1994.[37] The final passage of the new Constitution in 1997 and subsequent election of a Solidarity-led coalition to government in September of that year clearly marked a new stage of political development both for Poland and for Solidarity as its leading force for much of the recent period.

In Poland, as elsewhere in East-Central Europe, both party development and effective parliamentary government increasingly depend on the capacity to form and maintain coalitions in the course of regular political activity. This has not been easy to achieve, although the critical area has now moved from that of electoral coalition making to that of government formation and the maintenance of ruling coalitions. In the first year of Solidarity Electoral Action's governing coalition with the Freedom Union, as many as thirty distinct conflicts had arisen and numbers in the 201-strong parliamentary club originally formed by Solidarity's deputies had fallen by fifteen. In early 1999 the coalition was again announced to be on the brink of collapse, and the Freedom Union did indeed withdraw in June 2000, leaving AWS as a minority Government. Solidarity's parliamentary leadership also still faced the problems of developing a non-union base and building an alternative support organisation outside the legislature.

A Solidarity Social Movement intended to provide this was set up in December 1997 but achieved little growth in its first year, numbers reaching 30,000 rather than the 300,000 first aimed for.[38] Accompanying this development (or lack of it), the Solidarity union again declared at its tenth Congress in September 1998 its commitment to remaining essentially non-political as an organisation: holders of political office were required to resign from major union posts or, alternatively, to leave politics. The union was still concerned to protect its status as an interest group rather than blurring it with the identity of some kind of party, although the promotion of Solidarity's 'Social Movement' showed that the commitment to party development was still a qualified one.

The problems faced by the political leaders of Solidarity Election Action and the Social Movement in this respect were by no means unique, although the form it took in their case had specific historical roots. Low levels of party membership and scant material resources in the face of escalating costs meant that all parties placed great reliance on their parliamentary fraction in maintaining the identity of the party and its activities in the country at large. No clear and simple dividing line could be drawn between the kinds of party bureaucracy.[39] This is another major way in which Polish parties remain highly 'parliamentarised', although this feature is by no means a specifically Polish characteristic.[40] The continuing links both of Solidarity Election Action and the Democratic Left Alliance with the membership, personnel and material resources of a major trade union still disguise this institutional weakness to a large extent, and even the supposedly large membership of the Polish Peasant Party and its legacy from the former Communist Party ally present a different picture from that of wholly new organisations. Before the 1997 election, though, activists of the Union of Labour were clear about the party's slender chances of survival were it to lose its parliamentary representation.[41]

After ten years or so of democratisation, too, the record of East-Central European parliaments is a mixed one. They have grown organisationally and performed the necessary functions quite successfully, but clearly remain underdeveloped in some areas and continue to face major problems of institutionalisation. After five years' experience the region's parliaments were deemed (rather prematurely in human terms) to have entered their adolescence and, despite evident weaknesses, to have achieved quite encouraging results in terms of institutionalisation.[42] They had, moreover, to perform in this short time three extremely complex 'choreographies', which involved constitution building, liberalisation of economy and society in terms of simultaneous democratisation and marketisation, as well as the institutionalisation and regulation of their own internal procedures and political interactions.[43]

Contrasting views have been expressed about the role of parliaments in the different phases of the democratisation process. Key negotiations and political decisions as the Communist Party was removed from power generally occurred outside the existing legislature, and according to Olson it was only Hungary, 'in which the parliament itself was a major source of change', that constituted the exception to this rule of general passivity.[44] Another view argues more for a 'centrality of parliament' thesis in which Hungarian, Polish and Slovenian parliaments all participated actively in demolishing the authoritarian system; only in Czechoslovakia did parliament become a central site of political action after the obstacles to institutional reconstruction had been cleared.[45] From this perspective the salience of parliaments lessened during the process of post-Communist change and with the consolidation of a democratic order as parliaments become just one actor among many. Parliaments became less central to the pattern of change and the early 'over-parliamentarisation' of the post-Communist order declined as a form of 'rational parliamentarism' emerged.

But, regardless of the relative place of parliament and the party system in the political order as a whole, ambiguities remained in the relative position and role of these critical forms of democratic organisation in contemporary East-Central Europe. In some ways parliaments have had a clear priority in the democratisation process. But the parliamentary conditions of party development soon changed. As parliaments were 'rationalised' electoral thresholds were raised, which, combined with the benefits of prior organisation and the early occupation of prime ideological sites in the political arena, gave many of the parties formed during the first phase greater political impetus, a higher level of resources and more staying power than the late arrivals. The implications were in this area quite clear: parliamentary parties enjoy a definite comparative advantage. To this extent the new parliaments of the region, still relatively underdeveloped and in a state of early formation, found their activities increasingly limited both by more experienced executives and by the growing strength of the political parties increasingly well rooted within them.[46]

There is, however, something of a developmental paradox here. Party strength might be identified as one obstacle to the development of parliamentary autonomy, but deficiencies of party organisation within parliaments may also be seen as a major weakness in the further institutionalisation of post-Communist legislatures. They continue to occupy an 'ambiguous status', while the nature of party formation within them is still fluid and partial in character; they display a 'relative inability to control their own members', have weak discipline and form shifting alliances with other party groups.[47] Even though party groupings within the parliaments gain importance, the process of fraction institutionalisation is delayed and internal organisation remains partial.[48] The relationship between parties and parliaments as institutions remains an ambiguous one in the new democracies of East-Central Europe. Continuing party weakness is one aspect of the underdevelopment of post-Communist legislatures, but relative party strength may also be a challenge to the institutionalisation of parliaments' own practices.

The institutionalisation of a party democracy?

Organisational format

For AWS and SLD the issue of party organisation remained salient, since the 1997 Constitution specified the nomination of parliamentary candidates by 'political parties' and electors (Article 100, paragraph 1), and not as hitherto parties and 'social organisations'. Although the issue would not be settled until changes were made in the electoral system, needed first for the presidential election of 2000 and then for the parliamentary elections of 2001, both parties moved to reconsider the 'electoral party' format. AWS had been plagued from the outset by the issue of relations between the Solidarity trade union and its small political parties and groups, and from October 1997 also between the parliamentary party and the Government. The attempt to establish the AWS Social Movement (*Ruch Społeczny*) as the trade unionist party of AWS (12 December 1997) at first aroused little interest, though it rapidly became the largest element of AWS's parliamentary club. By the end of 1998 it embraced some 100 deputies.[49] By its first congress in January 1999 RS had gained considerable momentum as the 'party of power', and it incorporated a number of AWS's smallest groups. Since Solidarity had decided to separate party and union leadership, Prime Minister Buzek replaced Marian Krzaklewski as RS's leader. RS dominated AWS, which had been creeping

Table 16   *Changing attitudes (%) to the Government of Jerzy Buzek*

	December 1998	January 1999	February 1999	March 1999 (1)	March 1999 (2)
Supporters	40	36	36	35	27
Opponents	20	27	33	35	37
Indifferent	36	33	28	27	31
Hard to say	3	4	3	3	5

Sources: K. Pankowski, 'Stosunek do Rządu w Marcu', *Biuletyn informacyjny* 5 June (1999), Warsaw: CBOS, June 1999, Table 1, p. 21; CBOS data in *Polityka* 16, 1 May (1999).

hesitantly towards a formal federation. The Polish political sociologist Tomasz Żukowski said 'The (RS) Congress completes the building of the Polish party system. The Movement has occupied the last available political space.'[50]

Such a judgement seemed over hasty. RS had no public identity as a 'political party' separate from AWS. Its 'key issues' of mass distribution of state property (*powszechne uwłaszczenie*), a pro-family tax policy, and a 'less lenient' penal policy were those of the broad AWS programme and did not distinguish it from other AWS elements. Given its aspirations to attract a large trades unionist membership, its membership remained small (some 35,000), while its relationship with Solidarity was still highly opaque.

The conversion of AWS into a federal political party appeared no closer by the autumn of 2000, as a variety of tensions plagued the parliamentary club. One problem stemmed from the obvious asymmetry that developed between RS on the one hand and the Christian nationalist element (with about thirty-one deputies, mostly from the Christian National Union, ZChN); the Christian democratic element and the conservative Conservative–Peasant Party (*Stronnictwo Konserwatywno-Ludowy*, SKL, with about twenty-three) on the other. The latter elements had consistently demanded a greater role, but they had no options when threats to withdraw from AWS ('our patience is wearing thin', said Hall[51]) fell on deaf ears. The ZChN was left 'humiliated and insulted' as its two candidates were rejected for provincial governorships.[52] The issue of a presidential candidate also caused anxiety, and Solidarity leader Marian Krzaklewski was slow to declare his candidacy. Government popularity waned (see Table 16), while the president was highly regarded (see Table 17).

Moreover, efforts to increase mechanisms of party discipline had not been notably successful within AWS, with deputies submitting a vast array of individual legislative initiatives and not only individual deputies but even government ministers frequently voting against the Government. It remained unclear how this disparate grouping would respond to the vagaries of minority government after UW withdrew from the Government in the summer of 2000.

Table 17   *Attitudes (%) to state institutions (March 1999)*

Institution	Positive attitudes	Negative attitudes
President	64	17
Senate	20	47
Sejm	52	–
Government	18	56

Source: PBS data from *Rzeczpospolita* 72, 26 March (1999)

If the potential for some unravelling of AWS seemed considerable, the SLD appeared rather more secure. Unlike Solidarity, where AWS had stood on a common programme and where the trade union leaders created the new RS–AWS, the SLD was composed of thirty-two organisations, with the Social Democrat Party providing the political leadership. The process of government formation in 1993 had not depended (as with AWS) on attempts to placate the various wings of the electoral party. Tensions within SLD surfaced occasionally, but they were less public than those that convulsed the post-Solidarity camp from time to time. Moreover, SLD had already been tested over time, with its share of the vote increasing at successive elections from 1991. Indeed, the impetus to organisational change remained unclear, since the formal reason (the constitutional requirement) was not wholly convincing. Debate over the transformation of SLD had predated the Constitution, and the Social Democrat leader Leszek Miller had for some time advocated a single united political party (as distinct from a federation of parties, also mooted) to inject a new dynamism. In the event the new party, still called SLD, was established without incident and embraced most but not all existing affiliates to its progenitor.

By the time of the presidential election campaign in the summer of 2000, then, SLD was establishing its new organisational format, while AWS remained in turmoil. Each was all but assured of retaining the support of the two opposing trade union movements, part of the historical legacy carried forward throughout the first post-Communist decade. Some form of AWS and SLD would persist, but the short-term strategic decisions would reflect not only internal power relations within the two blocs but their perceptions of the implications of the new electoral system.

The electoral system

The need for a new electoral law stemmed from the extensive administrative reorganisation of 1998, with sixteen new provinces in place of the previous forty-nine and a second county tier. From 1993 electoral districts had been based on the provinces, not only for the Senate (which retained two senators from each province, but three each for Katowice and Warsaw) but now for the *Sejm* (one district per province, with two for Warsaw and three for Katowice). Although in its 1997 electoral programme AWS had campaigned in favour of a shift from a proportional to a majoritarian system, it could not alone amend the constitutional requirement for a proportional system. The small parties adamantly opposed such a change. At one time speculation centred on possible co-operation between AWS and SLD (as similarly mooted in the Czech Republic) with a view to further entrenching their dominance. This looked unlikely, not least because the chasm between the two remained as wide as ever. Indeed, SLD itself responded to AWS with an increasingly confrontational stance. Nor was AWS itself united on the majoritarian principle, with its conservative wing showing a degree of sympathy for the Freedom Union (UW).

By the summer of 2000 the shape of the new parliamentary electoral system remained an imponderable in the political equation. The absence of an agreed electoral law left the parties in a situation of uncertainty, compounding the organisational quandaries of the two major blocs. Overall uncertainty had greatly diminished after since 1991, for the political actors had gained a far better grasp of the ways in which electoral arrangements created incentives for political action, as well as a sense of the nature and distribution of their potential electoral support. At the same time voting patterns (and non-voting) could not be regarded as fully entrenched. The population was certainly less consumed by the historical–ideological divisions than was AWS. This was attested by the consistently large proportion of 'don't knows' or 'hard to says' in opinion polls regarding political attitudes and affiliations. It was also illustrated by persistently high levels of endorsement of Aleksander Kwaśniewski and his presidency, never sinking below a substantial majority. The ability of voters themselves to generate shocks to the political system should, however, not be ignored as a source of potential change in the evolving party system.

Electoral mobilisation

Following the onset of system change, observers remained divided in their assessments of the way in which the population itself might upset the applecart of democratisation. Some saw the process of building democracy in Poland as confounding this view. Others retained a persistent anxiety that a large group of disaffected elements of society remained available for potential anti-democratic mobilisation.[53] Two factors fed the latter view. One was the recurring waves of protest, notably in the summer of 1992 and again from the winter of 1998–99. Despite Poland's strong economic growth from 1993 onwards, strikes and demonstrations were frequent, especially by workers, peasants and public-sector employees. Yet Grzegorz Ekiert and Jan Kubik have argued forcefully that protest was not dysfunctional to the development of democracy; on the contrary it provided testimony to the vibrancy of democratic politics.[54] Protest was not 'anti-system' but rather a legitimate outlet

Table 18   *Voter turnout (1989–97)*

Type of election	Date	1st/sole ballot (%)	2nd ballot (%)
Parliamentary	June 1989	62.0	25.3
Local government	May 1990	42.3	
Presidential	Nov.–Dec. 1990	60.6	53.4
Parliamentary	October 1991	43.2	
Parliamentary	September 1993	52.1	
Local government	May 1994	33.8	
Presidential	November 1995	64.7	68.2
Referendum	February 1996	32.4	
Referendum	May 1997	42.8	
Parliamentary	September 1997	47.9	
Local government	October 1998	46.2[a]	

Note:
[a] Average for provincial, county and commune elections
Source: Compiled from data of the Państwowa Komisja Wyborcza (State Electoral Commission)

for the frustrations and dislocations of the process of economic transformation and the visible emergence of new social inequalities characteristic of post-Communist transformation.

The second factor was the large numbers who remained outside the electoral process. Only the 1995 presidential election generated participation even broadly commensurate with that of West European elections (see Table 18). The highest turnout – 68 per cent for the second ballot in 1995 – occurred in the close contest between Kwaśniewski and Wałęsa. The lowest was 25 per cent in the second ballot of the 'Round Table' election, when Solidarity had already triumphed. Excluding 1989, the lowest figure was 32.4 per cent for the abortive property rights referendum of 1996, initiated by President Wałęsa (a 50 per cent turnout was needed to bind parliament); here even informed observers failed to grasp its significance and implications. Historical 'Austrian Poland' had the highest turnout and 'Russian Poland' the lowest. Aside from this pattern, survey evidence indicates that non-voters neither knew nor cared much about politics, were rather pessimistic and did not participate in other forms of socio-political activity.[55] This did not make a sudden upsurge of mobilisation appear likely. However, the low levels of participation showed considerable potential for substantial changes in turnout with shifts in the public mood.

Conclusion

There is little doubt about the democratic nature of the electoral process in Poland after 1989. Many of the prerequisites of free elections were in place by

1989. After the distinctive semi-competitive election of June 1989, parliamentary, presidential and local elections confirmed the ease of 'electoral transition'. Elections were conducted fairly, without violence, intimidation or corruption. Every national election from 1989 to 1997 resulted in the peaceful transfer of power; in no case did the incumbents retain office. The electoral process itself was important in terms of the classical functions of liberal democracy. It was also the major motor of political party development. Changes in the electoral system contributed to the shaping of party behaviour and the voters' response. Election results and the consequent patterns of parliamentary representation eliminated some parties and forced others to rethink their strategies, their structures and their relationships with one another. There was no reason to suppose that this would not continue beyond the first decade. SLD in particular looked less likely to suffer a profound dislocation in the short term. AWS retained a greater heterogeneity. Both main 'parties' had peculiar features explicable by their origins. The institutional framework was not static either, with a future reshaping of the electoral system demanded by the changes in the country's administrative structure.

Poland clearly met conventional procedural criteria of consolidation, seen in terms of institutionalisation and the reduction of uncertainty. Elections became routinised. They fostered the development of an emerging party system based on stable patterns of interaction. Their rules were modified by elite consensus through processes of elite learning and adaptation. Within the evolving constitutional framework of parliamentary democracy elections determined government formation in predictable ways and legitimised the political institutions. The process was neither smooth nor inevitable: it was fraught with signs of instability and potential crisis. But it confounded the early views of many pessimists, who feared that the complexities and dislocations of multiple transition would undermine infant democratic practices and processes.[56] It is certainly the case that substantive flaws persist, as indeed elsewhere in Europe. It is also the case that the new democracy has not been tested by major crisis. Yet these democratic processes and practices were observable from 1989 onwards. Elites responded rapidly to the 'imperatives of democratisation'. There is no point at which it suddenly became something of a different order, 'consolidated' democracy. Democracy was from the outset the 'only game in town'.

Notes

Frances Millard would like to acknowledge the support of the ESRC's 'One Europe or Several?' programme in supporting the work for this paper as part of the Elections and Post-Communist Transformation Project (L213 25 2021).

1 Clive Tempest and Dean McSweeney, 'The political science of democratic transition in Eastern Europe', *Political Studies* 41: 3 (1993), pp. 408–19.

2 For example Samuel Huntington, *The Third Wave. Democratization in the Late Twentieth Century*, Norman, OK, and London: University of Oklahoma Press, 1991, pp. 266–7.

3 Juan Linz and Alfred Stephen, *Problems of Democratic Transition and Consolidation. Southern Europe, South America, and Post-Communist Europe*, Baltimore and London: Johns Hopkins University Press, 1996, p. 4. Frances Millard made this point in 'The Polish parliamentary elections of October 1991', *Soviet Studies* 44: 5 (1992), p. 837.

4 Linz and Stepan, *Problems of Democratic Transition*, p. 4.

5 Carole Pateman, *Participation and Democratic Theory*, Cambridge: Cambridge University Press, 1970.

6 Piotr Sztompka, 'The intangibles and imponderables of the transition to democracy', *Studies in Comparative Communism* 24: 3 (1991), pp. 295–311.

7 Bill Lomax, 'The strange death of 'civil society' in post-Communist Hungary', *The Journal of Communist Studies and Transition Politics* 13: 1 (1997), pp. 41–63.

8 See Leon D. Epstein, *Political Parties in Western Democracies*, rev. edn, New Brunswick and London: Transaction Publishers, 1980, pp. 19–45.

9 S. M. Lipset and Stein Rokkan, 'Cleavage structures and voter alignments: an introduction', in S.M. Lipset and Stein Rokkan (eds), *Party Systems and Voter Alignments*, New York: Free Press, 1967.

10 cf. Linz and Stefan, *Problems of Democratic Transition*, pp. 16–37.

11 J. Simon, 'Electoral systems and regime change in central and eastern Europe, 1990–1994', *Representation* 35: 2–3 (1998), pp. 122–3.

12 I. Jackiewicz and Z. Jackiewicz, 'The Polish parliament in transition: in search for a model', in A. Ágh and G. Ilonszki (eds), *Parliaments and Organised Interests: The Second Steps*, Budapest: Hungarian Centre for Democracy Studies, 1996, p. 366.

13 Eliza Orczyk, 'Założyciele odeszli', *Rzeczpospolita* 293, 15 December (1998).

14 See, for example, I. Krzemiński, 'Sami sobie damy radę?', *Rzeczpospolita* 283, 2 December 1992; J. Czapiński, 'Partie w (krzywym?) zwierciadle swoich zwolenników', *Rzeczpospolita* 302, 24–7 December 1992.

15 *Rzeczpospolita* 220, 20 September 1993; by law the findings could not be published before the election.

16 Excluding the virtually defunct ROP.

17 Herbert Kitschelt, 'Formation of party cleavages in post-communist democracies: theoretical propositions', *Party Politics* 1: 4 (1995), p. 449.

18 PBS data in *Rzeczpospolita* 221, 23–4 September 1995.

19 *Gazeta Wyborcza*, 17 April 1997.

20 Małgorzata Subotić, 'Nie mam dobrego słowa' (interview with Jadwiga Staniszkis), *Rzeczpospolita* 84, 10–11 April 1999.

21 'Program Akcji Wyborczej Solidarność. Lista nr 5' (leaflet), Warsaw, May 1997.

22 'Dobre Dziś-Lepsze Jutro'. Program wyborczy Sojuszu Lewicy Demokratycznej, Warsaw: Patria, 1997, p. 1.

23 *Unia Wolności, Wolność. Bezpieczeństwo. Rozwój. Program Unii Wolności*, Warsaw: Krajowy Sztab Wyborczy Unii Wolności, 1997, p. 7.

24 'Polskie Stronictwo Ludowe. Lista nr 7', Warsaw: PSL, 1997.

25 *Rzeczpospolita* 25 May 2000.

26 This is the view of Radosław Markowski, for example; see A. Kublik, 'Potencjał szantażu UW: Rozmowa z politologiem dr Radosławem Markowskim' (interview with Radosław Markowski), *Gazeta Wyborcza*, 15 October 1998.

27 This discussion refers to Hungary, Poland, Slovakia, Slovenia and the Czech Republic, a grouping which involves a broader geographical conception of the region than that used by some but one that makes good sense in contemporary political terms.

28 M. Cotta, 'Building party systems after the dictatorship', in G. Pridham and T. Vanhanen (eds), *Democratization in Eastern Europe*, London: Routledge, 1994, p. 100; P. Kopecky, *Parliaments in the Czech and Slovak Republics: Party Competition and Parliamentary Institutionalization*, Aldershot: Ashgate, 2001.

29 P. G. Lewis, 'Political institutionalisation and party development in post-communist Poland', *Europe–Asia Studies* 46: 5 (1994), pp. 785–94.

30 I. Panków, 'Posłowie Sejmu X Kadencji. Fenomenon tożsamości polityzcznej', in J. Wasilewski and W. Wesołowski (eds), *Początki parlamentarnej elity*, Warsaw: Wydawnictwo Instytutu Filosofii i Socjologii PAN, 1992, p. 240.

31 S. Gebethner (ed.), *Polska scena polityczna a wybory* Warsaw: Wydawnictwo Fundacji Inicjatyw Społecznych, 1993, p. 8.

32 T. Mołdawa, 'Parlament w systemie władz naczelnych Rzeczypospolitej', in R. Chruściak (ed.), *Polski system polityczny w okresie transformacji* Warsaw: Elipsa, 1995, p. 223.

33 M. D. Simon, 'Institutional development of Poland's post-communist Sejm: comparative analysis', in D. M. Olson and P. Norton (eds), *The New Parliaments of Central and Eastern Europe* London: Frank Cass, 1996, p. 79.

34 Jackiewicz and Jackiewicz, 'Polish parliament in transition', p. 377.

35 *Polityka*, 3 July 1999.

36 I. Jackiewicz, 'Solidarity in a double role: political representation and pressure group, 1991–1994', in *Parliaments and Organised Interests, The Second Steps*, pp. 122–4.

37 *Ibid.*, p. 127.

38 *Polityka*, 16 January 1999.

39 A. Szczerbiak, 'The 'professionalization' of party campaigning in post-communist Poland', in, P. G. Lewis (ed.), *Party Development and Democratic Change in Post-Communist Europe* London: Frank Cass, 2001.

40 I. van Biezen, 'The relationship between the party in public office and the extra-parliamentary party in new democracies', paper presented at the ECPR Joint Sessions, Warwick (1998).

41 A. Szczerbiak, 'Testing party models in East-Central Europe: local party organisation in post-communist Poland', *Party Politics* 5: 4 (1999), p. 532.

42 D. M. Olson and P. Norton (eds), *The New Parliaments of Central and Eastern Europe*, London: Frank Cass, 1996, p. 242.

43 D. Judge, 'East Central European parliaments: the first steps', in A. Ágh (ed.), *The Emergence of East Central European Parliaments: The First Steps*, Hungarian Centre of Democracy Studies, Budapest, 1994, p. 30.

44 D. M. Olson, 'The parliaments of new democracies and politics of representation', in S. White, J. Batt and P. G. Lewis (eds), *Developments in Central and East European Politics*, London: MacMillan, 1998, p. 129.

45 G. Ilonszki, 'From marginal to rational parliaments: a Central European regional view', in *The Second Steps*, p. 452.

46 Olson and Norton, *New Parliaments*, p. 241.

47 Olson, 'Parliaments of new democracies', pp. 135, 137–8, 143.

48 Ilonszki, 'From marginal to rational parliaments', p. 460.

49 M. D. Zdort, 'Nie musimy być w Akcji', *Rzeczpospolita* 298, 21 December 1998.
50 Quoted in Dorota Macieja, 'Ruch w Akcji', *Wprost* 4, 24 January 1999.
51 Quoted in *Rzeczpospolita*, 22, 27 January 1999.
52 Quoted in *Rzeczpospolita* 52, 3 March 1999.
53 See the views of Edmund Wnuk-Lipiński and Paweł Spiewak cited in Mariusz Janicki, 'Niezadowoleni', *Polityka* 24, 13 June 1998.
54 Grzegorz Ekiert and Jan Kubik, *Rebellious Civil Society. Popular Protest and Democratic Consolidation in Poland, 1989–1993*, Ann Arbor: University of Michigan Press, 1999.
55 K. Skarzyńska and K. Chmielewski, 'Obawy Polaków a preferencje wyborcze', *Rzeczpospolita* No. 247, 22 October 1991; Radosław Markowski, 'Milcząca Większość – O Bierności Politycznej Społeczeństwa Polskiego' in Gebethner (ed.), *Wybory . . . 1991 i 1993*, pp. 57ff.; CBOS, 'Nieobecni w wyborach – przyczyny absencji wyborczej', Komunikat z badań BS/132/132/97, Warsaw, CBOS, October (1997). One problem with survey data is the unwillingness of respondents to acknowledge non-voting; thus a poll conducted shortly after the 1997 election found responses indicating a turnout of 65 per cent compared to the actual figure of 47.9 per cent: see PBS data in Renata Wróbel, 'Raczej bierni niż zbuntowani', *Rzeczpospolita* 247, 22 October 1997.
56 Claus Offe, 'Capitalism by democratic design? Democratic theory facing the triple transition in East Central Europe', *Social Research* 58: 4 (1991), pp. 865–92; Grzegorz Ekiert, 'Democratization processes in East Central Europe: a theoretical reconsideration', *British Journal of Political Science* 21: 3 (1991), p. 309; A. Ágh, 'The transition to democracy in Eastern Europe', *Journal of Public Policy*, April/June (1991), pp. 133–51.

The path to democratic consolidation in the Czech Republic and Slovakia: divergence or convergence?

The Czech Republic and Slovakia are particularly valuable case studies in looking at democratisation and democratic consolidation because, as the state of Czechoslovakia, they had much in common for most of the twentieth century. Yet after the division of Czechoslovakia at the end of 1992, their trajectories have differed markedly. They can thus provide some interesting insights into the conditions which facilitate democratic development, since the similarities in their recent history make it easier to control the variables which may have led to the later divergence in their paths.

However, these paths have not been straightforward. In the 1990s, the Czechs appeared to be proceeding towards democratic consolidation,[1] while Slovakia was increasingly viewed as veering in a more authoritarian direction, variously described by political scientists as 'dysfunctional democratisation'[2] and 'nationalist populism'.[3] The Czechs' image had been helped in part by the fact that they took over the most positive symbols of post-1989 Czechoslovakia: the noble dissident playwright-president Václav Havel and, as prime minister, the dynamic economic reformer Václav Klaus. By contrast, the only famous and internationally revered Slovak, Alexander Dubček, had tragically died after a motorway accident in the autumn of 1992 and has therefore remained a symbol of the 1968 'Prague Spring', never entering the international consciousness as a Slovak politician. Instead, the single international image of Slovakia became Vladimír Mečiar, the Slovak prime minister who remained, into the new millennium, a symbol of all that was undesirable about the new Slovakia. Unlike Havel and Klaus, he had been (albeit very briefly) a member of the Communist Party, and was viewed as the man who had forced the division of Czechoslovakia by exploiting an unhealthy and intolerant Slovak nationalism inamicable to the post-Communist reform process.

The international images changed little in the mid-1990s. More complex analyses of the demise of Czechoslovakia began to prevail and it was recognised that Klaus's intransigence had precipitated the split at least as decisively as had Mečiar's pragmatic willingness to secure leadership by mobilising nationalism. But, by this point, Slovakia was already being viewed with suspicion because of developments after independence. Privatisation slowed down, and relations with the Hungarian minority deteriorated. Although Mečiar lost his parliamentary majority and was replaced as prime minister in March 1994, the electorate returned him to power in the autumn 1994 elections. Having, for more than two months, attempted to find more respectable partners, he finally formed a coalition Government with the Slovak National Party and the maverick far-left Workers' Association of Slovakia. This unfavourable constellation was to become the first Slovak government to remain in office for a full four-year term. In the Czech Republic, however, the centre-Right coalition Government led by Klaus which had been formed after the June 1992 elections not only lasted a full four years, but was re-elected in June 1996. This almost unique occurrence in the post-Communist world of the time was a reflection largely of the economic well-being felt by the Czechs, who enjoyed by far the lowest unemployment rate in East-Central Europe.

The difference in developments in the Czech and Slovak Republics was confirmed in July 1997, when the two states were placed in different groups in both the NATO and EU enlargements processes. The Czech Republic, Hungary and Poland were invited to negotiate NATO membership, and actually joined in March 1999, while Slovakia, which had originally also been one of the leading candidates, was excluded.[4] Similarly, the European Commission recommended that the EU should open entry negotiations with the Czech Republic, Estonia, Hungary, Poland and Slovenia, but placed Slovakia in the unaccustomed company of a 'second group' comprising Bulgaria, Latvia, Lithuania and Romania.[5] It should be noted that these were all states with radically lower standards of living than Slovakia.[6] Slovakia had been turned down by both NATO and the EU for political reasons.[7]

The divergence in the political and economic courses of the Czech and Slovak Republics seemed to provide a simple explanation for the division of Czechoslovakia: the two republics were clearly very different. However, the late 1990s saw the trajectories of the two suddenly turn towards convergence. The Czech Republic was hit by a crisis in 1997. The country's neglected economic weaknesses became obvious in May 1997, when it underwent a currency crisis: GDP growth rates approached nil, taking until 2000 to grow again; and unemployment began to rise. The Government fell apart in November 1997, as Klaus's party split and was abandoned by its coalition partners, and it was replaced by a 'technocratic' caretaker Government led by the governor of the Czech National Bank. Early elections were held in June 1998, and the Social Democrats came to power, albeit with a minority Government. However, the 'crisis' bore more resemblance to the sporadic crises faced at some point by most western democratic states,[8] rather than being a dramatic post-communist crisis likely to endanger democracy.[9] In general, the fact that alternation of power had taken place was positive, and the Czech Republic had also distinguished itself by producing the first 'real' Social Democrat Government in the post-Communist world – that is, one that was not led by a Communist successor party. Although a slowdown in preparations for EU membership led to rather negative reports by the European Commission in 1998 and 1999, and its place in the 'First Wave' of eastward enlargement appeared endangered, by 2000 the Czechs had corrected some of these failings and appeared to be back on course.

In Slovakia, the crucial year 1997 witnessed a turn away from the authoritarian direction. July 1997 – the month which saw the State's exclusion from the fast-track of the European integration process – was also marked by the formation of a coalition of five opposition parties in preparation for the 1998 general election. The Slovak Democratic Coalition, together with three further opposition parties, eventually defeated Mečiar and his allies and in October 1998 formed a Government with a majority above the 60 per cent necessary to change the constitution. The appointment of an ethnic Hungarian as deputy prime minister for human rights and minorities did much to alleviate concerns about the treatment of minorities, and Slovakia was invited to start full negotiations on EU accession in December 1999. However, the spectre of Mečiar's return was kept alive, particularly in the minds of the international community, by his standing (unsuccessfully) in direct elections for the presidency in May 1999, and the Government's domestic popularity inevitably declined somewhat as it had to tackle the economic problems inherited from its predecessor. The multi-party diversity of the coalition and a fractiousness deriving both from the politics of personalities and the coalition's inclusion of a broad Left–Right spectrum also created continued nervousness about its stability.

What, however, do these shifting trajectories in domestic politics, economics and international relations tell us about progress towards democratic consolidation in the Czech and Slovak Republics? In order to understand what has happened to each since 1989, and to predict likely developments in the future, it is necessary to look initially at what they had in common and what differentiated them in the decade when Czechoslovakia split. The first part of the chapter therefore examines the extent to which the prerequisites for establishing a stable democracy were dissimilar in its two constituent republics. In the second part of the chapter, the effect of these differences will be investigated, and the Czech and Slovak Republics will be measured against some of the criteria used to assess democratic consolidation.

Common inheritances and deep-rooted differences

A number of studies have examined the factors which lead to democratisation, and which facilitate the consolidation of democracy. Some of these apply to states democratising anywhere in the world, and deal with such factors as economic conditions, literacy and educational levels, and degree of urbanisation.[10] Others relate more specifically to post-Communist societies in the 'Third Wave' of democratisation,[11] and address modes of transition from Communism and the length of pre-Communist democratic experience, and decisions on institutional architecture.[12]

Despite the fact that for most of the twentieth century Czechs and Slovaks shared a common state, there were at times significant differences between the two parts of the country, apparent when one examines the factors listed above in more detail. There may have, therefore, been a different democratising potential in each when independence was finally negotiated in 1992. In order to highlight some of the variations between the Czech and Slovak Republics when the Communist regime crumbled, relevant factors have been grouped under five headings: history; economics; transition from Communism; political culture; and institutional architecture.

History

In common with much of the region, Czechoslovakia in the twentieth century was marked by profound discontinuity. Periods of foreign domination – by Austria-Hungary, Germany and the Soviet Union – alternated with independent government. However, Czechoslovakia differed from many other states that democratised in the late twentieth century in that its periods of self-rule – from 1918 to 1938, to a lesser extent from 1945 to 1948, and from 1989 onwards – were basically democratic. The experience of the Czech and Slovak parts of the country also differed from each other, so it is worth briefly recapping on the regimes to which they were subjected.

The Czechoslovak Republic was formed in November 1918 as a result of the disintegration of the Austro-Hungarian empire. In the spirit of the times, it was conceived as a 'nation state', embodying the Czechoslovak (or Czecho-Slovak) nation.[13] However, the Czechs and Slovaks had very different histories. The territory of Slovakia had been colonised by the Magyars in the tenth century, and remained under Hungarian rule until 1918. Whereas the Czechs had enjoyed opportunities of cultural development and some representation in the Austrian part of the Austro-Hungarian empire, the Slovaks, incorporated in the Hungarian part of the empire, had been subject to increasing attempts at Magyarisation from the *Ausgleich* of 1867 onwards. Without the debacle of the First World War and the dissolution of the Habsburg monarchy, they might well have been subjected to total assimilation and disappeared as a nation – something which more nationalist-inclined Slovaks in modern Slovakia are loathe to ignore.

Perhaps more crucial, however, for the development of the independent states in the 1990s was the Czechs' and Slovaks' different experience of statehood, and their differing historical self-images. The Kingdom of Bohemia, on which the Czech Republic could look back, had a glorious history from late

medieval times, which featured such individuals as the Holy Roman Emperor
Charles IV (who founded the Charles University in Prague in 1348) and the
Protestant martyr Jan Hus, who was burnt at the stake in 1415, before the
fateful Battle of White Mountain of 1620 led to the flight of the Bohemian aris-
tocracy and the subjection of the Czechs to Austrian rule lasting until 1918.
The Slovaks had nothing to compare with this, and there had been little Slovak
consciousness at all until the national awakening of the nineteenth century.
When Czechs and Slovaks were asked in a 1990 survey about the historical
periods of which they were proud, 28 per cent of Czechs but only 4 per cent of
Slovaks mentioned any historical periods before the end of the eighteenth
century. Indeed, more than half of Slovaks (though also one-third of Czechs)
were unable to think of any historical period at all of which they were proud.[14]

The first Czechoslovak Republic from 1918 to 1938 is a further example of
the far greater Czech experience in running a state. This was an age in which
the Czechs (but not the Slovaks) enjoyed one of the highest standards of living
in Europe, and where the philosopher–president Masaryk presided over the
only democracy in Central Europe not to collapse through internal weakness
in the interwar period.[15] But it was fundamentally a *Czech* state: the capital
was Prague, the agenda was set by Czechs, and power was largely shared
between the five political parties which formed the *pětka* – a shifting five-party
government coalition.[16]

Slovak perceptions of the First Republic were very different. Much of the
population remained in grinding rural poverty,[17] which they felt the Prague
Government did little to relieve. As the first generation of Slovak graduates
emerged, they perceived that their employment opportunities were blocked by
the Czech officials who had been moved to Slovakia to take over the running
of the State in place of Hungarians.[18] Also, over half the electorate in Slovakia
voted for parties that were almost perpetually excluded from power. While
some Slovaks voted for parties linked to the *pětka*, others voted for Hlinka's
Slovak People's Party, or for the Communist Party, or for Hungarian parties.[19]
Slovak elites hardly carried ultimate responsibility for the State.

It was Slovakia's misfortune that the first time in history when Slovaks were
able to run their own state without the intervention of Hungarians or Czechs
was during the Slovak Republic (commonly referred to as the 'Slovak state')
between 1939 and 1945. This was an unsavoury one-party dictatorship
beholden for its existence to the Nazis, who intervened massively both in its
creation, in March 1939, and in all its major policy decisions throughout its
short life.[20] Slovak popular attitudes to the Slovak state have remained ambivalent, but there is less doubt about the Slovak National Uprising of autumn
1944, when the Slovak Army and partisans rejected both the Slovak state and
German fascism, and led armed resistance against them. Although this failed
in the short term – and brought about direct German military occupation –
ultimately it provided an 'heroic' foundation on which Slovakia's self-image
could be based.[21]

The 1948 Communist takeover of the newly recreated Czechoslovakia ended the brief – three-year – democratic interlude and subjected the country to a Soviet-style socialism, which was particularly inappropriate for a society already as modern and developed as that of the Czech Lands. The Czechoslovak Socialist Republic was again a Czech-dominated state. This position changed somewhat after 1968, when federalisation became the only Prague Spring reform to survive the Warsaw Pact invasion, and a Slovak, Gustáv Husák, became both the leader of the Communist Party of Czechoslovakia and, in 1975, state president. However, Czechoslovak federalism remained largely asymmetrical. Although the Czech and Slovak Republics had their own governments, only the Slovaks had a separate, republic-level, Communist Party. This imbalance was crucial, since the party was the real repository of power in a Communist state. Slovaks tended to input into federal structures in Prague via Bratislava, while Czechs had more direct access.

The inexperienced democrats who took over Czechoslovakia after the Velvet Revolution of November 1989, overburdened as they were by the plethora of urgent decisions they faced, found this asymmetry of Czechoslovak federalism impossible to unravel.[22] The surprise decision in June 1992 to 'cut the Gordian knot' by splitting the State was largely accepted with passivity by its citizens. However, while both the Czech and Slovak Republics were technically successor states of Czechoslovakia, it was the Slovaks' status *vis-à-vis* the outside world that was shaken most dramatically. The Czechs and Slovaks had had an equal number of years of experience of living in a democracy, but only the Czechs had really had any experience of running one.

Economics

Economic development is a further factor which assists both democratisation and the consolidation of democracy. When Czechoslovakia was created in 1918, the Czech and Slovak parts of the country differed markedly in this respect. The Czechs had the good fortune to inherit the bulk of Austria's industry, whereas Slovakia – though not backward by *East* European standards – lagged far behind economically. In the Czech Lands the primary sector, agriculture, was already smaller than the secondary (industrial) sector, whereas in Slovakia three times more people were employed in agriculture than industry, as shown below in Table 19. Although this difference persisted throughout the interwar period, by the end of the Communist period, Slovakia had become almost as industrial as the Czech Republic, and urbanisation had increased commensurably.[23]

Standards of living also had nearly equalised by the 1980s.[24] Indeed, even after five years of rather different economic paths, following independence, the European Commission's 1997 opinions on the applications of the Central and East European countries to join the EU showed that the Slovak Republic was

Table 19 *Occupational structure (%) in the Czech Lands (CZ) and Slovakia (SK), 1921–89*

	Agriculture and Forestry		Industry		Services	
	CZ	SK	CZ	SK	CZ	SK
1921	36.6	65.0	46.2	20.9	17.2	14.1
1948	34.7	62.2	44.0	25.2	21.3	12.6
1970	15.9	25.7	55.0	46.9	29.1	27.4
1989	11.00	14.5	51.2	47.6	37.8	37.9

Source: J. Krejci and P. Machonin, *Czechoslovakia 1918–1992: A Laboratory for Social Change* (Basingstoke and London: Macmillan, 1996), pp. 119–20.

still nearer to the Czech standard of living than were either Hungary or Poland.[25] Educational levels had also improved markedly in Slovakia during the course of the Czechoslovak period – in this case, both in the interwar and in the Communist period.

It is at first sight something of an irony that Czechoslovakia split just when economic conditions in the Czech and Slovak Republics were more similar than at any other time since the state's foundation. However, to a certain extent the similarities between the Czech and Slovak Republics were only skin deep. The twentieth century experience in each part of the country had been very different. Precisely because Slovakia had industrialised under Communism it had a far less robust economic structure than the Czech Republic.[26] Many workers were employed in the 'industrial monocultures' created by the Communists whereby the majority of the workforce of a town was employed by a single enterprise. If this happened to be an arms factory whose products became obsolete at the beginning of the 1990s, as was the case in a number of Slovak towns, the social consequences of its closure were enormous. Likewise, the pace of urbanisation in Slovakia had been quite abnormally quick, with the population of Bratislava quadrupling in the second half of the twentieth century. As a result, many Slovaks with higher education, and part of the Slovak elites, were not only first-generation graduates but first-generation town-dwellers.

Both the Czech and Slovak Republics of the 1990s enjoyed levels of economic prosperity and modernisation that were conducive to the firm anchoring of democracy. However, in the Czech Republic it was more deeply rooted and less vulnerable than in Slovakia. In economics, as in politics, the new Czech state could reinforce its transition process by calling up positive memories of achievements under democratic government between the wars. In Slovakia, on the other hand, the Communist period had not been an unmitigated disaster in economic terms. Modernisation was not inextricably linked with democracy.

Transition from Communism

The lasting effect of the mode of transition from authoritarianism on the chances of a new democracy achieving consolidation has been the focus of much analysis of the 'Third Wave' of democratisation, including the post-Communist states. The initial impression that the collapse of Soviet-style socialism was a relatively similar process throughout all six Warsaw Pact states was replaced by a realisation that both the Communist leaderships and the opposition they faced were structured very differently throughout the Communist bloc, and that this affected the speed and the smoothness with which the regimes fell. In Poland and Hungary, 'negotiated transitions' took place in which reformists within the Communist Party agreed to contest elections with opposition forces, while in Czechoslovakia and the GDR intransigent, more hard-line, regimes responded only very reluctantly to Gorbachev's *perestroika*, and then simply collapsed when 'the people' finally came into the streets *en masse* to oppose them. At the end of this political spectrum, the dictator Ceauşescu was brought down and executed amid widespread bloodshed more resembling a classic revolution. However, on closer inspection of what followed (most particularly the 1990 elections), analysts inclined to the interpretation that events in both Romania and Bulgaria bore more similarity to a 'palace *coup*' in which the pre-emptive removal of a figurehead allowed the former Communist elites to remain in power. Lack of organised opposition in the Communist period had left few other alternatives.

Two issues cloud any assessment of the relevance of modes of transition from authoritarianism in the Czech and Slovak cases. First, it is not clear cut which mode is actually the more conducive to democratic consolidation. It has often been assumed, borrowing from experience in Latin America and Southern Europe, that 'pacted transitions', where reformers in the old regime find common ground with moderates among their opponents, are a more certain way of securing democracy since existing elites are not placed in such jeopardy that they rebel against democratic forces.[27] However, it has also been suggested, most notably in the post-Communist case by Herbert Kitschelt in his analyses of the emerging party systems, that in fact 'implosion', or the total collapse of the old elites, was more conducive than negotiated transition to the formation of programmatically structured party systems of the type normal in Western democracies.[28] There are logical reasons why observations based on other regions may not apply to the post-Communist world. The sheer diversity of the tasks faced in rebuilding democracy, a market economy and civil society in a post-totalitarian state means that the managerial and professional skills of old elites are neither indispensable nor transferable in the way they were in more straightforward cases of democratising authoritarian states. Therefore the quicker the old Communist elites disappear from power, the better.

The second difficulty in analysing the relevance of mode of transition on democratisation in the Czech and Slovak Republics is that doubts have been cast on whether both parts of Czechoslovakia were in fact subject to the complete implosion of Communist structures. It has frequently been suggested that the Velvet Revolution essentially emanated from Prague, and that Slovakia was initially merely dragged along in its wake. Thereafter, however, Slovak developments bore more resemblance to those in Bulgaria and Romania since there the old Communist elites were in fact able to remain in power.[29]

However, an alternative explanation of developments in Slovakia is that they were a variant of the Polish and Hungarian pattern. As in Poland and Hungary, it was recognised that there were external constraints on how much freedom could be permitted without attracting unwanted attention, but these were imposed by Prague as well as by Moscow. The Czechoslovak political agenda was dominated by the situation in Prague, where there was a vast gulf between an unimaginative Communist hardline leadership and outspoken dissidents who had been demonised by the regime and totally excluded from professional life. However, the post-1968 'normalisation' process was much less vicious in Slovakia than in the Czech Republic. Forward-looking Communists were not automatically expelled from the party, and the dissenting were less likely to be totally excluded from professional life, which increased the chances of meaningful dialogue. Accounts of negotiations between reform-minded Communists in Bratislava and members of the intelligentsia in the months before the Velvet Revolution suggest that, left to themselves, the Slovaks under *perestroika* conditions might have achieved a pacted transition.[30] Slovakia went on to develop a social-democratised Communist successor party which bore far more resemblance to its counterparts in Poland and Hungary than to the Communist Party of Bohemia and Moravia. The idea that Communist elites retained power in Slovakia is based rather on the influence of ex-Communists in Mečiar's HZDS. The Government Mečiar formed in 1994 contained only three members who had never held a Communist Party card.[31] However, the genesis of HZDS indicates that the circumstances of the division of Czechoslovakia were at least as important as the nature of the Velvet Revolution itself. It should also be noted that all Czech governments in the 1990s also contained some former Communist Party members.

In comparing the total influence of former Communist Party members in the Czech and Slovak Republics, it does appear to have been greater in Slovakia than in the Czech Republic. A multinational survey of economic, political and cultural elites in the Czech and Slovak Republics confirms this. The sample of the political elite in Slovakia contained nearly twice as many former Communists as in the Czech Republic (41 per cent compared to 27 per cent), and members of the Slovak elites were many times more likely to have held some kind of party office in the course of 1988.[32] These findings are consistent with the fact that the Czechoslovak Lustration Law, which excluded leading Communists from public office, was implemented almost exclusively in the Czech Republic, where it was also renewed after its initial five-year term expired.

However, this may tell us as much about the sort of society Slovakia was before the Velvet Revolution as about the kinds of changes that took place afterwards. Because of the less rigid normalisation process, the dichotomy between being a party member and refusing such a privilege was less stark. Later, interest in 'lustration' in Slovakia was less than in the Czech Republic because the issue of coming to terms with the Communist past had become less salient than the settling of scores between Mečiar's more nationalist supporters and his opponents. In the Czech Republic, on the other hand, the ideology of reform pursued by the Klaus Governments still required Communism as 'the enemy'. In summary, neither Communism nor the mode of extraction from Communist rule were the same in the Czech Republic and Slovakia, but differences should not be exaggerated. Slovak experiences were generally more in line with the Visegrad states than with the Balkans.

Political culture

The concept of 'political culture' assumes that individual attitudes towards democracy and the political process as a whole are influenced by an individual's background and will retain some constant traits regardless of the more ephemeral changes in political and personal circumstances to which they are subject. At the time of the division of Czechoslovakia, it was tempting to explain the event by differences in Czech and Slovak political culture, and to believe that the phenomenon of 'Mečiarism' was a product of deficient political culture among at least part of the Slovak population.

In fact, however, rigorous attempts to prove that the average Czech and the average Slovak have different 'mind-sets' have proved inconclusive. Many multinational surveys have demonstrated limited statistical differences between Czechs and Slovaks on such fundamental questions as whether democracy is preferable under any circumstances (see Table 8, p. 127). Other indicators show that Czechs have slightly more positive attitudes towards democracy than Slovaks, but that Slovak views are not out of line with those of the Visegrad Four as a whole.[33] Consequently, there is no obvious reason why Slovakia should have greater difficulties in moving towards democratic consolidation on these grounds.

There is evidence that the actual environment in which citizens live is more important in accounting for differences in views between Czechs and Slovaks than are underlying political attitudes. In a thorough analysis of data collected in 1994 carried out by Stephen Whitefield and Geoffrey Evans, it was found that there were differences in attitude between Czechs and Slovaks, but these correlated with differences in religiosity in the two states (and were actually less than might be expected given the much stronger influence of the Catholic Church in Slovakia), and also with economic circumstances.[34]

Slovak surveys throughout the 1990s also found that fundamental attitudes, termed 'professed principles of political life', were linked to individual reactions to the current political situation. For example, supporters of the parties which had formed the Mečiar Government showed less appreciation of the importance of 'the division of power, the role of the opposition, and the need to observe the law' than their opponents did. However, it was noticeable that after the 1998 elections, when Government and Opposition swapped roles, there was some convergence between the views of the two sides.[35] The conclusion was that the findings indicated that 'the commitment of party adherents to democratic principles is not an abstract issue, but is conditioned also by the concrete position of their political parties in the power apparatus'.[36] Furthermore, the same surveys have noted significant shifts in Slovak attitudes throughout the 1990s, so that towards the end of the decade Slovak responses were becoming similar to the more favourable ones measured in the Czech Republic in 1994.[37]

However, even if it cannot be proven that the Czechs and Slovaks have different cultures, for a discussion of success in attaining democratic consolidation it remains important that Czech and Slovak real-life experiences have been different, and that this gives rise to differing attitudes. New democracies are inherently fragile, and their survival may be endangered by a temporarily unfavourable constellation of factors.

This is particularly relevant because of one further consideration. This section has looked at the 'political mind-sets' of citizens as a whole in the Czech and Slovak Republics. However, analyses of events surrounding the division of Czechoslovakia and beyond suggest that it was in fact the behaviour and attitudes of the elites rather than public opinion that drove events.[38] The attitudes of the elites in each Republic are a composite phenomenon determined by history and economic structure as well as by political culture. The framework in which elites are able to influence democratisation is also vital in deciding whether their attitudes can be translated into actions which determine the further course of democratic development. The institutional architecture of Czechoslovakia and the Czech and Slovak Republics is therefore the final factor to be reviewed in this part of the chapter.

Institutional architecture

As in much of the post-Communist world, constitution building in the Czech and Slovak Republics was based initially on carrying out first urgent, and then more thorough, amendments of existing Communist constitutions. This happened in part because the change of regime occurred relatively quickly. In Czechoslovakia, a bare six weeks passed between the 17 November 1989 demonstration, which heralded the beginning of the Velvet Revolution, and the election of former dissident Václav Havel as president. Amending the existing

constitution was the simplest way of consolidating the far-reaching concessions that were being obtained from a crumbling regime. It was also possible
because Communist systems differed from those of other states which democratised in the Third Wave in that they boasted the infrastructure of democracy
– regular elections and parliaments – but had deprived these of democratic
content by constitutionally anchoring the leading role of the party. Restoring
their democratic content was quicker than building new institutions from
scratch.

Both post-Communist Czechoslovakia and the independent Czech and
Slovak Republics have benefited from democratic institutions particularly well
designed to assist the consolidation of democracy. Their electoral systems
have been based on proportional representation, and non-executive presidents
were initially elected by Parliament, which acted in the early years as a reasonably effective check on the concentration of power.[39] Some elements of this
system were adopted from Czechoslovakia's successful interwar democracy,
which provided a model not available to most post-Communist states.
Presidents had been elected by Parliament in the First Republic, and the
method had been carried over both into the Slovak state and the first (1948)
Communist Constitution.[40] The proportional representation system used in
the June 1990 elections, and in all other Czech or Slovak elections throughout
the 1990s, was also a revival from the First Republic, where PR had been
anchored in the Constitution. It was, however, refined to include a German-
style '5 per cent clause' to stop too many parties crossing the threshold into
parliament. It was hoped that this would avoid the party fragmentation and
complex coalition building behind closed doors which had marked the interwar period. Czechoslovakia also retained the traditional but rather idiosyn-
cratic three-fifths' 'special majority' for amending the Constitution, and, until
the late 1990s, the practice of voting on Friday afternoons and Saturday
mornings.

The new Czech and Slovak Constitutions created for the independent states
retained many of the constitutional choices originally made in 1990. The
Czech Constitution bore a stronger resemblance to the interwar Czechoslovak
Constitution than its Slovak counterpart, reflecting the far more positive
Czech attitudes to the First Republic. Most notably, it anchored PR elections
in the Constitution, and created a second chamber, the Senate. The Slovak
Constitution was passed several months earlier than the Czech one, but had
the major disadvantage that it was really the work of only one half of the
political spectrum, and not a product of broad political consensus. However,
although often criticised by the opposition, it did in fact prove during the third
Mečiar Government of 1994–98 to be reasonably functional in protecting
democracy. The single major change to the institutional architecture established by the Constitution was actually introduced by the Dzurinda
Government, which, using its three-fifths' parliamentary majority, introduced
the direct election of the president in the first half of 1999. However, as will

be discussed below, by the beginning of the new millennium it was the institutional structure of the Czech Republic that looked likely to undergo the most major changes.

Progress towards democratic consolidation in the Czech and Slovak Republics

Before attempting a more detailed assessment of the Czech and Slovak Republics' progress towards democratic consolidation, comment must be made on the different characterisations of this concept. One of the simplest is that a consolidated democracy is one where democracy is seen as 'the only game in town',[41] meaning that no major political actor considers that there is a realistic alternative to democratic methods in order to obtain power. Another succinct characterisation of a consolidated democracy is that it is 'likely to endure'.[42] It is possible for political parties to gain power democratically but then attempt to subvert the political process to retain power. A consolidated democracy therefore requires both institutionalised democratic rules – and political actors who adhere to them – and public attitudes that assume and demand adherence to them.[43] This elaboration is important in the case of post-Communist societies, since declared allegiance to democracy as the only alternative for the future of a state is exceptionally high, in part being linked to the cultural aspiration of a 'return to Europe'. What is crucial, however, is not only the declared aim of political actors but the internalised conception of what *democracy* means.

In view of these doubts about the operationalisation of 'democracy' by political actors in East-Central Europe, Samuel Huntington's 'two-turnover test' of a consolidated democracy is also useful. This states that

> a democracy may be viewed as consolidated if the party or group that takes power in the initial election at the time of transition loses a subsequent election and turns over power to those election winners, and if those election winners then peacefully turn over power to the winners of a later election.[44]

By this definition, it is clear that political factions which obtain power legally must accept the rules of the democratic game and be prepared to implement them in an impartial fashion which will – later if not sooner – oblige them to hand over power to their opponents.

However, this test is not as simple to apply as it at first sounds in the post-Communist case, since it relies somewhat on the finding from earlier democratic transitions in the 'Third Wave' that the first democratic elections tend to be 'founding elections' which had a major effect on the future shaping of the party system.[45] In post-Communism, however, the fluidity of identities and interests among post-Communist electorates which stemmed from the multifaceted nature of the transition led to a constant process of shifting and reshaping the party systems. As a result, post-Communist governments had a

tendency to collapse mid-term as it was sometimes shifts in the party allegiances of the deputies rather than of voters that changed a government.

Despite that caveat, however, this 'test' of democratic consolidation pro-
duces two interesting reflections. First, it reminds one of the vulnerability of
democratic consolidation in the Czech Republic, which really needs power to
be passed back from the Social Democrats to the centre-Right without the
rules of the 'electoral game' being changed in order for the test to be deemed
to be passed. Second, the 1998 Slovak election is a particularly interesting
illustration of the complexity the test can measure. There were grave doubts
about whether the election would be conducted fairly, in particular because of
the behaviour of the third Mečiar Government in relation to a referendum
called by the president in May 1997.[46] The reason that fair elections were held
and power changed hands was that the entire electoral process was conducted
in a environment where democracy was consolidating at a deeper level, and
the strength of civil society and its understanding of the principles of the rule
of law provided little scope for perverting the electoral process.[47]

The issue here is that the characteristics of democratic consolidation discussed so far measure largely what has variously been described as 'formal',
'procedural' or 'electoral' democracy.[48] For comparing the Czech and Slovak
Republics, it is useful also to look at the features of 'substantive democracy',[49]
which encompass a broader and deeper analysis of the way modern democracies function. In order to do this, the framework suggested by Juan J. Linz and
Alfred Stepan in their 1996 work *Problems of Democratic Transition and
Consolidation* will be employed. This starts from the premiss that 'consolidated democracies need to have in place five interacting arenas to reinforce one
another in order for such consolidation to exist'.[50] Prefaced by the prerequisite that 'no modern polity can become democratically consolidated unless it
is first a state', the five arenas are listed as:
- conditions for the development of a free and lively civil society;
- a relatively autonomous and valued political society;
- rule of law to ensure legal guarantees for citizens' freedoms and independent associational life;
- a state bureaucracy that is usable by the new democratic government; and
- an institutionalised economic society.[51]

This framework is particularly useful for assessing developments in a post-
Communist society because – like Claus Offe's earlier definition of the difficult 'triple transition' which such societies must master[52] – it can be used to
highlight the fact that post-totalitarian societies are radically different from
the states of Latin America and Southern Europe which also democratised in
the 'Third Wave'. They are constructing democratic institutions and multi-
party systems from a situation in which Communist Party rule has totally penetrated and distorted civil society, the legal system, the bureaucracy and the
economy. In the Czechoslovak case (and some other post-Communist examples), concepts of 'nation' and 'territory' were also renegotiated. A final differ-

ence (though scarcely a difficulty), which will be revisited in the conclusion of this chapter, is the international situation. The Warsaw Pact states all threw off foreign domination of their domestic political agendas when they escaped from Soviet-style socialism. They began to build up their new polities according to their own self-images as European democracies, and this, within a few years, led to the voluntary imposition of EU norms as a compulsory guiding model for the functioning of their polities, economies, legal systems and bureaucracies.[53]

Stateness

'Stateness' is held to be the prerequisite for consolidating democracy.[54] Although the Czech and Slovak Republics are both new states, neither has had a fundamental problem with this condition. Substantial numbers of citizens did not *want* Czechoslovakia to split, and the Hungarian ethnic minority in Slovakia had the gravest reservations about Slovak independence, but no group of citizens has seriously questioned the legitimacy of either the Czech or the Slovak Republic.[55] Both states were recognised as successors to Czechoslovakia by the major international organisations without problems early in 1993, and there have been few arguments about citizenship. Those that caused concern to the international community related solely to the granting of Czech citizenship to Roma born in Slovakia but living (whether legally registered there or not) in the Czech Republic. Since the Hungarians of Slovakia had been indigenous to the area long before the Communists came to power, and had enjoyed extensive rights in the interwar period, there were no questions about their entitlement to citizenship of the sort that were raised in relation to the recently settled Russian minorities of Estonia and Latvia. Consequently, although the precise cultural rights of Slovak Hungarians were a contentious domestic issue throughout the 1990s, these did not impinge on the Slovak Republic's stateness.

Initial difficulties in anchoring democracy in Slovakia did derive, however, from two rather different but related issues. One was the necessity of simultaneous state building and nation building. The preamble of the Slovak Constitution passed in September 1992 appears to define the Slovak nation in ethnic rather than civil terms, but there were doubts about what being a Slovak meant. As in 1939, the Slovaks had been rushed into statehood when their own agenda was more concerned with a lesser form of autonomy. Unlike the ethnic majorities in the Baltic states and Slovenia, Slovaks had not overwhelmingly endorsed independence as an integral part of escaping from the Communist yoke. This Slovak ambivalence led to insecurity. The more nationalistic parties accused their opponents of being enemies of Slovakia because they had not originally voted for the July 1992 declaration of Slovak sovereignty, and the unhelpful terms 'good Slovak' and 'bad Slovak' were often used.[56] Mečiar's opponents, on the other hand, felt anxious about democracy in the new

Slovakia. Ironically, the more numerous Czech supporters of the common state came to terms with the new independence much more quickly. The Czechs, with their centuries' long tradition of statehood, and past experience of running a democracy, were not faced by confusing uncertainty about *what* Czech democracy would mean.

The second Slovak difficulty related to the actual running of their state. The newly independent Slovak Republic faced some problems in finding qualified, experienced personnel to handle, in particular, its international relations. Slovaks as a whole had less knowledge of Western languages than did Czechs,[57] and a number of Slovaks who had been actively involved in running Czechoslovakia at the federal level, and therefore often having Prague-based families, chose to remain in the Czech Republic and took on Czech citizenship. This slowed down Slovakia's development – at a time when speed was of the essence – but none the less did not constitute a fundamental problem with stateness. Conditions for promoting Slovakia amid the complexities of joining international structures were not ideal, but they were not fundamentally flawed.

Civil society

Linz and Stepan define *civil society* as 'that arena of the polity where self-organizing groups, movements, and individuals, relatively autonomous from the state, attempt to articulate values, create association and solidarities, and advance their interests'.[58] It is a subject much discussed in relation to post-Communist societies, because Communism went so far towards homogenising society into a system where only one monolithic state- or party-led organisation existed to regulate and promote every possible activity, from trades union work to gardening. This contributed to the tendency for the political systems, most particularly the party systems, to be formed 'from above' (that is, from the parliament down), rather than 'from below', as structures representing competing interests in society.

For this reason, the international community has always laid great importance on the development of non-governmental organisations (NGOs) as a factor which would help the consolidation of democracy. Substantial financial support has been forthcoming from abroad for NGOs in both the Czech and Slovak Republics. For example, the two largest contributors to the Donors' Forum established in Slovakia in 1997 – the Open Society Foundation financed by the American businessman and philanthropist George Soros, and the EU Phare-funded Civil Society Development Foundation – provided about 120 million crowns (some 4 million Euros) in 1998.[59] While helpful in supporting local initiative, foreign sponsorship also makes it hard to evaluate the strength of NGOs, since it runs counter to the ethos of autonomy and self-help which underlies the very idea of civil society. Again, to some extent a degree of organisation, or impetus, is coming 'from above' instead of growing up from the grass roots.

Comparing the vitality of civil society in the Czech and Slovak Republics is complex. The number of civic associations and foundations is large in each: the European Commission cited 33,000 associations and 4,700 foundations in its 'opinion' on the Czech Republic in 1997,[60] and 12,000 NGOs in Slovakia.[61] Yet this tells us little about their membership and level of activity. Statistics show, however, that the largest organisation in Slovakia is the Confederation of Trades Unions of the Slovak Republic, with 830,542 members in 1998.[62] Its counterpart, the Czech and Moravian Confederation of Trades Unions, had 2.45 million members in 1995.[63] Both states are similar in that they have a tradition of tripartite agreements between government, trades unions and employers. In terms of NGOs as a whole, they also both started with similar legislation from the pre-1993 period, and both finally formalised these provisional measures with legislation in the 1996–98 period which was controversial in registering as 'foundations' (rather than 'civic associations') only organisations that possessed what were, in relation to local salaries, substantial resources to back them up.[64]

While the hostility of the Mečiar Government to non-governmental organisations was much publicised, the Dzurinda Government formed in late 1998 was much more open to ideas from think tanks, using, for example, research from Transparency International Slovakia as a basis for its anti-corruption campaign. The cooperation was, however, in part a legacy of the Mečiar period. The politicisation of state service had led many individuals interested in public service into the 'third sector', and NGOs had been very active in encouraging the high electoral turnout in 1998 which benefited the then opposition.[65] In the Czech Republic, Klaus had been perceived as hostile to NGO activity, but development was less polarised than in Slovakia.

Autonomous civic action requires support other than finance and a legislative framework on NGOs as well. Information is also essential. Both states benefited from diverse sources of information available to the public. Slovakia under Mečiar faced severe problems with biased political coverage on the state-run Slovak Television, and the press frequently felt under threat, most notably in early 1995.[66] However, society was strong enough to fight off these threats, which bodes well there for democratic consolidation. Both states also passed freedom of information legislation, partly to accord with EU norms. The Czech legislation came into force in January 2000, and amendments were soon planned to deal with ministries and public offices which proved reluctant to comply. Slovak legislation was passed in May 2000, to come into force in January 2001.

Finally, Linz and Stepan note that 'ordinary citizens who are not a part of any organisation' are also important.[67] Here, again, the strength of society is more noticeable in Slovakia than in the Czech Republic, having been subjected to the more severe tests. The total politicisation of Slovak society prior to the 1998 elections was remarkable, and the efforts of individuals to persuade their own relatives and friends in their voting intentions was as remarkable to an outside observer as the organised efforts of NGOs supported by the international community.[68] While Slovak society at times appears dangerously polarised, it has also benefited from a high level of public engagement, which contrasts with the greater level of passivity and acceptance of elite political decisions in the Czech Republic. At times of constitutional change, both prior to the split of Czechoslovakia in 1992 and when electoral system change was on the agenda at the end of the decade, debate within Slovakia has been much livelier. Nevertheless, indigenous organised civic activity and pressure groups remain underdeveloped in both the Czech Republic and Slovakia. This is not surprising, given the Communist legacy, and the ability of Slovak civil society to defend democracy under pressure shows the substantial progress that has been made. As long as progress continues, civil society in both states is generally supportive of democratic consolidation.

Political society

This is defined as 'the arena in which the polity specifically arranges itself to contest the legitimate right to exercise control over public power and the state apparatus'.[69] Political society is complementary to civil society, and essentially comprises the arena where political parties have developed to represent 'differences between democrats'. It also requires 'habituation to the norms and procedures of democratic conflict regulation'.[70]

Both the Czech and Slovak Republics still have shifting party systems, where parties split relatively frequently, and it is possible for a new party to gain enough votes to enter Parliament within six months of its foundation. All parliamentary parties pay lip service to democracy, but in practice, in the specific context of East-Central Europe at the turn of the millennium, it is possible roughly to divide them into two groups according to whether they are viable coalition partners for parties seriously seeking EU accession at the earliest possible date. Looking at all Czech and Slovak parties which entered Parliament at least twice in the three elections from 1992 to 1998, two in each state fail this test: the unreformed Communist Party of Bohemia and Moravia and the far-right Republicans in the Czech Republic; and the Movement for a Democratic Slovakia (HZDS) and the Slovak National Party, which were actually governing Slovakia when it was held to have 'failed' the EU's political (Copenhagen) criteria in 1997.[71] A major difference is the size of these parties. In 1998, the Czech Communists received 11 per cent of the vote, while the Republicans failed to cross the 5 per cent clause into Parliament.[72] In Slovakia, however, Mečiar's HZDS obtained 27 per cent of the vote, and the Nationalists gained 9 per cent.[73] Furthermore, in the direct presidential elections in 1999, Mečiar obtained 37 per cent of the vote in the first round and nearly 43 per cent in the second round run-off.[74]

There is a certain similarity in the demographic profiles of Czech Communist and HZDS voters: they tend to be older, and to have lower levels of education.[75] This group of 'residual voters' comprises transformation losers, who have found it difficult to come to terms with the rapid changes since 1989 and have less chance to benefit from them than younger and better-educated citizens. Their number is likely to undergo a natural decline over the years, but in Slovakia it remains high enough for HZDS and the Nationalists to re-enter government if – as in 1994 – a new maverick party enters Parliament.[76] In the Czech Republic, on the other hand, governments can alternate without the 'parties of the past' holding power.

Another worrying factor in both states is lack of agreement about the rules for conducting democratic competition in electing their parliaments and presidents. Both the Slovak Government prior to 1998 and the Czech Government after 1998 attempted to amend the electoral system in a manipulative fashion. Those who supported change did so because they believed a different system would increase their own power, and not because there was general consensus that current rules were dysfunctional. In the Slovak case, Mečiar began discussing the introduction of a majoritarian or mixed electoral system in 1996. On the 1994 elections' results, this would have allowed him to rule without coalition partners.[77] The attempt was abandoned when it became clear that the opposition was capable of uniting and, maybe, reaping the advantage of the new system. In any case, HZDS would have been hard-pressed to pass the necessary law because it was hostile towards the smaller coalition partners upon which it depended in government. In the end, the Government waited until May 1998, and made more minor amendments to the electoral law. The most notable insisted that electoral coalitions should obtain 5 per cent of the vote for *each* coalition partner in order to enter Parliament.[78] This was a perfectly sensible provision, removing a temporary concession which eased the entry of small parties into parliament in the wake of the Velvet Revolution, when they had had little time to organise themselves. However, it was clearly inappropriate to make such a correction a mere four months before the election as a reaction to the opposition forming a successful coalition. In fact, the opposition coalition circumvented the hurdle by registering as a political party called the Slovak Democratic Coalition. In one of its most significant acts ever, HZDS then attempted to have the Slovak Democratic Coalition banned by the Supreme Court on the grounds that it was a coalition and not a party. This was the clearest sign possible that the aim of HZDS was elimination of political competition and perpetuation of one-party rule.

In the Czech Republic, on the other hand, the aim of changes to the electoral system passed by Parliament in 2000 was the institutionalisation of alternating government between two parties, each of which should have its turn at ruling unhindered by coalition partners. Miloš Zeman's Social Democrats and Václav Klaus's Civic Democratic Party (ODS) had reached this deal when both were having problems trying to form a government in the wake of the 1998 elections, and they effectively ganged up against the smaller parties whose influence they agreed to reduce.[79] This 'opposition agreement' spoke pompously of the 'threat of political instability' and the 'preservation of basic democratic principles',[80] although arguably the major reason no majority government could be formed was nothing more dramatic than a personality clash between Klaus and the rest of the Czech centre-Right. However, the effective checks and balances in the existing system made changing the electoral law difficult. The British first-past-the-post electoral system favoured by Klaus was unconstitutional, since PR was anchored in the Czech Constitution. Amending the Constitution was in turn complicated by the fact that the composition of the Senate, where a three-fifths' majority was required, changed every two years. The Social Democrats and ODS therefore settled on a 'designer' electoral system with elements of PR specially tailored, almost, to eliminate the Communists.[81] However, because the results it was likely to produce were so *un*proportional, President Havel referred it to the Constitutional Court. Even if passed, the system's possible effects were unclear because a major flaw of electoral systems that produce unproportional results is that their outcomes overreact to relatively small shifts in electoral behaviour. A strand in Czech political culture favours the small man over the large bully boys, and such voters might rebel against attempts to concentrate the power of the powerful.

The situation with regard to the presidency remained confused. ODS supported a reduction in presidential powers while the office was held by Václav Havel, who was hostile to them, but clearly had designs on introducing direct elections and strengthening the office if ODS could change the Constitution and get its own Václav Klaus elected. The post-1998 Slovak Government's parties, on the other, introduced direct election of the president notwithstanding the fact that they had a sufficient majority to choose their preferred candidate in Parliament. They did so largely to keep the promise they had made to the electorate at a time when Slovakia was about to be left without a president because no candidate could muster the necessary three-fifths' majority after President Kováč's term in office ended in March 1998.[82] The man whom Dzurinda's Government finally put forward as its presidential candidate – the senior ex-Communist Rudolf Schuster – was scarcely the person it had in mind when it first promoted direct elections. In this case, direct election of the president was seen, primarily, as a means of checking and dispersing power rather than of concentrating it in the hands of a specific person. This is not uncommon in the post-Communist world, where a relatively high proportion of presidents without executive power are directly elected.

It appears, therefore, is that in both the Czech and Slovak Republics, sound institutional arrangements designed to prevent excessive concentration of power have so far been reasonably functional in preventing immature politicians manipulating the rules of the game in a self-seeking fashion. The most clearly undemocratic attempts at manipulation were undertaken in Slovakia by Mečiar's HZDS, which appeared to be looking for a way to perpetuate its own, unrestrained, one-party rule. The attempt failed, but HZDS was still far from accepting that others could have a legitimate right to rule. Despite the fact that the Dzurinda Government was supported by a parliamentary majority of over 60 per cent, HZDS forced a referendum on holding early elections in November 2000. The efforts of the Czech Social Democrats and ODS to manipulate the Constitution to their own ends were also worrying. Although they were a less direct attack on the fundamentals of democracy, in 2000 they still appeared to have a good chance of succeeding, thereby leaving Slovak democracy with the original Czechoslovak institutional rules more intact. What was also significant was that in the Czech case self-seeking rule amendment was being attempted by the two major political parties, which had together received the support of well over 60 per cent of voters. Although the constitutional changes appeared to be the result of consensus, it was a consensus between political elites – in some respects reminiscent of the interwar democracy – designed to close the political sphere to other actors.[83] It was also unclear how far the major parties would be prepared to go in changing the Constitution, since there was also talk of abolishing the Senate and establishing a unicameral parliamentary system.

Against this background, it is hard to talk of 'habituation to the norms and procedures of democratic conflict regulation' in either state. Full democratic consolidation in the Slovak Republic is hard to envisage while Mečiar remains a major political actor; and it cannot be completed in the Czech Republic while major changes of the constitutional rules for political competition are under way.

Rule of law

Respect for the rule of law is essential for both civil and political society to function, and it is vital for democratic consolidation. In examining the robustness of the rule of law in the Czech or the Slovak Republic, flaws can be found in its operation at three levels: observance of constitutional rules; the functioning of the police and judicial system; and everyday corruption.

The lack of consensus over the Constitution in the Czech and Slovak Republics has already been discussed. Notable in the Slovak case also are examples of governments ignoring decisions by the Constitutional Court. The most notorious was the Gaulieder case, where an elected parliamentary deputy who had defected from HZDS was stripped of his mandate on the basis of a dubious resignation letter.[84] The Mečiar Government's majority in Parliament refused to reinstate him in spite of a Constitutional Court decision condemning his expulsion. This introduced into Slovak politics the dangerous notion that Constitutional Court decisions do not have retrospective effect, and do not annul unconstitutional decisions made prior to the Court's judgment being published. Decisions on individual cases are therefore only binding in similar future cases.[85]

The functioning of the system of justice has been a major concern in most European Commission reports on post-Communist candidate states.[86] The police and the entire legal system were strongly subject to political influence under the Communist *nomenklatura* system. This was particularly true in the case of judges, who were initially difficult to replace in the post-Communist period because they are normally appointed from the most experienced members of the legal profession, who cannot be trained or retrained over-night. Furthermore, the introduction of a market economy, which brings with it a multitude of new legal subjects liable to require adjudication on contractual disputes, plus the specifically post-Communist problems of property restitution and privatisation, vastly increased the case loads on courts. The overburdening of courts, which was exacerbated by lack of clerical and technological support, led to excessive delays in judicial decision making which – together with a shortage in the legal expertise available to claimants – made recourse to the law an expensive, time consuming and consequently rather ineffectual option for ordinary citizens.

Neither the Czech nor the Slovak Republic had overcome this problem by the year 2000. The Czech Republic failed in successive attempts to pass legislation reforming the judiciary in 2000,[87] and the Slovak Republic required constitutional amendments in order to remove the system for appointing judges from overt political control.[88] The EU paid particular attention to the functioning of the judicial system, since current member states required evidence that candidates were able not only effectively to implement their own laws but to implement the EU's own extensive legal requirements.

The final area of concern, of vital importance to ordinary citizens, was the battle against corruption. The Czech Social Democrat Government introduced a 'clean hands' campaign in the second half of 1998, and adopted a programme for the fight against corruption in February 1999; the Slovak Government adopted a National Programme of Combating Corruption in June 2000. However, eradicating practices that had become a part of everyday life under the Communist regime was bound to be a long process. The Transparency International corruption perception rankings in 2000 showed the Czech Republic as the forty-second least corrupt state of ninety, while Slovakia as the fifty-second was ten places behind.[89] (It is perhaps significant that, unlike economic indicators, the Transparency International rankings from 1998 onwards have consistently arranged the ten CEE countries negotiating EU membership in the same order in which negotiations had started: Slovenia, Estonia, Hungary, the Czech Republic and Poland ahead of Lithuania, Slovakia, Latvia, Bulgaria and Romania. It is also notable that Italy and Greece, the lowest-ranking EU member states, are only just ahead of the Czech Republic.) The Transparency International rankings largely coincided with the popular perceptions which emerge in opinion surveys, whereby Slovaks believe corruption to be more prevalent than do the Czechs.[90]

Bureaucracy

Linz and Stepan note that a modern democracy 'needs a functioning state and a state bureaucracy considered usable by the new democratic government'.[91] Post-Communist states all suffered from the problem that state bureaucracy was totally penetrated by the control of the single 'party'. Furthermore, since employment by the state was the norm rather than the exception in Communist countries, no civil service laws existed to differentiate the conditions of employment of bureaucrats from those of the rest of the population.

This was problematic in both the Czech and Slovak Republics, where the new private sector offered salaries sometimes several times higher than those available in the state sector, and where supplementing an unsatisfactory standard of living provided by the salary from one's full-time employer through other means was common practice. Legislation preventing secondary employment by civil servants could not, therefore, credibly be implemented unless such persons received salaries commensurate with their qualifications and were provided with other advantages such as job security. Neither situation was easy to create in a time of severe budgetary constraints.

Both the Czech and Slovak Republics belonged to post-Communist states that had still not introduced a civil service law by the year 2000. In Slovakia, it had been recognised by the Dzurinda Government from its inception that such legislation was a priority for securing EU accession, and a draft Civil Service Act was under discussion in 2000. It was delayed, however, in part by the continued failure to complete the restructuring of public administration as a whole. This involved both decentralising competences, and transferring functions from the central authorities to elected local government bodies. Legislation passed by the Mečiar Government in 1996 had created 8 regions and 79 districts for state administration, while local government remained weak, with no units larger than the municipality (that is, often the village council). Interestingly, however, Slovakia – unlike the Czech Republic – had directly elected mayors, and perhaps because of this the Association of Slovak Towns and Villages (ZMOS) became one of the most organised pressure groups in the country, willing to defend local interests against governments of any political complexion. Since the regional structure created by Mečiar was controversial, the Dzurinda Government sought to rearrange state administration while also establishing regional units of local government. However, the Government was barely able to agree on the number and shape of the new regions among its own coalition partners, let alone with the opposition. Without structures having been agreed in purely geographic terms, it was hard to deal constructively with the more detailed questions of how public administration functioned.

More progress was made in the Czech Republic. Václav Klaus had, like Mečiar, been rather hostile to decentralisation of political power and happy to leave local government at a level where councils had neither the financial resources nor the political power to threaten the authority of central government. Under his successors, the creation of fourteen regions was agreed, with elections to regional parliaments scheduled for November 2000 (except in Prague, where they were due a year later). However, the introduction of a civil service law was delayed, so that it would not come into force before 2002. It was, however, increasingly appreciated that a depoliticisation of the civil service was necessary so that the work of ministries was not disrupted every time a new minister was appointed.

In terms of the functioning of the bureaucracy, the Czech Republic had two advantages over Slovakia. One was the strong bureaucratic tradition under Austrian rule (notwithstanding its flaws in terms of complexity and lack of transparency). However, this was undermined both by the decades of Communist rule and by the very low status of public service under the Klaus Governments, which conjured up a Czech self-image deifying the small businessmen of the First Republic. The second was that, while the Czech civil service was politicised, political competition in the Czech Republic was not marked by quite the same level of enmity as in Slovakia.

Economic society

'Economic society', in Linz and Stepan's definition of a consolidated democracy, mediates between state and market, and comprises 'sociopolitically accepted norms, institutions and regulations'.[92] Both the Czech and Slovak Republics faced particularly difficult tasks in transforming themselves from Soviet-style command economies to democratically regulated market economies because they had been among the most rigidly state-controlled economies in the Warsaw Pact, and did not – unlike their Visegrad Four neighbours Hungary and Poland – experience an increase in independent economic activity and cooperation with Western firms in the 1980s. The Czechs, however, embarked on independence in 1993 with two advantages over the Slovaks. The first was that they were the most prosperous and modern nation ever to have been subjected to Communism, which enabled Klaus to convert private enterprise into a form of ideology which would provide simple solutions to complex problems. The Czech economy had been less distorted by Communism in its industrialisation patterns, and the development of a thriving service sector – an overdue development long held up by the previous regime – also helped absorb employees made redundant in the early years of transition. Second, the Czech Republic benefited from being surrounded on three sides by Western democracies, which facilitated the cross-border flow of Western cash both from casual tourists from the West and from Czechs working there, and also made the country an attractive goal for foreign investment. On top of this, Slovakia was badly damaged in terms of investor confidence by the political antics and untransparent privatisation projects of the third Mečiar Government from 1994 to 1998.

By the year 2000, the balance sheet was mixed. The flaws of Klaus's once much-heralded voucher privatisation had become clear, but the Czech Republic appeared to be emerging from the economic downturn of 1997. The European Commission decided that it was a functioning market economy in its first 'opinion' on the Czech Republic's EU membership application in 1997. Slovakia, on the other hand, was still waiting for such an accolade more than two years later, although the European Commission's October 1999 'progress report' stated that it was 'close to being a functioning market economy'.[93] The Dzurinda Government on coming to power in 1998 inherited an unfortunate economy legacy, particularly in terms of the 'crony capitalism' of Mečiar's privatisation policies. Since the Mečiar Government in its last months had resorted to borrowing on unfavourable terms to prevent an economic downturn becoming manifest shortly before the election, the new Government found itself with a devaluation of the Slovak crown and a sharp decline in GDP growth rates as soon as it was elected and before it was even sworn into office.

What both states clearly lacked was the institutionalisation of the rules for the conduct of economic affairs. Banks collapsed, the pursuit of debtors through court action proved difficult, governments ministers were suspected of privatisation-linked crimes, and there was a general public perception that success in business and legal–moral behaviour were incompatible. The Czech lead over the Slovaks was perhaps not as great as one might have expected given the structural differences in their economy at the outset and the political difficulties in Slovakia in the mid-1990s. In the end, the strongest guarantee that economic structures, regulations and enforcement procedures would consolidate in a democratic fashion likely to gain the confidence of citizens came from the fact that the European Union was extremely precise about the standards it expected.

Conclusion

The first part of this chapter looked at the underlying structural differences between the Czech and Slovak Republics which might affect their chances of achieving democratic consolidation. In two of the categories – *history* and *economics* – Slovakia suffers distinct disadvantages. It has a far less clear and self-confident historically based image of its national identity, and less practical experience of exercising governmental responsibility. Economically, history has left it more backward than the Czech Lands, and it was therefore more marked by the distorted Communist modernisation process, as well as having geographical disadvantages in terms of markets. On other indicators, the divergence is less marked. It is hard to conclude that the *modes of transition* from Communist rule were much more than reflections of differences deriving from history and economic structures. Likewise, any differences in *political culture* appear largely to be products of the fact that Slovakia remains a more rural Catholic society. The *institutional architecture* for the conduct of politics is a major similarity between the states. It served both well in the early post-Communist years, and has shown some resistance to manipulative change by self-interested sectors of the political elites.

In attempting to measure progress towards democratic consolidation in the areas of *civil* and *political society*, the *rule of law*, the *bureaucracy* and *economic society*, it is notable that in many formal respects the Slovak Republic seems to be only one or two years behind the Czech Republic. What one sees after the division of Czechoslovakia is not so much a fundamental parting of ways – although Slovakia did indeed appear to be setting off on a divergent trajectory in the mid-1990s – but rather a pattern whereby Slovakia trails behind the Czech Republic. The metaphor of Slovakia as the 'little brother' seems apt, if rather patronising.[94]

Two additional factors which go some way to explaining the pattern of divergence and convergence during the 1990s need a mention. The first is the role of elites. The monolithic and undemocratic nature of Warsaw Pact regimes, plus their subordination to an alien (Soviet) force, produced both inexperienced elites and inexperienced citizens unused to holding their rulers to account. In Czechoslovakia, this contributed to the division of the state, which in turn slowed down the process of democratic consolidation, most particularly in the Slovak Republic. The division of the state also created two 'founding fathers' – Klaus and Mečiar – who are the only two prime ministers (as opposed to presidents) in the entire post-Communist world who can be regarded as their state's towering political figure of the 1990s. This led to a personalisation of politics more usual in presidential systems. By the beginning of the new millennium, both were still active opposition leaders, with evident designs on somehow becoming an executive president who could wisely lead their fellow citizens without being troubled by the chaos of the pluralist interests inherent in a democratic political system. This was not particularly helpful to the development of substantive democracy.

However, by the beginning of the new millennium, both Klaus and Mečiar, ten years older than when they first became prominent in politics, increasingly appeared anachronistic symbols of a bygone and more ideological age. Patterns of leadership were therefore likely to change. Furthermore, a new generation, with skills honed predominantly in a more open society, was increasingly taking over the reins of government as both states grappled with the intricate process of EU accession. Because of the complexity of the multi-layered post-Communist transition process, the whole of the 1990s had been a transition period. All skills acquired in the Communist period, both political, economic, social and cultural, were becoming increasingly antiquated, but the younger generation, equipped with Western-oriented training, was approaching the point where it constituted a critical mass able to take over the running of society. From the moment Slovakia obtained independence, its younger generation had received particular attention from the international community in the provision of training opportunities. This is likely to produce a convergence in outlook among the younger, more cosmopolitan generations in both the Czech Republic and Slovakia. Both will be broadly supportive of democratic consolidation.

The second major factor in the transition process, which became predominant in the second half of the 1990s, is the influence of the European Union as a driving force providing momentum to all aspects of the reform process. Here, again, the Czech Republic and Slovakia are subject to equal conditions. Slovakia was certainly slower in completing the transition to democracy, and fulfilling the conditions of a procedural or formal democracy. This was reflected in the fact that the European Commission deemed it to have fulfilled the first political (Copenhagen) conditions two years later than the Czech Republic. However, the consolidation of democracy is a more complex process. This complexity is reflected in the EU's third Copenhagen criterion, 'the ability to take on the obligations of membership'. Although a simple phrase, it embraces myriad intricate conditions affecting almost every aspect of political and economic life. It relates not just to legislative measures, but to the efficacy of structures and the procedures for their implementation and for monitoring implementation. It also assumes that all candidate states, regardless of divergent historical and economic inheritances, have the capacity to adapt to the EU's membership conditions and are not prisoners of their past. By the end of the 1990s, the Parliaments of the Czech and Slovak Republics had legislative programmes dominated by the exigencies of EU accession. As long as the desire to 'return to Europe' remains, the EU's membership conditions do not permit deviation from the path to successful democratic consolidation.

Where, then, does this leave the Czech and Slovak Republics? The Slovak Republic is slightly behind the Czech Republic in most areas of democratic consolidation, but its democratic institutions have demonstrated a remarkable robustness under considerable pressure. Czech institutions, on the other hand, have been subjected to less severe tests. While their healthy history of democratic precedents bodes well, any tendency in Czech society towards civic passivity is worrying, particularly given their twentieth-century track record of never fighting to preserve their freedom. However, as NATO and (almost certain) EU members, they are unlikely ever again to need to do so.

Whether Czech and Slovak trajectories will again diverge may well depend on two factors. Firstly, as mentioned earlier, the proportion of Slovak voters with a backward-looking political agenda which does not prioritise EU membership is a slowly decreasing minority, but it nonetheless appears to be at least twice as large as that in the Czech Republic. The Communists are very much less likely to come to power in the Czech Republic than is HZDS in Slovakia. Particularly given the weaker economy, the Slovaks remain more likely than the Czechs to produce a government that would endanger their chances of EU membership fundamentally, thereby producing a double jeopardy of the process of democratic consolidation being derailed.

Secondly, the influence of the EU as a guiding force for democratic consolidation makes candidate states vulnerable to shifts in EU policy on enlargement. The two years which Slovakia lost in opening negotiations on EU accession could prove a major and lasting setback if it does not join in the First Wave of EU eastward enlargement *and* if the EU experiences difficulties with First Wave countries which stall the further enlargement process.

While Czech democracy has its flaws, on all counts its chances of democratic consolidation are high, particularly because external factors are currently very conducive to such a development. The Slovak Republic is also likely to consolidate democracy, but, as in its entire history, it remains susceptible to outside influences. The unfortunate behaviour of inexperienced Slovak elites in the mid-1990s, which derived from a constellation of historical and structural factors, should prove to have been a temporary setback following its unexpected attainment of independence. However, the future remains uncertain.

Notes

1 See, for example, J. Elster, C. Offe and U. K. Preuss, *Institutional Design in Postcommunist Societies: Rebuilding the Ship at Sea* (Cambridge: Cambridge University Press, 1998), which states that the Czech Republic fares 'extraordinarily well on three criteria of consolidated democratic societies' (p. 279), and ranks it first in the countries studied, ahead of Hungary as well as Slovakia and Bulgaria (p. 305).
2 C. Skalnik Leff, 'Dysfunctional democratization? Institutional conflict in postcommunist Slovakia', *Problems of Post-Communism* 43:5 (1996), pp. 36–50.
3 M. Carpenter, 'Slovakia and the triumph of nationalist populism', *Communist and Post-Communist Studies* 30:2 (1997), pp. 205–19; also W. Merkel, *Defective Democracies* (Madrid: Juan March Institute Working Papers, 1999), p. 2.
4 For a detailed account of Slovakia's path to exclusion from NATO, see M. Bútora and F. Šebej (eds), *Slovensko v šedej zóne? Rozširovanie NATO, zlyhania a perspektívy Slovenska* (Bratislava: Inštitút pre verejné otázky, 1998).
5 European Commission, 'Agenda 2000. For a stronger and wider Union', *Bulletin of the European Union* (1997), Supplement 5/97.
6 *Ibid.*, p. 138.
7 For an analysis of the political developments leading to EU exclusion, see Karen Henderson, 'Slovakia and the democratic criteria for EU accession', in K. Henderson (ed.), *Back to Europe: Central and Eastern Europe and the European Union* (London: UCL Press, 1999), pp. 221–40.
8 See J. Horváth, 'The May 1997 currency crisis in the Czech Republic', *Post-Communist Economies*, 11:3 (1999), pp. 277–98, which describes the Czech events as 'the first typical currency crisis in the advanced part of the Second World'.
9 This view is put in P. Fiala and F. Mikš, *Úvahy a české politické krizi* (Brno: CDK, 1998).
10 See for example S. M. Lipset, 'Some social requisites of democracy: economic development and political legitimacy', *American Political Science Review* 53:1 (1959), pp. 69–105; D. A. Rustow, 'Transitions to democracy', *Comparative Politics*

2:3 (1970), pp. 337–63; T. Vanhanen and R. Kimber, 'Predicting and explaining democratization in Eastern Europe', in G. Pridham and T. Vanhanen (eds), *Democratization in Eastern Europe* (London: Routledge 1994), pp. 63–98.

11 The term is taken from S. P. Huntington, *The Third Wave: Democratization in the Late Twentieth Century* (Norman and London: University of Oklahoma Press, 1991), and refers also to democratisation in Latin America and Southern Europe.

12 See H. Kitschelt, 'Party systems in East Central Europe: consolidation or fluidity?', *Studies in Public Policy*, no. 241 (Glasgow: University of Strathclyde, 1995); H. Kitschelt, 'Formation of party cleavages in post-communist democracies: theoretical propositions', *Party Politics* 1:4 (1995), pp. 447–72.

13 In 1921, this actually comprised a mere 64 per cent of the population; Germans, concentrated primarily in the Czech lands, formed a further 23 per cent, while Hungarians constituted 5 per cent of the Czechoslovak population, but 20 per cent of citizens in Slovakia. The *raison d'être* for the notion of the Czechoslovak 'nation' was partly pragmatic: if the Slovaks had been recognised as a separate 'nation' from the Czechs, then Czechs would have formed barely half the population of Czechoslovakia, and the Germans would have been the second largest national grouping. The myth of the 'nation state' would therefore have been unsustainable.

14 P. Frič, Z. Bútorová and T. Rosová, 'Česko-slovenské vzťahy v zrkadle empirického výskumu', *Sociológia* 24:1–2 (1992), 43–74.

15 For views of Czechs and Slovaks on the First Republic, see *ibid.*; also Institut pro výzkum veřejného mínění, 'Názory obyvatel na tři historická období vývoje naší republiky', *Informace* 1:17 (1990).

16 On parties in interwar Czechoslovakia, see Eva Broklová, *Československá demokracie: politický systém ČSR 1918–1938* (Prague: Slon, 1992).

17 The most extensive statistics on prewar Slovak poverty are given in A. J. Chura, *Slovensko bez dorastu* (Bratislava: Roľnícka osveta, 1936).

18 This impression may have been false, since the period concerned coincided with the Depression. See O. V. Johnson, *Slovakia 1918–1938: Education and the Making of a Nation* (New York: Columbia University Press, 1985).

19 See James Ramon Felak, *Hlinka's Slovak People's Party, 1929–1938* (Pittsburgh and London: University of Pittsburgh Press, 1994).

20 Ivan Kamenec, *Slovenský štát* (Prague: Anomal, 1992).

21 For public opinion assessments of the interwar period, see Z. Bútorová and M. Bútora, 'Events and personalities in Slovakia's history', in Z. Bútorová (ed.), *Democracy and Discontent in Slovakia: A Public Opinion Profile of a Country in Transition* (Bratislava: Institute for Public Affairs, 1998), pp. 191–202; 'Hodnotenie úlohy Slovenského štátu v dejinách Slovákov', *Názory* 2:3 (1991), 41–2.

22 See Karen Henderson, 'Czechoslovakia: the failure of consensus politics and the break-up of the federation', *Regional and Federal Studies*, 5:2 (1995), pp. 111–33.

23 The 1991 Census showed that 65 per cent of Czechs and 56 per cent of Slovaks lived in settlements with more than 5,000 inhabitants. Český statistický úřad, *Statistická ročenka České republiky* (Prague: Český statistický úřad/Český spisovatel, 1993), p. 405.

24 Jozef Žatkuliak, 'Čo otvoril November 1989 vo sfére politickej, ekonomickej and štátoprávnej', in J. Pešek and S. Szomolányi (eds), *November 1989 na Slovensko: Súvislosti, predpoklady a dôsledky* (Bratislava: Nadácia Milana Šimečku, 2000), pp. 76–91; P. Machonin, 'Česko-slovenské vztahy ve světle dat sociologického

výzkumu', in F. Gál a kol., *Dnešní krize česko-slovenských vztahů* (Prague: Sociologické nakladatelství, 1992), pp. 97–101. More detailed historical comparisons can be found in Federální statistický úřad, *Historická statistická ročenka ČSSR* (Prague: SNTL/ALFA, 1985).

25 European Commission, 'Agenda 2000', p. 138. By 1999, Hungary had overtaken Slovakia.

26 See Jiri Musil, 'Czech and Slovak society', *Government and Opposition* 28:4 (1993), pp. 479–95.

27 See e.g. T. L. Karl and P. C. Schmitter, 'Modes of Transition in Latin America, Southern and Eastern Europe', *International Social Science Journal* 128 (1991), pp. 269–84.

28 Kitschelt, 'Party Systems in East Central Europe', p. 11.

29 *Ibid.*, p. 13.

30 See accounts of 1989 in Ingrid Antalová (ed.), *Verejnosťproti násiliu 1989–1991* (Bratislava: Nadácia Milana Šimečku, 1998) and Fedor Gál, *Z prvej ruky* (Bratislava: Archa, 1991). See also S. Szomolányi, 'November 1989: otvorenie kľukatej cesty k demokracii', in Pešek and Szomolányi (eds), *November 1989*, pp. 92–110.

31 By comparison, the Czech Social Democrat Government formed in 1997 contained only seven ex-Communists, all but one of whom had parted ways with the party soon after 1968; and Dzurinda's post-1998 Government had eleven former Communists from twenty members.

32 A. Róna-Tas, J. Bunčák and V. Harmadyová, 'Post-Communist transformation and the new elite in Slovakia', *Sociológia* 31:3 (1999), pp. 235–62.

33 See R. Rose and C. Haerpfer, 'New democracies' Barometer V', *Studies in Public Policy*, no. 306 (Glasgow: University of Strathclyde, 1998).

34 Stephen Whitefield and Geoffrey Evans, 'Political culture versus rational choice: explaining responses to transition in the Czech Republic and Slovakia', *British Journal of Political Science* 29:1 (1999), pp. 129–54. For the religious composition of the Czech and Slovak Republics, see 1991 census figures in Český statistický úřad, *Statistická ročenka*, p. 413. The major difference is the number of citizens stating they had no confession: 39.9 per cent of Czechs and 9.8 per cent of Slovaks.

35 Z. Bútorová, O. Gyárfášová and M. Velšic, 'Public Opinion', in G. Mesežnikov, M. Ivantyšyn, and T. Nicholson (eds), *Slovakia 1998–1999: A Global Report on the State of Society* (Bratislava: Institute for Public Affairs, 1999), pp. 137–66.

36 *Ibid.*, p. 151.

37 Z. Bútorová, 'Public reactions to domestic political issues', in Bútorová (ed.), *Democracy and Discontent*, pp. 111–33; FOCUS, *Aktuálne problémy Slovenska December 1994* (Bratislava: FOCUS, 1994), p. 65.

38 Henderson, 'Czechoslovakia'; P. Kopecky and C. Mudde, 'Growing apart: explaining the different paths of democratization in the Czech and Slovak Republics', paper presented at the 94th Annual American Political Science Convention, Boston, MA, 3–6 September 1998.

39 For analysis of the advantages of such an institutional combination, see A. Stepan and C. Skach, 'Constitutional frameworks and democratic consolidation: parliamentarianism versus presidentialism', *World Politics* 46 (1993), pp. 1–22; Arend Lijphart, 'Democratization and constitutional choices in Czecho-Slovakia, Hungary and Poland, 1989–91', *Journal of Theoretical Politics* 4:2 (1992), pp. 207–33.

40 There were also immediate reasons for having Havel elected by Parliament in

December 1989: getting rid of President Husák was too urgent a task to await popular elections. See M. Calda, 'The Roundtable talks in Czechoslovakia', in J. Elster (ed.), *The Roundtable Talks and the Breakdown of Communism* (Chicago and London: University of Chicago Press, 1996), pp. 135–77.

41 J. J. Linz, 'Transition to democracy', *The Washington Quarterly* 13:3 (1990), pp. 143–64.

42 G. O'Donnell, 'Illusions about consolidation', *Journal of Democracy* 7:2 (1996), pp. 34–51.

43 J. J. Linz and A. Stepan, *Problems of Democratic Transition and Consolidation: Southern Europe, South America, and Post-Communist Europe* (Baltimore and London: Johns Hopkins University Press, 1996), p. 6.

44 Huntington, *The Third Wave*, pp. 266–7.

45 G. O'Donnell and P. C. Schmitter, *Transitions from Authoritarian Rule: Tentative Conclusions about Uncertain Democracies* (Baltimore and London: Johns Hopkins University Press, 1986), p. 58.

46 For details of the 'spoilt' referendum, see G. Mesežnikov and M. Bútora (eds), *Slovenské referendum '97: zrod, priebeh, dôsledky* (Bratislava: Inštitút pre verejné otázky, 1997).

47 For a detailed analysis of democratic consolidation and the 1998 Slovak elections, see K. Henderson, 'Problems of democratic consolidation in the Slovak Republic', *Society and Economy in Central and Eastern Europe* 3 (1999), pp. 141–78.

48 This is usually defined with reference to Robert Dahl's definitions in *Dilemmas of Pluralist Democracy: Autonomy vs. Control* (New Haven and London: Yale University Press, 1982), p. 11; *Democracy and its Critics* (New Haven and London: Yale University Press, 1989), p. 21; also *Polyarchy: Participation and Opposition* (New Haven and London: Yale University Press, 1971), p. 3.

49 See M. Kaldor and I. Vejvoda, 'Democratization in central and eastern Europe', *International Affairs* 73:1 (1997), pp. 75–88.

50 Linz and Stepan, *Problems of Democratic Transition*, p. 7.

51 *Ibid.*

52 C. Offe, 'Capitalism by democratic design? Democratic theory facing the triple transition in East Central Europe', *Social Research* 58:4 (1991), pp. 865–92.

53 K. Henderson, 'The challenges of EU eastward enlargement', *International Politics*, 37:1 (2000), pp. 1–18.

54 Linz and Stepan, *Problems of Democratic Transition*, p. 7.

55 For shifts in Czech and Slovak attitudes towards their newly independent states, see FOCUS, *Aktuálne problémy Slovenska*, p. 37; Z. Bútorová, 'Transformation challenges in public perception', in Bútorová, *Democracy and Discontent*, pp. 21–36.

56 See, for example, M. Bútora and Z. Bútorová, 'Slovakia's democratic awakening', *Journal of Democracy* 10:1 (1999), pp. 80–95.

57 FOCUS, *Aktuálne problémy Slovenska*, p. 25; European Commission, *Central and Eastern Eurobarometer* 8 (1998), Annexe Figure 55; Róna-Tas *et al.*, 'Post-Communist Transformation', pp. 256–7.

58 Linz and Stepan, *Problems of Democratic Transition*, p. 7.

59 P. Demeš, 'The third sector and volantarism' in G. Mesežnikov *et al.*, *Slovakia 1998–1999*, pp. 347–63.

60 European Commission, 'Agenda 2000. Commission opinion on the Czech

Republic's application for membership of the European Union', *Bulletin of the European Union* (1997), Supplement 14/97, p. 18.

61 European Commission, 'Agenda 2000. Commission opinion on the Slovakia's application for membership of the European Union', *Bulletin of the European Union* (1997), Supplement 9/97, p. 18.

62 Štatistický úrad Slovenskej republiky, *Štatistická ročenka Slovenskej republiky 1999* (Bratislava: VEDA, 1999), p. 523.

63 L. Brokl (and collective), *Reprezentace zájmů v politickém systému České republiky* (Prague: Slon, 1997), p. 157.

64 For details of the Czech law, see J. Hurdík and I. Telec, *Zákon o nadacích a nadačních fondech* (Prague: C. H. Beck, 1998); for the Slovak law, see P. Demeš and M. Bútora, 'Tretí sektor a dobrovoľníctvo', in M. Bútora and M. Ivantyšyn (eds), *Slovensko 1997: Súhrnná správa o stave spoločnosti a trendoch na rok 1998* (Bratislava: Inštitút pre verejné otázky, 1998), 637–56.

65 M. Bútora and P. Demeš, 'Civil society organizations in the 1998 elections', in M. Bútora, G. Mesežnikov, Z. Bútorová and S. Fisher (eds), *The 1998 Parliamentary Elections and Democratic Rebirth in Slovakia* (Bratislava: Institute for Public Affairs, 1999), pp. 155–67.

66 On 6 March 1995, the daily newspapers *Sme, Pravda, Národná obroda, Nový čas, Új Szó , Smena* and Práca, plus a number of weekly magazines and regional dailies, appeared with an almost blank front page bearing a stark message headed *znepokojenie* (anxiety, concern) to express worry about a planned tax rise apparently designed to put them out of business.

67 Linz and Stepan, *Problems of Democratic Transition*, p. 8.

68 See Henderson, *Problems of Democratic Consolidation*, pp. 159–60.

69 Linz and Stepan, *Problems of Democratic Transition*, p. 8.

70 *Ibid.*, p. 10.

71 The Copenhagen European Council of June 1993, at which the European Community first committed itself politically to eastward enlargement, laid down the three membership conditions which are repeated at the beginning of EU reports on the candidate states. The first condition related to stability of institutions guaranteeing democracy, the rule of law, human rights and respect for and protection of minorities; the second, to the existence of a functioning market economy and capacity to cope with competitive pressures; and the third, to the ability to take on the obligations of membership.

72 *Parlamentní zpravodaj* 4:16 (1998), pp. 368–9.

73 Štatistický úrad Slovenskej republiky, *Výsledky hlasovania vo voľbách do Národnej rady Slovenskej republiky 25–26. september 1998* (Štatistický úrad Slovenskej republiky: Bratislava, 1998).

74 Štatistický úrad Slovenskej republiky, *Výsledky hlasovania vo voľbe prezidenta Slovenskej republiky* (Štatistický úrad Slovenskej republiky: Bratislava, 1999).

75 For the profile of HZDS voters, see *Volebný výskum*, Medzinárodný republikánsky inštitút/Agentúra FOCUS, 25.-26. September 1998; Vladimír Krivý, 'Election results' in M. Bútora *et al.*, *The 1998 Parliamentary Elections*, pp. 63–78. For the profile of KSČM voters, see *Parlamentní zpravodaj* 4:16 (1998), pp. 376–7.

76 The decline in the 'wasted vote' does, however, reduce somewhat the chance of this happening again, since wasted votes increase the number of parliamentary seats a party with more than 5 per cent receives for each per cent of the vote.

77 See V. Krivý, V. Feglová and D. Balko, *Slovensko a jeho regióny: Sociokultúrne súvislosti volebného spravania* (Bratislava: Nadácia Médià, 1996), pp. 352–62.
78 For the election law, see D. Šveda, M. Petrlová and L. Skultétyová, *Parlamentné voľby* (Bratislava: Epos, 1998).
79 See K. Henderson, 'Social Democracy comes to power: the 1998 Czech elections', *Labour Focus on Eastern Europe* 60 (1998), pp. 502
80 For the text of the 'opposition agreement' (officially entitled 'Agreement on the creation of a stable political environment in the Czech Republic concluded between the Czech Party of Social Democracy and the Civic Democratic Party') see *Parlamentní zpravodaj* 4:17 (1999), p. 550.
81 See *Hospodářské noviny* (31 May 2000), pp. 1–2. For the calculations used to tailor the system, see Tomáš Lebeda, 'Vládní stabilita v České republice a volební systém poměrného zastoupení II: Modelování výsledků voleb do Poslanecké sněmovny z roku 1998', *Politologický časopis* 6:2 (1999), pp. 146–61; the first part of the article is in *Politologický časopis* 5:2 (1998).
82 On the advantages and disadvantages of directly electing the president in the Slovak case, see K. Henderson, 'Don't blame the constitution . . .', in *The New Presence*, September (1999), pp. 10–11.
83 For example, in September 2000, the Czech Parliament overrode a presidential veto and passed a law removing all state finance from parties receiving less than 5 per cent of the vote. This would tend to 'freeze' the party system around those parties currently in parliament.
84 For details of the Gaulieder case, see *Sme*, 28 July (1997), p. 5.
85 M. Galanda, A. Földesová and M. Benedik, 'Rule of law, legislation and constitutionality', in G. Mesežnikov *et al.*, *Slovakia 1998–1999*, pp. 83–94.
86 For the European Commission's 1998 and 1999 progress reports on the Czech and Slovak Republics, see Commission of the European Communities, *Regular Report from the Commission on Czech Republic's (Slovakia's) Progress Towards Accession*, COM(1998) 708 (703) final and *Regular Report from the Commission on Czech Republic's (Slovakia's) Progress Towards Accession*, COM(1999) 703 (711) final.
87 *Lidové noviny*, 10 September (2000), p. 2.
88 *Report on the Slovak Republic's Progress in its Integration into the European Union September 1999–June 2000*, p. 12.
89 www.transparency.sk/index-cpi.htm
90 See Ase B. Grodeland, Tatyana Y. Koshechkina and William L. Miller, 'Foolish to give and yet more foolish not to take: in-depth interviews with post-Communist citizens on their everyday use of bribes and contacts', *Europe–Asia Studies* 50:4 (1998), pp. 651–77, for focus group research results; and for USIA figures, www.governnment.gov.sk/bojprotikorupcii/sk_prieskum01.shtml
91 Linz and Stepan, *Problems of Democratic Transition*, p. 11.
92 *Ibid.*, p. 12.
93 Commission of the European Communities, *Regular Report from the Commission on Slovakia's Progress* (1999), p. 29.
94 This metaphor was used most controversially by the Czech writer Ludvík Vaculík in a December 1990 article in *Literární noviny* which suggested that the little brother should leave home if he didn't like it – the line effectively implemented by Klaus in June 1992.

Index